INTERNATIONAL BUSINESS MANAGEMENT

Rexcel Lagare

TAP

Toronto Academic Press

International Business Management

Rexcel Lagare

Toronto Academic Press
224 Shoreacres Road
Burlington, ON L7L 2H2
Canada
www.tap-books.com
Email: orders@arclereducation.com

ISBN: 978-1-77469-728-3

ABOUT THE AUTHOR

Rex is an MBA graduate from Arizona State University's Thunderbird School of Global Management, ranked No. 1 in the world for international trade by the QS International Trade Rankings, ahead of Cambridge, Harvard, and Stanford. Arizona State University ranked No. 1 as the "Most Innovative School" in the nation by U.S. News & World Report for eight years in succession. Rex graduated magna cum laude with a bachelor's degree in accounting from the University of San Carlos in the Philippines. Spanning over a decade of experience in finance, supply chain & operations projects with Fortune 500 clients and Business World's Top 1000 Corporations, as well as with startup and midsize companies, Rexcel Lagare is proficient in guiding clients enhance their business performance in his role as a management consultant.

Contents

2 Theories of International Trade 39

3 International Business Environment 71

List of Figures

List of Tables

List of Abbreviations

AMA	American Marketing Association
BP	British Petroleum
CFIUS	Committee on Foreign Investment in the United States
CISG	Contracts for the International Sale of Goods
CSR	Corporate Social Responsibility
DSS	Decision Support System
ESOMAR	European Society for Opinion and Marketing Research
EU	European Union
FAO	Food and Agricultural Organization
FDI	Foreign Direct Investment
FPI	Foreign Portfolio Investment
FSIA	Foreign Sovereign Immunities Act
GATT	General Agreement on Tariffs and Trade
GDSS	Group Decision Support System
GNI	Gross National Income
GSP	Generalized Preferences of System
HP	Hewlett-Packard
ICC	International Chamber of Commerce
ICJ	International Court of Justice
ILO	International Labor Organization
IMF	International Monetary Fund
IMR	International Marketing Research

IPO	Import Promotion Office
IPR	Intellectual Property Rights
ITC	International Trade Center
JIT	Just-In-Time
JV	Joint Venture
LCDs	Less-Developed Countries
LMICs	Lower Middle-Income Countries
M&A	Mergers and Acquisitions
MIS	Management Information System
MNCs	Multinational Corporations
MNEs	Multinational Enterprises
MRS	Market Research Society
NAFTA	North American Free Trade Agreement
NAICS	North American Industry Classification System
NDRC	National Development and Reform Commission
OECD	Organization for Economic Cooperation and Development
PPF	Production Possibility Frontier
PSAs	Production-Sharing Arrangements
R&D	Research and Development
SMEs	Small and Medium-Sized Enterprises
TNC	Transnational Corporation
TPP	Trans-Pacific Partnership
TPS	Transaction Processing System
TQM	Total Quality Management
TV	Television
UAE	United Arab Emirates
UNC	Unemotional Company
UNCTAD	United Nations Conference on Trade and Development
WTO	World Trade Organization

PREFACE

International business refers to the act of conducting business operations beyond the borders of one's own country. It is a glamorous and tempting field for those interested in expanding their markets globally and increasing the economic growth of their nation. Today, international business has become a topic of debate and discussion as it brings raw materials, human skills, technology, creativity, innovations, and other resources to host nations. With the lowering of international barriers and good relationships with governments across borders, international business is rapidly growing and touching the shores of every country.

However, the global economy has faced challenges such as world economic growth, trade tensions, monetary policy tightening, and the COVID-19 crisis, leading to a fall in consumer trust and affecting the export and tourism industries. All businesses must adapt to shifts in political, economic, cultural, and technological factors to maintain their competitive advantage in local and global markets. Factors such as different cultures, languages, ethnicities, religions, national work systems, values, and standards also affect global business expansion, requiring attention from all participants to ensure the organizational culture, employee behavior, customer satisfaction, and stakeholder satisfaction.

This book focuses on the worldwide economy, globalization, and the global market, providing students with a balanced perspective on business in a global environment. It covers the fundamental challenges and emerging trends in international business, highlighting the differences between local, national, and international business. The book is divided into seven chapters, each of which covers a different aspect of international business. Chapter 1 introduces the concept of international business, defines its key terms, and highlights the characteristics that distinguish it from domestic business. Chapter 2 explores the various theories of international trade that help explain why countries engage in international business and how they can benefit from it. Chapter 3 delves into the international business environment, examining the political, legal, economic, and cultural factors that can affect business operations and outcomes. Furthermore, Chapter 4 discusses different entry strategies that companies can use when expanding into foreign markets, such as exporting, licensing, franchising, joint ventures, and strategic alliances.

Chapter 5 focuses on foreign direct investment (FDI), which involves investing in and controlling business operations in foreign countries. Chapter 6 examines multinational corporations (MNCs), which are large companies that operate in multiple countries and often face unique challenges related to international business management. Finally, Chapter 7 covers marketing research in international business, explaining how companies can gather and analyze data to better understand their foreign markets and make informed decisions.

The book explores implications for multinational companies in developed and emerging markets, providing valuable insights for those interested in pursuing international business.

–Author

CHAPTER 1

INTERNATIONAL BUSINESS: CONCEPT, DEFINITION, AND CHARACTERISTICS

UNIT INTRODUCTION

Globalization and international business have enabled companies from different countries to collaborate and work together in various ways. This has resulted in the production and distribution of goods and services across borders.

For example, a beverage company in India may collaborate with a company from the United States to produce and distribute its products globally. The tea used in the production of the beverage may be sourced from Sri Lanka, while the technology used in the manufacturing of the product may come from Japan.

This type of collaboration and exchange of resources has become increasingly common in today's global economy. It allows companies to leverage each other's strengths and expertise to produce high-quality products and services that meet the needs of consumers around the world.

The rapid growth of the international business has been one of the most significant trends in the past two decades. The expansion of markets and the globalization of goods and services have led to increased world product trade, which has grown more than six percent a year since 1950. Financial instruments, especially in the global forex markets, have seen the most dramatic increase in globalization.

The global forex market is where billions of dollars are transacted each day, with over 90% of these transactions being financial and unrelated to trade or investment. Much of this activity takes place in the Euromarkets, which are markets outside the country whose currency is used. These markets have grown rapidly due to the increasing globalization of financial transactions.

The growth of the international business has been driven by a variety of factors, including technological advancements, increased access to information, and changes in government policies. Advances in technology have made it easier and faster to communicate and transfer money across borders. Increased access to information has made it easier for businesses to understand and enter new markets. Changes in government policies, such as the removal of trade barriers, have made it easier for businesses to operate globally.

As international business continues to grow, it is important for businesses to understand the risks and challenges that come with operating in a global market. These risks include political instability, currency fluctuations, and changes in government policies.

The increasing interdependence of economies through international trade and capital flows has made it difficult for any country to avoid external impacts on its economy. In particular, massive capital flows can lead to exchange rate fluctuations that can affect a country's competitiveness in the global market.

If a country's economic policies or performance diverge from those of other countries in the short run, it can result in significant external impacts on its economy. For example, if a country experiences a sudden decline in economic growth or increased inflation, investors may withdraw their investments, leading to a depreciation of the country's currency. This, in turn, can lead to higher prices for imports and lower prices for exports, making it more difficult for the country to compete in the global market.

To address these challenges, countries may implement policies such as currency interventions or capital controls to stabilize their exchange rates and reduce the impact of external factors on their economy. However, such policies can have unintended consequences, such as reducing the attractiveness of the country as an investment destination or increasing the volatility of its currency.

The rapid dissemination of new technologies has increased the pace at which countries must adjust to external events. This is particularly true for smaller, more open economies that have long given up the illusion of domestic policy autonomy.

However, even large and apparently self-contained economies, such as the United States, are now significantly affected by the global economy. The increasing integration of trade, investment, factor flows, technology, and communication has created linkages between economies that were not present before.

For example, technological advancements in one part of the world can quickly spread to other countries, affecting industries and jobs across borders. Similarly, changes in global financial markets can have significant impacts on the domestic economy of a country, even if it is seemingly self-contained.

As a result, countries must increasingly consider the impact of global events and trends on their domestic policies and economic performance. They must also work collaboratively with other countries to address global challenges such as climate change, cybersecurity, and economic inequality.

The changes in the global economy are the result of several interconnected factors, including technological advancements, changes in international trade and investment policies, and the emergence of corporate empires.

In recent decades, scientific and technological developments have facilitated the globalization of production. This has enabled corporations to leverage the benefits of global supply chains, with different parts of the production process taking place in different countries based on cost and efficiency considerations.

As a result of this globalization of production and cooperation among global productive units, large-scale capital exports and the "export of production" have come to the forefront as a dominant feature of the world economy. In other words, corporations are now exporting production capabilities, rather than just exporting finished goods.

This trend has been facilitated by changes in international trade and investment policies, which have made it easier for corporations to establish operations in multiple countries. For example, the rise of free trade agreements has reduced barriers to trade and investment, while the liberalization of capital flows has made it easier for corporations to move capital across borders.

Indeed, global corporations have redefined the boundaries of production and markets. They are no longer confined to a single country or region but consider the whole world as their production place as well as their market. They seek to optimize the combination of factors of production by moving them to wherever they can be most efficiently utilized. This mobility is facilitated by the revolution in communication and transportation technology, which has made it possible to instantly connect with anyone, anywhere in the world.

Global corporations are also characterized by its transnational ownership and management structure. Their management teams are composed of individuals from different countries, and their ownership is spread across multiple countries. This allows them to operate seamlessly across borders, transcending individual national boundaries. They are domestic in each place they operate, and foreign in none.

The free mobility of management, technology, and capital has become the modern agent for stepped-up economic growth, transcending individual national boundaries. This has led to greater interdependence among nations and reduced the economic, social, and political insularity of the peoples of the world. Globalization has brought about a more interconnected world, where the actions of one country can have a significant impact on the economies and societies of other countries.

Learning Objectives

After completing this chapter, you should be able to:

- Understand the concept of international business.
- Identify the different types of international business activities.
- Describe the benefits and challenges of engaging in international business activities.
- Understand the role of cultural differences in international business.
- Analyze the impact of international trade agreements and regulations on international business.

Key Terms

- Cross-cultural communication
- Currency exchange rates
- Export
- Foreign direct investment (FDI)
- Free trade
- Globalization
- Import
- International business strategy
- International marketing
- International trade
- Multinational corporations (MNCs)

1.1. MEANING AND DEFINITION OF INTERNATIONAL BUSINESS

In recent decades, there has been a significant shift in the way countries produce and market goods and services, which has led to increased interdependence between countries. This shift has been driven by factors such as advances in transportation and communication technology, the liberalization of trade policies, and the rise of MNCs.

As a result of these changes, many countries that previously pursued self-reliance are now more dependent on others for the procurement and supply of goods and services. For example, many countries now import raw materials, components, and finished goods from other countries, and rely on international trade to support their economies.

In addition to increased trade, there has also been a rise in cross-border investments, with companies from one country investing in businesses in other countries. This has led to a more interconnected global economy, where countries are no longer isolated and must compete and collaborate with each other to succeed.

The development of communication technology and transportation infrastructure has been a key driver of the radical change in the way countries produce and market goods and services. Advances in communication technology, such as the internet, mobile phones, and social media, have made it easier for people to connect and communicate across borders. This has facilitated the exchange of ideas, information, and business transactions, making it easier for countries to trade with each other (Figure 1.1).

Figure 1.1. An illustration of international business.

Similarly, the development of faster and more efficient means of transportation, such as air travel and container shipping, has made it easier and cheaper for goods and people to move across borders. This has increased a country's ability to participate in global trade and supply chains, even if they are geographically distant from one another.

The increased interaction between countries has also been facilitated by improvements in infrastructure, such as the construction of ports, airports, and highways. This has made it easier to transport goods and people across borders, further promoting economic integration and interdependence.

The World Trade Organization (WTO) has been a significant contributor to the increased interactions and business relations among nations. The WTO was established in 1995 to promote free trade and reduce barriers to trade between countries. The WTO has helped to reduce tariffs and other trade barriers, making it easier for businesses to trade across borders.

In addition to the WTO, many countries have implemented economic reforms aimed at promoting greater international trade and investment. These reforms have included the liberalization of trade policies, the privatization of state-owned enterprises, and the deregulation of industries.

As a result of these changes, the obstacles to the cross-border movement of goods and people have substantially come down, and national economies are increasingly becoming borderless and integrated into the world economy. This has led to the development of a global village, where business is no longer restricted to the boundaries of the domestic country.

This has presented firms with numerous opportunities for growth and increased profits, as they can now access a larger market and take advantage of comparative advantages in other countries. However, it has also led to increased competition, as firms from different countries now compete in the same market. The reduction of obstacles to the cross-border movement of goods and people, along with the integration of national economies into the world economy, has led to the development of a global village.

This has presented firms with numerous opportunities for growth and increased profits, as they can now access larger markets and take advantage of comparative advantages in other countries. This has led to an increase in international business, as more and more firms seek to expand their operations beyond the boundaries of their domestic country.

The development of the global economy has brought both opportunities and challenges for businesses and individuals alike. It has enabled firms to access new markets and customers but has also increased competition and led to greater economic interdependence among countries.

1.1.1. Domestic vs. International Business

Domestic or national business refers to business transactions that take place within the geographical boundaries of a country. It involves the buying and selling of goods and services within the domestic market and is also referred to as internal business or home trade.

Domestic business can be conducted by both large and small firms and can take place across different industries and sectors. It is typically subject to domestic regulations and laws and can be influenced by domestic economic conditions such as inflation, interest rates, and consumer demand.

Examples of domestic business transactions include a consumer purchasing groceries from a local supermarket, a small business owner selling handmade crafts at a local market, and a large corporation buying raw materials from a domestic supplier.

While the domestic business may not involve the same level of complexity and risk as international business, it still plays a critical role in the overall economy of a country. Domestic businesses contribute to employment, economic growth, and the development of local communities.

International business refers to the manufacturing, trade, and other business activities that take place beyond the boundaries of one's own country. It involves the movement of goods and services, capital, personnel, technology, and intellectual property across national borders.

International business is typically conducted by firms of all sizes, ranging from small businesses to MNCs. It can involve a variety of activities, such as exporting and importing goods, establishing foreign subsidiaries or joint ventures (JVs), licensing technology or intellectual property to foreign firms, and participating in international trade agreements (Figure 1.2).

International business can present numerous challenges, including navigating complex regulatory frameworks, managing cultural differences, and dealing with exchange rate fluctuations and other economic risks. However, it also offers many opportunities for firms to access new markets, take advantage of comparative advantages in other countries, and tap into global networks of suppliers and customers.

Remember

The increased integration of national economies has led to greater competition among firms. As firms from different countries now compete in the same markets, they must innovate and improve their products and services to remain competitive.

Figure 1.2. Schematic representation of types of international business.

Most people think of international business as international trade. That's a very important point to make. International trade is a significant aspect of international business, but it is not the only one. In recent years, the scope of international business has indeed expanded to include a broader range of activities beyond just the import and export of goods.

For example, the international business now includes FDI, where a company sets up operations in a foreign country, such as opening a subsidiary or acquiring a local company. It can also involve licensing agreements, where a firm grants another company the right to use its intellectual property, or franchising, where a company allows a foreign partner to use its business model and brand.

International business can also involve the movement of people, such as when a company sends employees to work in a foreign country, or when a firm hires workers from different countries to work remotely.

In short, international business encompasses a wide range of activities beyond just international trade. It involves the movement of goods, services, people, capital, and ideas across national borders, and is a key driver of economic growth and development in the globalized world. Indeed, international business is a vast and diverse field that encompasses a range of activities beyond just the exchange of goods and services across borders. It includes FDI, licensing agreements, franchising, movement of people, and other activities that involve companies operating across national borders. The objective of international business is to help companies achieve their goals of growth and profitability by tapping into foreign markets and resources, and by creating a global presence that enables them to serve customers more effectively and efficiently.

1.1.2. Definition of International Business

There are various definitions of international business in the business literature. Some definitions focus on the activities involved, such as trade, investment, and production, while others emphasize the geographical scope of the business. Generally speaking, international business refers to any business activity that involves the crossing of national borders. This can include activities such as importing and exporting goods and services, investing in foreign markets, establishing JVs with foreign partners, and setting up subsidiaries or branches in other countries. The scope of international business can vary widely, from small-scale operations between two countries to large MNCs with a global presence. The increasing globalization of markets and the growth of digital technologies have further expanded the scope of international business, making it an increasingly important and complex field.

Here are some different definitions of international business by several authors:

- According to Charles Hill, international business refers to any commercial transaction that crosses the borders of two or more nations.
- According to Michael Czinkota and Ilkka Ronkainen, international business is defined as the performance of trade and investment activities by firms across national borders.
- According to John Daniels and Lee Radebaugh, international business refers to all commercial transactions, including sales, investments, and transportation of goods and services, that take place between two or more countries.
- According to Alan Rugman and Richard Hodgetts, international business involves the performance of business activities that involve exchanges across national borders, including trade, investment, and licensing.
- According to Richard M. Hodgetts, international business is a multidimensional concept that encompasses all forms of commercial transactions and interactions that take place between two or more countries.
- According to S. Tamer Cavusgil, international business involves the conduct of commercial transactions between firms that are based in

different countries and the coordination and management of these activities across national borders.

Different definitions of international business can focus on different aspects of the business activity and its geographical scope. The broadest definition of international business is any business activity that involves transactions across national borders, regardless of the organizational structure of the company. This definition can include both small and large firms that engage in cross-border trade, investment, or production.

On the other hand, a narrower definition of international business might focus on large MNCs that have operating units or subsidiaries in multiple countries. This definition emphasizes the complexity and scale of international business activities that involve significant investments, global supply chains, and diverse customer bases.

Did you get it?

In 1958 historian Hal Bridges finds that the most vehement and persistent controversy in business history has been that waged by the critics and defenders of the 'robber baron' concept of the American businessman.

However, there are also many hybrid forms of international business that fall between these two extremes. For example, JVs or strategic alliances with foreign partners may involve some managerial control of business activity in other countries, but may not involve full ownership or control of foreign operations.

Indeed, international business has become a major force in shaping the global economy and influencing political and social developments. With the growth of MNCs and the increasing globalization of markets, the impact of international business is felt in nearly every corner of the world. The study of international business has become an important field of inquiry for scholars, policymakers, and business practitioners alike, as it seeks to understand the complex interactions between different countries and the role of MNCs in shaping the global economy. Comparative business studies play an important role in this field, as they help to identify patterns and best practices across different countries and regions and provide insights into the challenges and opportunities of operating in a globalized world.

Foreign operations and comparative business are related fields of study but differ from international business in their focus. Foreign operations refer to domestic operations within a foreign country, while comparative business focuses on similarities and differences among countries and business systems. These fields of inquiry do not center on the special problems that arise when business activities cross national boundaries, unlike international business, which deals with issues such as potential conflicts between the nation-state and multinational firms.

Foreign operations and comparative business are focused on the domestic operations of businesses within a foreign country or the similarities and differences among countries and business systems, respectively. These fields of inquiry do not necessarily consider the special issues that arise when businesses operate across national boundaries, such as conflicts between the nation-state and MNCs. This is why international business is a distinct field of study with its own unique set of concerns and challenges.

1.2. EVOLUTION OF INTERNATIONAL BUSINESS

While international trade has been around for centuries, the growth of multinational companies is a relatively recent phenomenon. The post-World War II period, in particular, saw a significant expansion of national companies into international or multinational companies. This was driven by factors such as the liberalization of trade policies, advances in transportation and communication technologies, and the emergence of new markets in developing countries.

In the 1990s, globalization intensified even further with the rise of the internet and the increasing ease of global communication and collaboration. This led to a proliferation of new business models and a further blurring of national boundaries. Today, international business is a crucial component of the global economy, and it continues to evolve and adapt to new challenges and opportunities.

The term "international business" has been in use for much longer than two decades. It refers to any business activity that involves cross-border transactions, including international trade, foreign investment, and global supply chain management.

While it's true that the term "international marketing" came into use before "international business," the two terms refer to different aspects of cross-border business. International marketing refers specifically to the process of promoting and selling products and services in foreign markets, while international business encompasses a broader range of activities, including not only marketing but also production, finance, and logistics.

The term "export marketing," refers specifically to the process of selling goods and services in foreign markets. It is a subset of international marketing, which in turn is a subset of international business.

For example, when companies started exporting their products to far-off countries, they realized the need to adapt their marketing strategies to suit the cultural and economic differences of the target markets. This led to the evolution of the concept of international marketing, which involved customizing the marketing mix (product, price, promotion, and place) for each target market.

Eventually, companies began to expand their operations beyond just exporting and started establishing subsidiaries, JVs, and strategic alliances with foreign companies, leading to the emergence of international business as a distinct field.

As economies develop, they tend to move from exporting raw materials and basic goods to more value-added and sophisticated products and services. This is known as the product cycle theory, which suggests that countries tend to start with exporting goods that require abundant natural resources and low-skilled labor, and then gradually move towards producing and exporting more complex products that require higher-skilled labor, technology, and innovation. The export marketing efforts, as mentioned, play a crucial role in creating demand and expanding the market for these products.

This shift from just marketing products in foreign countries to producing them in foreign countries is often referred to as "FDI." Multinational companies began to invest in foreign countries to take advantage of lower labor costs, favorable tax policies, and other benefits. This allowed them to produce goods more efficiently and cost-effectively, and to better serve local markets. FDI has been an important driver of international business growth over the past few decades.

For example, Unilever established its subsidiary company in India, i.e., Hindustan Lever Limited (HLL). HLL produces its products in India and markets them in Bangladesh, Sri Lanka, Nepal, etc. The establishment of subsidiaries or JVs in foreign countries and the production of goods or services in those countries, followed by marketing those products in other foreign countries, is an example of the expansion of international trade into international marketing and eventually into international business. This trend has continued to grow in recent years, leading to an increase in the number of multinational companies and their global operations.

1.2.1. Timeline

- **Ancient Times:** Trading networks emerged along the Silk Road, connecting China, India, the Middle East, and Europe. Phoenician merchants conducted maritime trade in the Mediterranean Sea.
- **Middle Ages:** Trade between Europe and the Middle East expanded, including the import of silk, spices, and other luxury goods from the East. The Hanseatic League, a confederation of merchant guilds in Northern Europe, established trading posts and controlled maritime trade in the Baltic and North Seas.
- **Age of Exploration:** European nations began exploring and colonizing the Americas, Africa, and Asia, leading to the development of global trade networks. The Dutch East India Company and the British East

India Company were formed to trade with Asia.

- **Industrial Revolution:** The introduction of new manufacturing technologies and transportation systems enabled the mass production and distribution of goods. The growth of MNCs began with companies like Standard Oil, founded by John D. Rockefeller in 1870.
- **Post-World War II:** The Bretton Woods Agreement established a stable international monetary system and the General Agreement on Tariffs and Trade (GATT) facilitated the reduction of trade barriers. MNCs expanded rapidly, and international trade grew significantly.
- **Late 20th Century:** Globalization accelerated, driven by advancements in technology, transportation, and communication. The rise of emerging markets in Asia and Latin America created new opportunities for international business. The establishment of the WTO in 1995 further facilitated global trade.

According to year:

- **1492:** Christopher Columbus sets sail and discovers the New World, opening up new trade routes and opportunities for international business.
- **1600:** The British East India Company is formed and becomes one of the earliest and most successful MNCs, involved in trade and commerce across Asia.
- **1815:** The Congress of Vienna is held to redraw the political map of Europe after the Napoleonic Wars. The resulting political stability in Europe leads to increased trade and economic growth, laying the foundation for modern international business.
- **1870s-1914:** The "first wave" of globalization takes place, characterized by the spread of industrialization and trade across Europe, North America, and Asia. Advances in transportation and communication technology make it easier and faster to conduct international business.
- **1914–1945:** The "interwar period" and World War II disrupt international trade and business, as protectionist policies and war itself makes it difficult to conduct cross-border commerce.
- **1945–1970s:** The "second wave" of globalization takes place, characterized by the reconstruction of Europe and Japan after World War II, the rise of the United States as a dominant economic power, and the spread of trade and investment across the world.
- **1970s–Present:** The world economy becomes increasingly integrated and interdependent, as technology, deregulation, and globalization enable businesses to operate across borders more easily than ever before. The rise of China and other emerging markets creates new opportunities and challenges for international business.

1.3. REASONS FOR THE EMERGENCE OF INTERNATIONAL BUSINESS

The unequal distribution of natural resources and differences in productivity levels are among the main reasons why countries engage in international trade and business. Each country has its own unique set of resources, capabilities, and expertise, which gives it a comparative advantage in producing certain goods or services more efficiently and cost-effectively than other countries.

By engaging in international trade and business, countries can specialize in producing the goods and services they are best at, and exchange them with other countries for the products they need but cannot produce as efficiently themselves. This can lead to increased efficiency, lower prices, and a wider range of products available for consumers.

In addition to natural resources and productivity, other factors that drive international business include differences in consumer preferences, technology, government policies, and currency exchange rates. All of these factors can impact a country's competitiveness in the global marketplace and influence the types and volumes of trade and investment flows between countries.

The availability of various factors of production such as labor, capital, and raw materials can differ among nations, which can impact their ability to produce goods and services efficiently and cost-effectively. For example, some countries may have an abundance of natural resources, such as oil or minerals, while others may have a highly skilled workforce or advanced technology.

Labor productivity and production costs can also vary among nations due to various socio-economic, geographical, and political factors. For example, countries with high levels of education and training for their workforce may have higher labor productivity, while countries with lower levels of education and training may have lower productivity. Similarly, countries with favorable government policies, such as low taxes or subsidies, may have lower production costs than those with less favorable policies.

These differences in labor productivity, production costs, and other factors of production can create comparative advantages for countries in producing certain goods and services. By specializing in the production of goods and services that they can produce efficiently and cost-effectively, countries can benefit from international trade and business. They can export their specialized goods and services to other countries and import the goods and services that they cannot produce efficiently themselves.

Due to the differences in labor productivity, production costs, and other factors of production among nations, it is not uncommon to find one particular country in a better position to produce goods and services of higher quality and/

or at lower costs than other nations. This phenomenon is known as comparative advantage and is a key driver of international trade and business. Each country has its own unique set of resources, capabilities, and expertise, which gives it a comparative advantage in producing certain goods and services more efficiently and cost-effectively than other countries. By specializing in the production of goods and services in which they have a comparative advantage, countries can increase their efficiency and lower their costs of production, leading to increased competitiveness in the global marketplace.

For example, a country with abundant natural resources such as oil may have a comparative advantage in producing oil-based products, while a country with a highly skilled workforce may have a comparative advantage in producing high-tech products. By specializing in these areas, each country can benefit from international trade and exchange goods and services with other nations, resulting in mutual gains from trade.

Countries trade with each other and engage in international business because each country has its own unique set of resources, capabilities, and expertise, which gives it a comparative advantage in producing certain goods and services more efficiently and cost-effectively than other countries.

By specializing in the production of goods and services in which they have a comparative advantage, countries can increase their efficiency and lower their costs of production, leading to increased competitiveness in the global marketplace. This allows them to produce certain goods and services more effectively and efficiently at home while procuring the rest through trade with other countries that can produce those goods and services at lower costs.

This creates mutual gains from trade, as each country can benefit from the exchange of goods and services with other countries, resulting in increased efficiency, lower prices, and a wider range of products available for consumers. Therefore, international business is an important aspect of the global economy, as it allows countries to specialize in the production of goods and services in which they have a comparative advantage, leading to increased efficiency and economic growth.

The principle of territorial division of labor is applicable both at the domestic and international levels. Just as states or regions within a country tend to specialize in the production of goods and services for which they are best suited, countries also tend to specialize in the production of goods and services in which they have a comparative advantage.

Geographical specialization is a natural outcome of the differences in factors of production, labor productivity, and production costs among countries. Each country tends to specialize in the production of goods and services in which it has a comparative advantage, based on its unique set of resources, capabilities, and expertise. This allows countries to increase their efficiency and lower their costs of production, leading to increased competitiveness in the global marketplace.

For example, some countries are rich in natural resources, such as oil or minerals, and tend to specialize in the production of commodities based on these resources. Other countries may have a highly skilled workforce or advanced technology and tend to specialize in the production of high-tech products or services. By specializing in the production of goods and services in which they have a comparative advantage, countries can increase their efficiency and competitiveness, leading to economic growth and development.

International business is therefore a natural outcome of geographical specialization and the territorial division of labor at the international level. Countries engage in international trade and exchange of goods and services based on their comparative advantages, leading to mutual gains from trade and economic growth for all countries involved.

Developing countries that are labor-abundant tend to specialize in the production and export of labor-intensive goods such as garments, footwear, and textiles. Since they lack capital and technology, they often import machinery and equipment from developed nations that are more advanced in the production of capital-intensive goods.

The developed nations, in turn, are able to produce capital-intensive goods more efficiently due to their advanced technology, skilled workforce, and access to capital. They tend to specialize in the production and export of capital-intensive goods such as machinery, equipment, and high-tech products.

By engaging in trade and exchange of goods and services based on their comparative advantages, both developed and developing countries can benefit from the exchange. Developing countries can access the capital and technology they need to develop their industries and increase their efficiency, while developed countries can access the lower-cost labor and resources they need to produce goods more cost-effectively. This leads to mutual gains from trade and economic growth for all countries involved. However, it is important to ensure that trade is conducted in a fair and balanced manner, with appropriate policies in place to protect workers' rights, the environment, and the interests of all parties involved. Firms engage in international business not only to import goods and services at lower prices from other countries but also to export goods and services to other countries where they can fetch better prices for their products. This allows firms to expand their customer base and increase their revenue and profitability.

In addition to price considerations, there are several other benefits that nations and firms can derive from international business. These include:

- **Access to New Markets:** International business allows firms to access new markets and customers, which can help to increase their sales and revenue.
- **Diversification:** International business can help firms to diversify their operations and reduce their reliance on a single market or product. This can help to reduce risks and increase stability.
- **Access to Resources:** International business can provide firms with access to new resources, such as raw materials, labor, and technology, which can help to increase their efficiency and competitiveness.
- **Learning Opportunities:** International business provides firms with opportunities to learn from other cultures, business practices, and technologies, which can help them to improve their operations and products.
- **Brand Building:** International business can help firms to build their brand and reputation in new markets, which can help to increase their competitiveness and customer loyalty.

Let's discuss some other benefits that nations and firms can derive from engaging in international business:

- **Increased Economic Growth:** International business can stimulate economic growth by increasing exports, creating new jobs, and generating more revenue for businesses and governments. This can lead to higher standards of living and greater prosperity for citizens.
- **Access to Larger Markets:** International business provides firms with access to larger markets, which can help to increase sales and revenue. This is particularly important for small and medium-sized enterprises (SMEs), which may struggle to compete in their domestic markets.
- **Lower Costs:** International business can help firms to lower their production costs by accessing cheaper inputs such as raw materials, labor, and technology from other countries.
- **Improved Competitiveness:** International business can help firms to improve their competitiveness by exposing them to new technologies, business practices, and ideas. This can help firms to innovate and improve their products and processes.
- **Risk Diversification:** International business can help firms to diversify their risks by expanding their operations into multiple markets. This can help to reduce their dependence on any single market and protect them from economic downturns or other risks.
- **Improved Diplomatic Relations:** International business can help to improve diplomatic relations between nations by promoting cooperation and collaboration. This can help to reduce tensions and promote peace and stability.

Engaging in international business can bring many benefits to nations and firms. However, it is important to recognize that there are also risks and challenges associated with international business, such as currency fluctuations, political instability, and cultural differences. Therefore, it is important for nations and firms to carefully evaluate the costs and benefits of engaging in international business, and to develop strategies to manage risks and maximize benefits.

1.4. BENEFITS OF INTERNATIONAL BUSINESS

Several benefits of international business are discussed below (Figure 1.3).

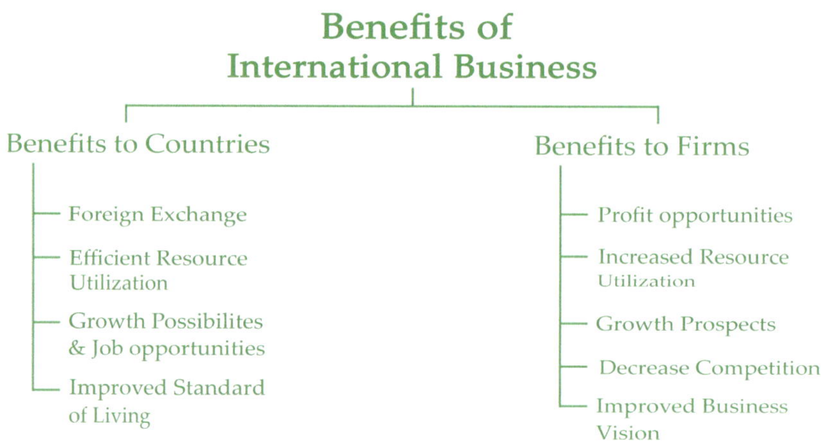

Figure 1.3. *Benefits of international business.*

1.4.1. Benefits to Countries

International business brings many benefits to countries, including:

- **Foreign Exchange:** International business can help countries earn foreign exchange through exports of goods and services, which can then be used to import capital goods, technology, and other products from foreign countries. This can contribute to the economic growth and development of the country by facilitating access to new markets, resources, and technologies.
- **More Efficient Resource Utilization:** International business is based on the theory of comparative advantage, which suggests that countries should specialize in producing goods and services in which they have a lower opportunity cost compared to other countries, and then trade those

goods with other countries. This will lead to a more efficient allocation of resources, increased overall global output, and higher standards of living for people in all participating countries.

By focusing on producing what they can produce more efficiently, countries can use their limited resources to their fullest potential and maximize their productivity. By trading with other countries, they can acquire goods and services that they may not be able to produce efficiently themselves, which can benefit their consumers and businesses. International business also promotes competition, which can drive innovation, improve efficiency, and lead to better quality products and services. Additionally, it can foster cultural understanding and promote peaceful relations between nations by encouraging communication and collaboration between people from different countries.

- **Growth Possibilities and Job Opportunities:** External trade can increase a country's manufacturing capacity and provide opportunities to supply goods to other countries, which can help to increase production levels and contribute to economic growth. When a country is able to export its goods, it can generate revenue and increase its GDP, which can improve its standard of living.

Increased production and external trade can also lead to job creation, as companies may need to hire more workers to meet the increased demand for goods and services. This can have a positive impact on the economy, as it can help to reduce unemployment rates and increase overall prosperity.

However, it is important to note that the benefits of international business may not be evenly distributed across all sectors or regions within a country. Certain industries or regions may benefit more from international trade, while others may experience negative effects. Therefore, it is important for governments to ensure that the benefits of international business are shared equitably and that policies are in place to address any negative impacts on workers or communities.

- **Improved Standard of Living:** International business allows individuals to consume goods and services from other countries, which can improve their standard of living. By importing goods and services that are not available or not produced efficiently domestically, individuals and businesses can have access to a wider range of products at competitive prices. This can lead to a higher standard of living, as people can enjoy greater choices and better quality products and services.

In addition, international business can lead to improvements in technology and innovation, which can further enhance the quality of goods and services available to consumers. By sharing knowledge and expertise across borders, businesses can develop new products and technologies that can improve people's lives.

1.4.2. Benefits to Firms

- **Profit Opportunities:** International business can indeed be more profitable than local business in certain situations. One of the main reasons for this is that businesses can take advantage of price differences between domestic and international markets.

For example, if a business produces goods or services that are in high demand in other countries, and if the prices for those goods or services are higher in those countries than in the domestic market, the business can sell its products at a higher price and make a larger profit. This is known as price arbitrage.

Additionally, international business can provide opportunities to access larger markets, which can increase sales and revenue. By expanding into new markets, businesses can also benefit from economies of scale, which can help to lower production costs and increase profitability.

Though, it is important to note that international business can also be more complex and risky than a local business, as it involves dealing with different cultures, languages, laws, and regulations. Businesses must be prepared to invest time, resources, and expertise into understanding and adapting to these differences in order to be successful in international markets.

- **Increased Resource Utilization:** Many companies anticipate international growth and seek to expand their business by setting up production capabilities in foreign markets. This can enable them to better utilize their excess resources and take advantage of opportunities in new markets.

By setting up production capabilities in foreign markets, companies can take advantage of lower costs of labor, raw materials, or other factors of production. This can lead to cost savings and increased profitability. Additionally, producing goods locally can help companies to overcome trade barriers and regulatory hurdles, such as tariffs or quotas, which can limit access to certain markets.

Setting up production capabilities in foreign markets can also help companies to better understand local markets, cultures, and consumer preferences. By being closer to their customers, companies can respond more quickly to changing market conditions and develop more effective marketing strategies. On the other hand, setting up production capabilities in foreign markets can also be challenging and costly. Companies must be prepared to invest significant resources into research, development, and logistics to ensure that their production facilities are efficient, cost-effective, and comply with local laws and regulations.

- **Growth Prospects:** When demand falls or the domestic market reaches saturation point, businesses may explore opportunities to expand internationally in order to sustain growth and increase their market share. By expanding into new international markets, businesses can tap into new sources of demand and increase their growth potential significantly.

Expanding internationally can also help businesses to diversify their revenue streams and reduce their exposure to domestic market fluctuations. By operating in multiple international markets, businesses can spread their risk and reduce their dependence on any one market.

In addition, international expansion can help businesses to access new technologies, talent, and resources that may not be available domestically.

- **Decrease Competition:** Fierce domestic competition can motivate businesses to explore opportunities to expand into overseas markets in order to achieve success and required growth. By expanding into international markets, businesses can tap into new sources of demand and reduce their dependence on the domestic market.

Furthermore, expanding internationally can also help businesses to gain a competitive advantage over their domestic rivals. By offering unique products or services that are not available domestically, businesses can differentiate themselves from their competitors and gain market share.

International expansion can also help businesses to leverage economies of scale and reduce their costs of production. By producing goods and services in larger volumes, businesses can benefit from lower production costs and achieve higher profit margins.

- **Improved Business Vision:** For many firms, their existence, and goodwill depend on their ability to expand their worldwide business. The desire to expand and diversify, as well as to take advantage of the strategic advantages of internationalization, is often expressed in the desire to become more international.

International expansion can provide firms with access to new markets, customers, and revenue streams, as well as help them to diversify their operations and reduce their risk. By operating in multiple international markets, firms can spread their risk and reduce their dependence on any one market.

International expansion can also help firms to access new technologies, talent, and resources that may not be available domestically. This can lead to increased innovation, improved product quality, and enhanced competitiveness in both domestic and international markets.

Moreover, expanding internationally can also help firms to build their brand and reputation globally, and increase their ability to attract international partners, investors, and customers.

1.5. FEATURES OF INTERNATIONAL BUSINESS

Some of the key features of international business are shown in Figure 1.4.

Figure 1.4. *Features of international business.*

1.5.1. Large Scale Operations

International business often involves large-scale production and marketing activities. Companies that engage in international business typically have operations in multiple countries and sell their products or services in multiple markets around the world.

In many cases, companies will first sell their goods or services in their home country or local market. If they have excess production capacity or if demand in their local market is limited, they may then export their products to other countries where demand is higher.

To facilitate these operations, companies may need to establish distribution channels and logistics networks in multiple countries, and they may need to adapt their products or marketing strategies to meet the needs and preferences of customers in different markets.

1.5.2. Integration of Economies

International business often involves the integration of economies across multiple countries. Companies that engage in international business may use finance, labor, and infrastructure from different countries to design, produce, and sell their products or services. For example, a multinational company may obtain financing from banks in one country, hire workers from another country, and use infrastructure such as factories or transportation systems in a third country. The company may then design its products in one country, produce components in multiple countries, and assemble the final product in yet another country. The finished product may then be sold in many different countries around the world.

This kind of global integration can bring a number of benefits, such as lower costs, access to specialized resources, and the ability to tap into new markets. However, it also requires careful management and coordination to ensure that different operations and activities are aligned and working together effectively.

1.5.3. Dominated by Developed Countries and MNCs

It is true that multinational companies based in developed countries such as the United States, Europe, and Japan play a dominant role in international business. These companies often have access to greater financial resources, advanced technology, and other advantages that can give them a competitive edge in the global marketplace.

However, it is also worth noting that developing countries are playing an increasingly important role in international business. Many developing countries have been experiencing rapid economic growth in recent years, which has created new opportunities for businesses to expand into these markets. Moreover, advances in technology and communications have made it easier for companies in developing countries to connecting with customers and partners around the world.

In addition, there are a number of multilateral organizations and agreements that have been established to promote international trade and business opportunities for developing countries. For example, the WTO provides a forum for member countries to negotiate and enforce rules for international trade, with the goal of creating a more level playing field for businesses around the world.

1.5.4. Benefits to Participating Countries

International business can bring benefits to all participating countries, although the distribution of these benefits may not always be equal. Developed countries may be better positioned to capture a larger share of the benefits, given their greater resources and expertise in global markets. However, developing countries can also gain from international business in a number of ways.

One of the primary benefits that developing countries can gain from international business is access to foreign capital and technology. Foreign companies may invest in developing countries, which can help to spur economic growth and development. This investment can also bring new technology and expertise, which can help to modernize industries and improve productivity.

International business can also create new employment opportunities in developing countries. This can be particularly important in regions where traditional industries may be in decline, or where there are limited opportunities for workers. By attracting foreign investment and expanding export markets, international business can help to create new jobs and spur economic growth.

As a final point, international business can also help to promote greater economic integration and cooperation between countries. By increasing trade and investment flows, international business can help to create closer ties between countries and foster greater understanding and collaboration on issues that extend beyond economic affairs.

1.5.5. Keen Competition

Developing countries may face challenges in competing with developed countries due to differences in factors such as technology, infrastructure, and access to capital. However, developing countries can also gain a competitive advantage by specializing in producing goods and services that they can produce more efficiently and effectively, as well as by implementing policies that encourage foreign investment and trade. Additionally, international organizations such as the WTO can help level the playing field and promote fair trade practices.

1.5.6. The Special Role of Science and Technology

The international business facilitates the transfer of technology from developed countries to developing countries. This transfer of technology can enable developing countries to improve their production methods and increase their productivity, leading to faster economic growth and development. In addition, international business provides opportunities for developing countries to acquire new technologies and knowledge, which can be adapted and applied to their own unique circumstances. This can lead to innovation and improvements in products and services, as well as in manufacturing and distribution processes.

1.5.7. International Restrictions

An international business faces various restrictions and barriers that can limit the flow of capital, technology, and goods between countries. These restrictions can take the form of tariffs, quotas, embargoes, trade barriers, and foreign exchange controls. Governments may use these restrictions to protect their domestic industries and markets, but they can also create difficulties for international businesses by limiting their ability to expand into new markets, import necessary inputs or technologies, or compete effectively against domestic firms.

International organizations such as the WTO work to promote free trade and reduce trade barriers between countries, but the issue remains complex and politically sensitive.

1.5.8. Sensitive Nature

International business is influenced by various external factors such as changes in economic policies, technological advancements, political environment, cultural differences, etc. These factors can have a significant impact on the operations and profitability of international businesses. Hence, it is important for companies to conduct thorough market research and analysis to stay informed about any changes in the external environment and adapt their business strategies accordingly. Failure to do so can lead to loss of market share, decreased profitability, and even failure of the business. Therefore, companies operating in international markets must be vigilant and agile in responding to changes in the environment.

1.5.9. Accurate and Timely Information

Accurate and timely information is crucial for the success of the international business. This includes information about the economic, political, and social conditions in different countries, as well as information about competitors, suppliers, and customers. International businesses must be able to gather, analyze, and interpret data from a variety of sources, including government reports, market research studies, and industry publications, in order to make informed decisions about where to invest, what products to sell, and how to market their goods and services. Inaccurate or incomplete information can lead to poor decisions, which can result in financial losses and damage to the company's reputation.

1.5.10. Segments of Their Markets Based on the Geographic Market Segment

International business houses do segment their markets based on geographic market segments. This is because different countries and regions have unique characteristics and cultural differences that affect consumer behavior and preferences. Therefore, businesses need to tailor their marketing strategies to meet the specific needs and preferences of each geographic market segment. For example, a product that may be popular in one country may not be popular in another country due to cultural differences or preferences. By segmenting the market geographically, businesses can effectively target their marketing efforts and increase their chances of success in different regions.

1.6. SCOPE OF INTERNATIONAL BUSINESS ACTIVITIES

International businesses operate in multiple countries and conduct transactions of goods and services on a global scale. They are often large in size and have a significant impact on the economies of the countries where they operate. By earning foreign currency, they contribute to the balance of payments of their home country and provide employment opportunities to a large number of people. International business involves the study of the unique challenges and opportunities that arise when a business operates across borders. These challenges can include dealing with different legal systems, currency exchange rates, cultural differences, and varying economic conditions. Successful international business operations require a deep understanding of these factors and the ability to adapt and navigate complex international environments.

International businesses are indeed dominated by MNCs from developed countries such as the United States, Japan, and European nations. However, there are also MNCs from developing countries such as China, India, and Brazil that are increasingly becoming major players in international business.

International businesses do indeed employ highly skilled workers and have access to the best technological facilities. However, the salaries and benefits of their employees can vary widely depending on factors such as location, industry, and the level of skills and expertise required. Additionally, some international businesses have faced criticism for exploiting workers in developing countries and not providing fair wages or working conditions.

For example, Hewlett-Packard (HP) and Microsoft are both MNCs with operations in many countries around the world, making them examples of international businesses. HP is a technology company that specializes in personal computers, printers, and related products and services, while Microsoft is a software company known for its Windows operating system, Office software suite, and other applications. Both companies are headquartered in the United States but have a global presence with offices, manufacturing facilities, and distribution channels in many countries.

The scope of international businesses include:

- Importing And Exporting
- Licensing
- Franchising

- Contract Manufacturing/Outsourcing
- Joint Ventures
- Foreign Direct Investment
- Growth Opportunities
- Multinational Corporations
- Integration Of Economies

Did you get it?

The WTO officially commenced on 1 January 1995 signed by 123 nations on 15 April 1994 in Marrakesh at the end of the Uruguay Round negotiations, replacing the General Agreement on Tariffs and Trade (GATT), which was established in 1947.

1.6.1. Importing and Exporting

Importing and exporting are important activities in international business. Importing refers to the process of bringing goods or services from a foreign country into a domestic market while exporting refers to the process of selling goods or services produced in a domestic market to foreign countries. Both activities require knowledge of international trade laws, tariffs, exchange rates, and cultural differences. Companies engage in importing and exporting to gain access to larger markets, increase profitability, and acquire new sources of supply or production.

1.6.2. Licensing

Licensing is indeed another scope of international business. Licensing is a contractual agreement between a company (licensor) that owns a technology or trademark and another company (licensee) that wants to use that technology or trademark. The licensee pays the licensor a fee for the right to use the technology or trademark. This allows the licensee to enter the international market with a minimum investment in research and development (R&D) or marketing. It is a popular strategy for companies looking to expand their global reach.

1.6.3. Franchising

Franchising is a popular method for companies to expand globally as it allows them to use the expertise and resources of local partners while maintaining control over the brand and product quality. It also provides a low-risk entry into international markets for franchisees, as they benefit from an established brand and business model. Many companies such as KFC, McDonald's, and Holiday Inn are good examples. Franchising allows companies to expand their brand and reach new markets without having to invest heavily in new infrastructure or personnel. It also allows local entrepreneurs to benefit from an established brand and business model, while still maintaining some degree of independence and control over their operations. This can be a win-win situation for both the franchisor and the franchisee.

1.6.4. Contract Manufacturing/Outsourcing

Outsourcing is a common practice in various industries, including the clothing industry. Outsourcing enables companies to lower their production costs and increase their profit margins. However, it also has some potential drawbacks, such as the loss of jobs in the domestic market and dependence on foreign suppliers. Nonetheless, outsourcing remains an important scope of international business.

Contract manufacturing and outsourcing are common strategies used by companies to reduce costs and increase efficiency in their operations. By outsourcing manufacturing or services to foreign companies, companies can take advantage of lower labor costs, favorable tax policies, and other benefits in those countries. This can lead to cost savings, higher profits, and improved competitiveness in the global market. For instance, India has become a center for software development for many American companies.

1.6.5. Joint Ventures

JVs are a popular way for companies to enter foreign markets and share the risks and rewards of the venture with a local partner. In a JV, two or more companies come together to form a new entity, sharing ownership, control, and profits. This can be particularly useful in situations where a foreign company lacks the local knowledge, contacts, or infrastructure necessary to operate effectively in a new market. By partnering with a local company, the foreign firm can gain access to valuable resources and expertise, while the local partner can benefit from the foreign company's technology, management skills, and marketing savvy.

1.6.6. Foreign Direct Investment

Foreign Direct Investment (FDI) refers to the investment made by a company or an individual in a foreign country, usually in the form of establishing new operations or acquiring an existing business. FDI is a major component of international business and plays a significant role in global economic development. It allows companies to expand their business operations beyond their domestic borders, access new markets, take advantage of lower labor and production costs, and benefit from favorable tax and regulatory environments.

1.6.7. Growth Opportunities

International businesses can bring about growth opportunities for both the home country and the host country. For the home country, international business provides an opportunity for businesses to expand beyond their domestic market, access new customers and markets, and diversify their revenue streams. For the host country, foreign investment by multinational companies can bring about job creation, transfer of technology, and an increase in economic activity. It can also help to develop local industries and infrastructure, as well as enhance the country's competitiveness in the global market.

1.6.8. Multinational Corporations

MNCs are companies that have operations in multiple countries and engage in international business activities such as importing, exporting, FDI, licensing, franchising, and JVs. They are often large and powerful companies that have the ability to adapt to different cultural and economic environments, and they play an important role in the global economy.

1.6.9. Integration of Economies

International businesses create employment opportunities in the host countries, contribute to technological advancements, and facilitate the transfer of knowledge and skills between countries. They also generate foreign exchange earnings for the host country through exports and foreign investments. Furthermore, international businesses promote competition and innovation, which leads to improved quality of goods and services and lower prices for consumers.

Companies like Nike and Timberland often source raw materials from different countries and then manufacture their products in factories located in other countries where labor and production costs are lower. These products are then exported and sold to various other countries, including their home country. This enables these companies to take advantage of the different strengths and resources that different countries offer and also allows them to reach a global market.

1.7. INTERNATIONAL BUSINESS VS. DOMESTIC BUSINESS

Conducting and managing international business operations is indeed more complex than domestic business operations due to several reasons such as:

1. **Differences in Political and Legal Systems**: Political systems and

legal frameworks differ significantly from country to country. A company must abide by the rules and regulations of each country it operates, and these rules may vary widely.

2. **Cultural and Social Differences**: The cultural and social differences between countries can affect the way business is conducted, including communication styles, business etiquette, and values.
3. **Economic Differences**: Economic systems vary across countries, with different levels of development, infrastructure, and access to resources. Economic differences also affect currency exchange rates, which can impact the cost of doing business.
4. **Language Barriers**: Communication is crucial in business, but language barriers can make it challenging to communicate effectively with customers, suppliers, and other stakeholders in different countries.
5. **Supply Chain Complexities**: Supply chain management becomes more complicated when dealing with international markets, especially when dealing with multiple suppliers and distributors across different countries.

Due to these factors, companies need to develop different strategies for international business operations than domestic business operations. They need to conduct extensive research, understand local laws and regulations, and develop a strong understanding of the local culture to be successful in international markets.

Companies that operate internationally must be able to adapt to the local environment, including political, social, cultural, and economic factors. This requires a deep understanding of the target market, as well as the ability to tailor business strategies and plans to meet the unique needs and preferences of local consumers. For example, a product that sells well in one country may not be as successful in another due to differences in cultural preferences, regulatory requirements, or competitive landscape. Therefore, companies must be willing to invest time and resources in market research and product development to ensure that their offerings are well-suited to the target market.

Key aspects in respect of which domestic and international businesses differ from each other are discussed below:

- **Nationality of Buyers and Sellers:** In international business, buyers and sellers may come from different countries with different cultural, legal, and economic backgrounds. This can create additional challenges in terms of communication, negotiation, and understanding of business practices. Companies must be aware of and adapt to these differences in order to effectively do business in international markets. This often involves hiring staff or working with local partners who have a better understanding of the local business culture and customs.

Language barriers, differences in cultural values and business practices, and varying legal and regulatory frameworks can all make it challenging for participants in international business deals to communicate effectively and understand each other's needs and expectations. As a result, cross-cultural communication and negotiation skills are often essential for success in international business.

- **Nationality of Other Stakeholders:** In international business, stakeholders such as employees, suppliers, shareholders/partners, and the general public come from diverse backgrounds and cultures. This makes decision-making more complex as the values, norms, and expectations of these stakeholders can vary significantly across different countries. Business firms have to take into account these diverse perspectives and find ways to balance them while making decisions. Failure to do so can result in misunderstandings, conflicts, and even business failure. Therefore, effective cross-cultural communication and understanding are essential for the success of international businesses.
- **Mobility of Factors of Production:** Different countries have their own policies and regulations with regard to foreign investment, employment, and business operations. This can further complicate the movement of factors like labor and capital across borders. In some countries, foreign investors may face restrictions on the amount of equity they can hold in a company or may be required to partner with a local company. Similarly, the employment of foreign workers may require specific permits or visas, which can be difficult to obtain. All these factors can make it more challenging for international businesses to mobilize factors of production across countries.
- **Customer Heterogeneity Across Markets:** Customer heterogeneity refers to the differences in customer preferences, behavior, and needs across different markets. It is an important consideration for companies engaging in international business as they need to adapt their products and marketing strategies to suit the specific requirements of the target markets.

  For example, McDonald's is a fast-food chain that operates in many countries around the world. While the core menu items like the Big Mac and fries are the same in all countries, the company adapts its menu to suit local tastes and preferences. In India, for example, McDonald's offers the McAloo Tikki burger, which is a vegetarian burger made with a spicy potato patty. This product is tailored to the Indian market where many people are vegetarian. Similarly, in Japan, McDonald's offers a teriyaki burger which is adapted to suit local tastes. This is just one example of how companies need to adapt their products to suit the preferences of different markets. Customer heterogeneity is a key consideration for international businesses as it can have a significant impact on the success or failure of their operations in different countries.

- **Differences in Business Systems and Practices:** Countries have their unique socio-economic and cultural backgrounds that shape their business systems and practices. These differences may include legal and regulatory frameworks, taxation policies, labor laws, financial systems, communication infrastructure, and market structures. International businesses need to adapt their operations to these different systems and practices if they want to succeed in foreign markets. This requires a deep understanding of the local market conditions and the ability to tailor business strategies accordingly.

  For example, the business practices in Japan are vastly different from those in the United States. In Japan, business decisions are based on long-term relationships and group consensus, while in the US, decisions are more individualistic and can be based on on a short-term business horizon. Similarly, in some countries, bribery and corruption may be common practices, while in others, such practices are strictly enforced against. The differences in business systems and practices can also impact the way companies structure their organizations and manage their employees. For instance, in some countries, labor laws and regulations may be more restrictive than in others, which can impact hiring and compensation practices.

- **Political System and Risks:** Political factors in international business can be much more complex and challenging compared to domestic business. In international business, a company has to deal with the political environment of different countries and regions, each with its own political system, policies, regulations, and cultural nuances. Political instability, changes in government policies, and differences in political ideologies can significantly affect the operations and profitability of an international business. For instance, a sudden change in government policies on import or export tariffs can adversely affect a company's supply chain or pricing strategy. Similarly, political risks such as expropriation, nationalization, terrorism, and war can threaten the existence and growth of an international business.

  A major problem with a foreign country's political environment is a tendency among nations to favor products and services originating in their own countries over those coming from other countries. This is commonly known as protectionism, where governments use policies such as tariffs, quotas, and regulations to give an advantage to domestic businesses over foreign competitors. Protectionism can make it difficult for foreign firms to compete in the local market, as they face higher costs and barriers to entry. It can also lead to trade disputes and tensions between countries. To overcome protectionist measures, firms need to carefully study the local market and regulatory environment, and devise strategies that comply with local laws and regulations while remaining competitive.

- **Business Regulations and Policies:** Business regulations and policies in domestic and international business differ significantly. Domestic business regulations and policies are governed by the laws of the home country, and businesses have to comply with them. In contrast, international business is governed by various laws, policies, and regulations of the host country, as well as the home country. The home country's regulations and policies also play a significant role in international business operations.

  Domestic business regulations and policies are designed to ensure fair competition, protect consumer rights, and ensure environmental and social sustainability. They cover various aspects such as product safety and labeling, labor laws, taxes, trade policies, and environmental regulations. Compliance with these regulations and policies is mandatory for businesses.

  In contrast, international business regulations and policies can vary significantly across countries. Businesses have to comply with the regulations and policies of the host country, which can be different from those of the home country. These regulations and policies can include trade restrictions, tariffs, quotas, labor laws, environmental regulations, and investment policies. Businesses need to be aware of these regulations and policies and ensure compliance to operate smoothly in international markets.

  Moreover, international business regulations and policies are subject to frequent changes, which can make it difficult for businesses to keep up with them. These changes can have a significant impact on the operations and profitability of businesses in the international markets.

- **Currency Used in Business Transactions:** International business transactions involve the use of different currencies, which can lead to currency exchange rate risk. The exchange rates between currencies can fluctuate rapidly, leading to a significant impact on the cost of goods and services. International businesses must carefully consider exchange rate risk when pricing their products or services and consider implementing strategies to hedge against currency fluctuations. These strategies may include the use of forward contracts, currency options, or other financial instruments that provide protection against exchange rate risk.

1.8. APPROACHES TO INTERNATIONAL BUSINESS

The four approaches to international business were proposed by Douglas Wind and Raymond P. Pelmutter in their article "The Emergence of the Global Factory" published in Harvard Business Review in 1982.

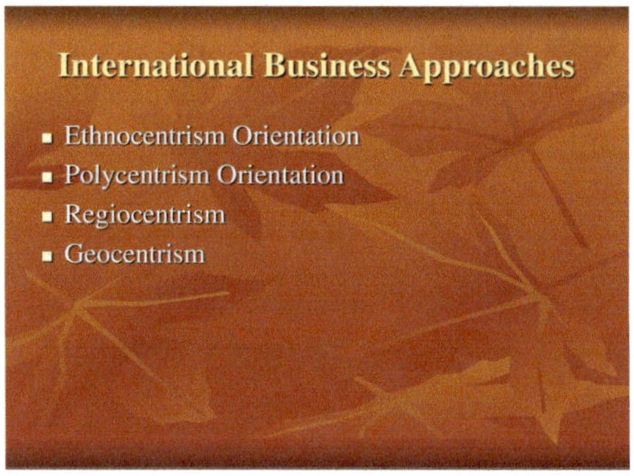

The four approaches are:

- Ethnocentric Approach;
- Polycentric Approach;
- Regiocentric Approach; and
- Geocentric Approach.

1.8.1. Ethnocentric Approach

The ethnocentric approach to international business is a domestic-oriented approach where companies formulate strategies, product designs, and operations based on the norms and practices of their home country. In this approach, the company's focus is on exporting the same products and services designed for the domestic market to foreign countries. The company views its home country's practices and norms as superior and adapts them to the foreign market.

1.8.2. Polycentric Approach

The polycentric approach is an international business strategy where a company adapts its products, services, and management practices to meet the needs and preferences of the local markets where it operates. In this approach, the company gives more autonomy to its foreign subsidiaries, and decision-making power is largely delegated to local managers. The company also hires host-country nationals to fill top management positions and key positions. The Polycentric Approach recognizes the diversity of local markets and allows for greater local customization, leading to higher levels of customer satisfaction. It also reduces cultural barriers, as local managers understand the local language, customs, and business practices. However, it may result in a lack of coordination between headquarters and subsidiaries and may limit the transfer of knowledge and skills across borders. It may also lead to the duplication of efforts and the inability to achieve economies of scale.

1.8.3. Regiocentric Approach

The regiocentric approach is a strategy in international business where a company groups its operations and resources by region rather than by country. In this approach, the company considers a region as a single market and tailors its products, services, and marketing strategies to the needs and preferences of that region. The regiocentric approach combines the benefits of both the geocentric and polycentric approaches while minimizing their drawbacks.

For example, a company that operates in the Asia-Pacific region may create a regional management team that is responsible for developing and implementing strategies that are specific to the region. This team may be made up of executives from different countries in the region who have a deep understanding of the local market conditions and cultural differences. The company may also develop products and marketing strategies that are customized for the region, rather than trying to apply a one-size-fits-all approach across all countries.

1.8.4. Geocentric Approach

The geocentric approach is an international business approach that considers the entire global market as one unit and develops standardized products, marketing strategies, and management practices that are applicable across different countries and regions. In this approach, the company does not differentiate between the home country and the foreign country markets, but rather it adopts a global perspective. The geocentric approach involves hiring and promoting employees based on their skills and competencies, irrespective of their nationality, and also transferring employees across different countries to gain global experience and expertise. The company also develops a global supply chain to source materials and components from different regions to optimize costs and quality.

The geocentric approach is considered to be the most advanced and mature approach to international business as it allows companies to leverage global resources and create a unified corporate culture that can support the company's global strategy. However, this approach requires a high level of coordination and integration across different regions, which can be challenging to achieve.

Examples of companies that have adopted a geocentric approach to international business include:

1. **Coca-Cola:** The beverage giant operates in over 200 countries and employs local managers in each country who have a deep understanding of the local market.
2. **Unilever:** The consumer goods company operates in over 190 countries and has a geocentric approach to staffing. The company believes in hiring the best talent regardless of their nationality and promoting a diverse and inclusive culture.
3. **IBM:** The technology company operates in over 170 countries and has a geocentric approach to management. IBM believes in creating a global culture that is based on collaboration, innovation, and customer satisfaction.
4. **Nestle:** The food and beverage company operates in over 190 countries and has a geocentric approach to management. Nestle believes in hiring local talent who have a deep understanding of the local market and can help the company tailor its products to local tastes and preferences.
5. **Procter & Gamble**: The consumer goods company operates in over 180 countries and has a geocentric approach to management. Procter & Gamble believes in hiring the best talent from around the world and promoting a diverse and inclusive culture that reflects the company's global footprint.

REVIEW QUESTIONS

1. What are the key characteristics of international business, and how do they differ from domestic business?
2. How does globalization impact international business? Explain.
3. What role do governments and international institutions play in regulating international business?
4. What are the key drivers of international business, and how have they evolved over time?
5. How do cultural differences affect international business practices and strategies?
6. What are the major risks and challenges faced by MNCs operating in foreign markets?
7. What are some of the emerging trends and opportunities in international business?

MULTIPLE CHOICE QUESTIONS

1. What is the definition of International Business?

a. The process of conducting trade and investment activities between two or more countries

b. The process of conducting trade and investment activities within one country

c. The process of conducting trade and investment activities within one region

2. What are the factors that primarily influence international business?

a Cultural, political, and economic factors

b. Technological, environmental, and social factors

c. Legal, marketing, and organizational factors

3. Which of the following is NOT an entry mode for international business?

a. Exporting

b. Licensing

c. Franchising

d. Outsourcing

4. Which of the following is an example of a trade barrier?

a. Tariffs

b. Cultural norms

c. Technological advancements

5. What is the purpose of the World Trade Organization (WTO)?

a. To promote free trade and reduce trade barriers between member countries

b. To promote protectionism and increase trade barriers between member countries
c. To regulate only international financial transactions

Answers to Multiple Choice Questions

1. (a); 2. (a); 3. (d); 4. (a); 5. (a)

REFERENCES

1. Cavusgil, S. T., Knight, G., & Riesenberger, J. R., (2018). *International Business: The New Realities* (5th edn., Vol. 1). Pearson Education, Inc.
2. Chadha, N. K., (2018). *International Business Management: A Managerial Perspective*. Vikas Publishing House.
3. Cherunilam, F., (2017). *International Business Management: Text and Cases*. Himalaya Publishing House.
4. Cullen, J. B., & Parboteeah, K. P., (2018). *International Business: Strategy and the Multinational Company* (2nd edn., Vol. 2). Routledge.
5. Daniels, J. D., Radebaugh, L. H., & Sullivan, D. P., (2018). *International Business: Environments and Operations*. Pearson Education.
6. Deresky, H., (2020). *International Management: Managing Across Borders and Cultures* (10th edn.). Pearson Education.
7. Hill, C. W. L., & Hult, G. T. M., (2019). *Global Business Today* (11th edn., Vol. 1). McGraw-Hill Education.
8. Hill, C. W. L., & Hult, G. T. M., (2021). *International Business: Competing in the Global Marketplace* (12th edn., Vol. 2). McGraw-Hill Education.
9. Kuthiala, B. K., & Kuthiala, D., (2017). *International Business Management: Theory and Practice*. Excel Books.
10. Luthans, F., & Doh, J. P., (2020). *International Management: Culture, Strategy, and Behavior* (10th edn., Vol. 2). McGraw-Hill Education.
11. Sharma, K., & Dubey, A., (2017). *International Business Management: Globalization and Beyond*. Pearson India.
12. Wild, J. J., Wild, K. L., & Han, J. C. Y., (2017). *International Business: The Challenges of Globalization* (9th edn., Vol. 1). Pearson Education, Inc.

CHAPTER 2

THEORIES OF INTERNATIONAL TRADE

UNIT INTRODUCTION

International trade is a major contributing factor in global economic activity and a catalyst for economic growth in both developing and developed countries. The differences in various conditions, such as resource availability, natural climatic conditions, cost of production, etc., act as a motivation behind trade between countries.

International trade allows countries to specialize in the production of goods and services that they can produce efficiently and at a lower cost, and trade them with other countries for goods and services that they cannot produce efficiently or cost-effectively. This leads to the optimal utilization of resources, increased efficiency, and higher productivity, which in turn leads to economic growth and development.

International trade also promotes competition, which encourages firms to innovate and improve the quality of their products and services. This can lead to lower prices, increased consumer choice, and higher standards of living for people in both importing and exporting countries.

Furthermore, international trade can also help to create jobs and increase wages, as firms that engage in trade often require more workers and pay higher wages than firms that only operate domestically. This can help to reduce poverty and inequality in both developed and developing countries.

International trade has been a major contributor to the growth of GDP and the rising living standards of people all over the globe. It has provided a large number of employment opportunities and several goods and services for the consumer, which has led to increased economic activity and growth.

International trade has been a part of human civilization for a very long time, but in recent decades, there has been rapid development in cross-border trading. This has been made possible due to advancements in transportation, communication, and technology, which have made it easier and faster to trade goods and services across borders.

Imports and exports have played a significant role in the growth of GDP, as they allow countries to specialize in the production of goods and services that they can produce efficiently and trade them with other countries for goods and services that they cannot produce efficiently.

International trade theories provide a framework for understanding the patterns and benefits of international trade. These theories help in explaining the reasons behind the exchange of goods and services between countries and how it affects their economic growth and development.

Having a clear understanding of international trade theories is essential for countries to make informed decisions about their trade policies and to achieve long-term financial stability. For instance, protectionist policies like tariffs or quotas, which restrict imports or exports, can have negative consequences for a country's economy in the long run, as it reduces competition, hampers innovation, and may lead to retaliation from trading partners.

On the other hand, policies that promote free trade, based on the principles of international trade theories, can lead to increased efficiency, productivity, and competitiveness, and can also benefit consumers by providing them with a wider variety of goods and services at lower prices.

Learning Objectives

After completing this chapter, you should be able to:

- Understand the historical development of trade theories, from mercantilism to the Heckscher-Ohlin model.
- Familiarize yourself with modern trade theories
- Identify and evaluate the factors that affect international trade
- Understand the implications of trade theories for policymakers and business leaders.
- Assess the limitations and criticisms of trade theories

Key Terms

- Absolute advantage
- Capital
- Chance events
- Comparative advantage
- Domestic market conditions
- Free trade
- Government policies
- Heckscher-Ohlin model
- Labor
- Mercantilism
- Natural resources
- Porter's Diamond Model
- Protectionism

2.1. WHAT IS INTERNATIONAL TRADE THEORY?

International trade is indeed the exchange of goods and services across international borders, and it has become increasingly regulated over the past few hundred years. These regulations are put in place to protect domestic industries and ensure that trade is conducted fairly and efficiently.

In addition to regulations, there have been many developments in business models that help businesses use their resources more efficiently in international trade. For example, many companies now use just-in-time (JIT) inventory management systems to minimize the amount of inventory they need to keep on hand, which can reduce costs and improve efficiency. Other companies use global supply chain management techniques to coordinate production and distribution across multiple countries.

While it is true that international trade theory has traditionally focused on how countries can efficiently use their natural resources, the goals of international trade have evolved over time. Today, many economists and policymakers see international trade as a means of achieving broader economic objectives, such as increasing productivity, promoting economic growth, and improving living standards for people around the world (Figure 2.1).

Figure 2.1. Illustration of international trade.

In terms of whether a country should try to end its reliance on imports, there is no simple answer. While it is true that relying heavily on imports can make a country vulnerable to changes in global markets, it is also true that no country can produce everything it needs entirely on its own. In practice, most countries seek to strike a balance between producing goods domestically and importing goods from other countries.

As for what kinds of products can be imported, this largely depends on a country's needs and comparative advantage. For example, a country with a strong agricultural sector may choose to import manufactured goods while exporting agricultural products. Similarly, a country with abundant natural resources may choose to export raw materials while importing finished goods that require those materials. International trade theory does have practical implications for countries, both at the micro and macro levels. As pointed out, countries must make decisions about how much of their resources to allocate to different industries, based on their comparative advantage, in order to maximize their overall welfare.

Did you get it?

International trade has a rich history starting with the barter system being replaced by Mercantilism in the 16th and 17th Centuries.

For example, if Country X has a comparative advantage in producing technology products, then it may be more efficient for it to allocate some of its resources to producing those products for export, and use the revenue generated to import the food it needs. This is known as trade specialization, and it is one of the main principles of international trade theory.

However, the exact amount of resources that should be diverted to different industries will depend on a variety of factors, including the availability of resources, the cost of production, and the demand for goods and services in different markets. This is why policymakers need to carefully analyze these factors before making decisions about trade policy. In addition to trade specialization, international trade theory also has implications for policies such as tax cuts and subsidies. These policies can be used to incentivize firms to develop products for export, as you mentioned. However, policymakers need to be careful to avoid distorting market incentives or creating trade imbalances that could ultimately harm their country's economy.

2.1.1. Why Is International Trade Theory Important?

International trade theories provide a framework for understanding and facilitating international trade, and a misguided or ill-informed approach to trade can have negative consequences for a country's financial stability in the long run.

Regarding the issue of banning products from other countries that are produced through the use of slavery or child labor, different international trade theories may have different perspectives. For example, some theories may focus solely on economic efficiency and argue that banning such products would be inefficient, as it could reduce consumer welfare and increase the cost of production.

However, other theories may take a broader perspective that considers social and ethical factors, and argue that allowing the trade of products made using forced labor would be morally unacceptable and could harm the reputation of the country. In this case, a country may choose to ban such products in order to uphold its values and protect its reputation, even if it may have short-term economic costs.

Different trade theories may have different perspectives on the issue of trade founded on slavery or child labor. One perspective might be that allowing trade in products made using forced labor would have long-term negative consequences for both the importing and exporting countries, as it could lead to social and economic instability, damage the reputation of the countries involved, and ultimately harm their long-term welfare.

Another perspective might be that trade founded on slavery or child labor is not inherently good or bad but rather depends on the specific circumstances of each case. For example, a country that is exporting products made using forced labor may have few other options for economic development, and banning such products could do more harm than good by pushing workers into even worse forms of exploitation or poverty.

Classical Country-Based Theories	Modern Firm-Based Theories
Mercantilism	Country Similarity
Absolute Advantage	Product Life Cycle
Comparative Advantage	Global strategic Rivalry
Heckscher-Ohlin	Porter's National Competitive Advantage

Figure 2.2. International trade theory.

Ultimately, the issue of trade and forced labor is a complex one that requires policymakers to carefully consider a range of economic, social, and ethical factors. While trade can be an important driver of economic growth and development, it is important to ensure that it is conducted in a way that upholds basic human rights and dignity, and promotes the long-term welfare of all parties involved (Figure 2.2).

2.2. MERCANTILISM

Mercantilism was the dominant economic theory during the 16th to 18th century, and it focused on accumulating wealth through trade surpluses, particularly in the form of gold and silver. In this way, the country would accumulate precious metals and become wealthy. Mercantilists believed that a nation's economic strength and military power were closely linked and that a strong economy was essential for national security. The policy of mercantilism led to the development of protectionist policies such as tariffs and quotas to restrict imports and promote exports. However, this approach has been criticized by later economic theories, such as the theory of comparative advantage, which emphasizes the benefits of free trade and specialization.

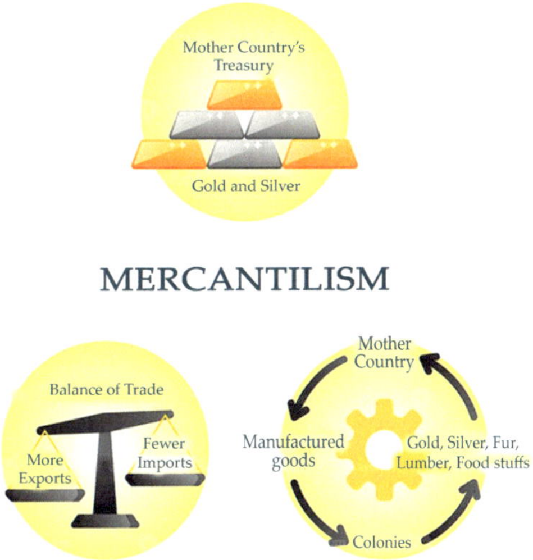

This theory is often called the protectionist theory because it mainly works on the strategy of protecting oneself. Protectionist policies are still used by many countries today, including China, Japan, and Taiwan, among others. These policies are often implemented to protect domestic industries from foreign competition, and they can take many forms, such as tariffs, quotas, subsidies, and regulations.

While protectionism can be beneficial for some industries in the short term, it can also have negative effects on the overall economy, such as higher prices for consumers, reduced competition and innovation, and trade retaliation from other countries.

On the other hand, free trade policies can lead to lower prices for consumers, increased competition and innovation, and greater economic growth and cooperation between countries. However, free trade can also lead to job losses in certain industries and can create winners and losers in the global marketplace.

There is a balance between protectionism and free trade that needs to be struck, depending on the specific needs and circumstances of each country. Many countries today employ a mixture of protectionist and free trade policies to achieve this balance and promote the growth of their economies.

Remember

The theory emphasized the importance of exports over imports and suggested that countries should strive to maintain a positive balance of trade by exporting more than they import.

2.2.1. Limitations

- Under the Mercantilist theory, the accumulation of wealth in one country was believed to come at the expense of another trading partner. This view led to the belief that international trade was a zero-sum game, where one country's gain was another's loss. However, this view has been challenged by more modern economic theories such as the theory of comparative advantage, which shows that countries can benefit from trade even if they have an absolute disadvantage in producing all goods. According to the theory of comparative advantage, countries should specialize in producing goods that they can produce more efficiently than other countries and trade with those other countries for goods that they cannot produce as efficiently. This leads to gains from trade for involved countries and results in an overall increase in global wealth. Therefore, while Mercantilism may have viewed international trade as a zero-sum game, more modern economic theories suggest that international trade can be a positive-sum game, where both countries can benefit and contribute to global wealth.
- David Hume's Price-Specie-Flow doctrine states that in the long run, a country's trade surplus or deficit would automatically be eliminated due to the adjustment of prices and exchange rates. If a country has a trade surplus and receives more gold than it spends, its domestic prices will increase, making its exports more expensive and its imports cheaper. This would lead to a decrease in exports and an increase in imports, which would eventually eliminate

the surplus. Similarly, if a country has a trade deficit and spends more gold than it receives, its domestic prices will decrease, making its exports cheaper and its imports more expensive. This would lead to an increase in exports and a decrease in imports, which would eventually eliminate the deficit.

- In modern times, national foreign exchange reserves are typically held in a variety of currencies, including but not limited to gold. The main purpose of these reserves is to provide a cushion to the economy in case of external shocks or to facilitate international trade. Governments may also use foreign exchange reserves to influence exchange rates, such as by buying or selling currencies in the foreign exchange market.
- Mercantilism, as a theory, was based on the idea that a country's wealth was solely determined by its gold and silver holdings. It focused on increasing exports and restricting imports, but it failed to take into account other factors that could contribute to a country's wealth. For example, a country with abundant natural resources and skilled labor could still be wealthy, even if it did not have a large amount of gold or silver. Moreover, the theory did not take into account the impact of technological advancements and innovations on a country's wealth.
- If all countries adopt protectionist policies and impose barriers to trade, it would lead to a decrease in international trade and result in a highly restrictive environment for trade. This could have adverse effects on global economic growth and development. It could also lead to retaliatory actions by other countries, triggering a trade war, which would negatively impact the economies of all countries involved. Therefore, it is important for countries to strike a balance between protecting their domestic industries and promoting international trade.
- The emphasis on trade surpluses and the accumulation of precious metals led to the exploitation of the colonies by colonial powers. The colonies were used as sources of cheap raw materials, and the finished goods were sold back to them at higher prices. This led to the underdevelopment of the colonies, as they were not allowed to develop their own industries and infrastructure. The colonies were forced to remain dependent on the colonial powers for their economic development, which perpetuated their poverty.
- Some countries continue to promote exports and restrict imports, often as part of their development strategy. This can be seen in the policy of import substitution, where a country tries to produce domestically what it would otherwise import from abroad. This strategy was popular in many developing countries during the mid-20th century, as a way to reduce dependence on foreign imports and promote domestic industries. However, it has been criticized for being inefficient and leading to a lack of competition in domestic markets. In recent years, many countries

have moved away from import substitution and towards more open trade policies, promoting exports while also allowing for greater imports and foreign investment.

2.3. THEORY OF ABSOLUTE COST ADVANTAGE

In "The Wealth of Nations," Adam Smith argued that specialization and division of labor can lead to greater productivity and efficiency, ultimately resulting in economic growth. Smith believed that countries should focus on producing goods and services in which they have an absolute advantage, and this can be achieved by producing the goods or services more efficiently than other countries. As a result, they can trade with other countries and both parties can benefit from the exchange.

Adam Smith believed that specialization and the division of labor would increase productivity, leading to economic growth and an improvement in living standards. He argued that countries should focus on producing goods and services in which they have an absolute advantage – that is, they can produce these goods more efficiently than other countries. In this way, countries can trade with each other and benefit from the differences in production costs, leading to gains from trade.

Adam Smith believed that government intervention in the market would lead to inefficiencies and distortions. He argued that the market mechanism, based on the principles of supply and demand, was the most efficient means of allocating resources and determining prices. He also believed that the role of the government should be limited to providing a stable legal and institutional framework that would facilitate free trade and competition. Smith's theory of free trade and laissez-faire economics laid the foundation for modern international trade theory.

Exactly, Smith argued that trade should be based on mutual benefit and voluntary exchange and that by focusing solely on exports and restricting imports, countries would miss out on the benefits of specialization and comparative advantage. He believed that countries should focus on producing and exporting the goods in which they have a comparative advantage and import goods that can be produced more efficiently by other countries. In this way, both countries can benefit from trade and increase their overall wealth.

Smith believed that competition in the market was crucial as it ensures the best quality products at the lowest possible prices. Hence, restrictions on imports would reduce competition, leading to higher prices for consumers and ultimately leading to a decline in the standard of living. Moreover, Smith argued that restrictions on imports could cause retaliatory measures from other countries, leading to a trade war, and ultimately causing harm to both countries involved. Smith also believed that free trade would result in benefits for all countries involved, and that government intervention in trade would only lead to inefficiencies and negative consequences. He argued that individuals and businesses are best suited to make decisions about what goods and services to produce and trade, rather than the government.

2.3.1. Assumptions

Here are the most significant assumptions underlying the theory of absolute advantage proposed by Adam Smith (Figure 2.3):

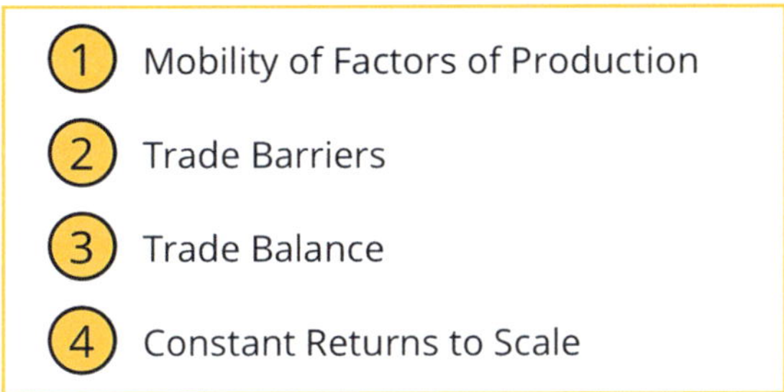

Figure 2.3. Theory of absolute advantage.

Here are the most significant of these assumptions:

1. **Lack of Mobility for Factors of Production:** Adam Smith's theory of absolute advantage assumes that factors of production are immobile between countries, meaning that they cannot easily move from one country to another. This implies that each country's Production Possibility Frontier (PPF) remains fixed and does not change after the trade. However, in reality, factors of production can be mobile, and trade can lead to changes in the PPF of each country as resources are allocated more efficiently. This is known as the theory of comparative advantage, which is an extension of Smith's theory.
2. **Trade Barriers:** Trade barriers can come in various forms, such as tariffs, quotas, embargoes, and regulations, and they can be implemented by governments to protect domestic industries, reduce trade deficits, or for political reasons. However, these barriers can also limit competition, increase prices for consumers, and reduce the overall benefits of trade.
3. **Trade Balance:** Smith's theory of absolute advantage assumes that the balance of trade, or the difference between a country's exports and imports, will always

be balanced. In other words, a country will only export as much as it imports. This is because, in Smith's view, countries will only trade goods in which they have an absolute advantage, and they will trade these goods for goods that other countries have an absolute advantage in producing. This will lead to a balanced trade, with both countries benefitting from the exchange. However, in reality, trade imbalances do occur, with some countries exporting more than they import, while others import more than they export.

4. **Constant Returns to Scale:** Adam Smith's assumption of constant returns to scale means that the cost of producing an additional unit of a good remains the same, regardless of the level of output. However, in reality, many industries experience economies of scale, which means that the cost of producing additional units decreases as production increases. For example, if it takes 2 hours to make one loaf of bread in country A, then it should take 4 hours to produce two loaves of bread. Consequently, it would take 8 hours to produce four loaves of bread. This can give some countries an advantage in producing certain goods and can affect the patterns of trade that emerge between countries.

2.3.2. Absolute Advantage Example

Here is an example of an absolute advantage:

Let's consider two countries: Country A and Country B. They both can produce two goods: Wheat and cloth. The table below shows the number of units of each good that each country can produce per hour of work.

Country	Wheat	Cloth
A	6	2
B	4	1

From the table, we can see that Country A has an absolute advantage in both wheat and cloth production because it can produce more of both goods in an hour than Country B. Specifically, Country A can produce 6 units of wheat or 2 units of cloth per hour of work, while Country B can produce only 4 units of wheat or 1 unit of cloth per hour of work.

Therefore, according to the theory of absolute advantage, Country A should specialize in producing wheat, while Country B should specialize in producing cloth. As a result, both countries can benefit from trade because they can exchange the goods they specialize in for the goods they do not specialize in and get more of both goods than if they tried to produce both goods themselves.

2.4. THEORY OF COMPARATIVE ADVANTAGE

David Ricardo's theory of comparative advantage is one of the most important and influential theories in the field of international trade. David Ricardo was a British economist who lived in the 19th century and is known for his work on international trade, especially the theory of comparative advantage. In his book "Principles of Political Economy and Taxation," he argued that countries could benefit from trade even if one country was more efficient at producing all goods than another.

He demonstrated that it was advantageous for countries to specialize in producing the goods they could produce most efficiently and to trade with other countries for goods they could not produce as efficiently. Unlike Adam Smith's theory of absolute advantage, which argues that countries should specialize in producing goods they are most efficient at producing,

Ricardo's theory argues that even if a country is less efficient at producing all goods than another country, it can still benefit from trade by specializing in producing the goods in which it has a comparative advantage, i.e., the goods in which its opportunity cost of production is lower than in other goods compared to other countries.

A classic example of the theory of comparative advantage involves two countries, Portugal and England, and two goods, wine, and cloth.

Let's assume that Portugal can produce wine more efficiently than England, while England can produce cloth more efficiently than Portugal.

In the absence of trade, Portugal would produce both wine and cloth, but it would have to sacrifice more cloth production to produce a given amount of wine than England would. Similarly, England would have to sacrifice more wine production to produce a given amount of cloth than Portugal would.

Now, if the two countries specialize in producing the good that they are relatively more efficient in, and then trade with each other, both countries can benefit from the trade. Portugal will focus on producing wine, and England will focus on producing cloth.

Assuming that the terms of trade are mutually beneficial, Portugal will be able to get cloth cheaper from England than it would have cost to produce it itself, while England will be able to get wine cheaper from Portugal than it would have cost to produce it itself. This means that both countries can enjoy a higher standard of living by trading than they would have had without trade. The table below, for example, represents the Production Possibilities Frontiers (PPFs) for two countries Portugal and England. In this example, Portugal specializes in wine, which it can produce at a lower opportunity cost than cloth. England specializes in cloth, which it can produce at a lower opportunity cost than wine. As a result, the total production of both goods increases, and both countries are better off through trade.

Table 2.1. The Hypothetical Production Possibility Frontier (PPF) for Portugal and England

	Cloth (yards)	Wine (gallons)
Portugal (PPF)	80	120
England (PPF)	100	60
Specialization		
Portugal	0	200
England	120	0
Total	120	200

Ricardo's theory of comparative advantage suggests that countries should specialize in producing and exporting goods that they can produce at a lower opportunity cost (in terms of other goods that they could have produced instead) compared to other countries, and import goods that they cannot produce efficiently, even if they have an absolute advantage in producing them. This leads to a more efficient allocation of resources and increased overall global productivity, and benefits all countries involved in the trade.

2.4.1. Assumptions of Comparative Advantage

The Ricardian doctrine of comparative advantage is built upon several assumptions that must hold true for the theory to be valid. These assumptions are:

1. **There Are Only Two Countries and Two Goods**: This is a simplifying assumption to help us better understand the theory. In reality, there are many countries and many goods traded globally.
2. **Labor Is the Only Factor of Production**: This assumption simplifies the theory by assuming that only labor is used to produce goods. In reality, other factors such as capital and technology also play a role in production.
3. **Labor Is Homogeneous Within a Country but Heterogeneous Between Countries**: This assumption means that labor has the same skills and productivity within a country, but different levels of productivity between countries.
4. **No Transportation Costs or Trade Barriers**: This assumption means that there are no costs associated with transporting goods between countries and no barriers to trade such as tariffs or quotas.

5. **Constant Returns to Scale:** This assumption means that as a country produces more of a good, the opportunity cost of producing that good remains constant. In reality, there may be increasing or decreasing returns to scale depending on the industry.

These assumptions are necessary for the theory of comparative advantage to hold true, and deviations from these assumptions can affect the validity of the theory in practice.

2.4.2. Criticisms of Comparative Advantage

There are several criticisms of the theory of comparative advantage. Here are some of them:

1. **Unrealistic Assumptions**: The theory assumes that there are no transportation costs, trade barriers, or other obstacles to trade. In reality, these factors can significantly impact the flow of goods between countries.
2. **Immobile Factors of Production**: The theory assumes that capital, labor, and other factors of production cannot move between countries. In reality, these factors can and do move across borders, which can impact comparative advantage.
3. **Lack of Consideration for Domestic Industries**: The theory assumes that countries should specialize in certain goods and import others, but this can lead to the neglect of domestic industries that could be competitive if given the chance to develop.
4. Unequal Distribution of Gains: The theory assumes that all countries benefit from trade, but in reality, the gains from trade may not be evenly distributed among individuals or within a country.
5. **Short-Term Pain for Long-Term Gain**: The theory assumes that the adjustment to trade will be smooth and that there will be no short-term pain for countries that must adjust to changes in trade patterns. In reality, the adjustment can be painful for some individuals and industries, which can lead to resistance to trade liberalization.
6. **Failure to Account for Externalities**: The theory assumes that the production of goods has no impact on the environment or society. In reality, the production of some goods can have negative externalities, such as pollution or exploitation of workers.
7. **Limited to Trade in Goods**: The theory focuses on trade in goods, but in today's world, trade in services and intellectual property is becoming increasingly important.

2.5. HECKSCHER-OHLIN THEORY (FACTOR PROPORTIONS THEORY)

Smith and Ricardo's theories focused on the idea of absolute advantage and comparative advantage, respectively. Absolute advantage suggests that a country should specialize in producing goods that it can produce more efficiently than any other country, while comparative advantage suggests that a country should specialize in producing goods that it can produce more efficiently than any other country, even if it does not have an absolute advantage in producing them.

The theories of Smith and Ricardo were criticized because they did not take into account the differences in resources and factors of production between countries. Heckscher and Ohlin's theory addressed this criticism by emphasizing the importance of factor endowments, or the availability of different types of resources in different countries, in determining comparative advantage.

Heckscher-Ohlin theory, also known as the Factor Proportions theory, is an economic theory that explains international trade patterns based on the relative abundance of factors of production, such as labor, capital, and land, in different countries. The theory was developed by two Swedish economists, Eli Heckscher, and Bertil Ohlin, in the early 20th century.

The basic idea behind the Heckscher-Ohlin theory is that countries have different endowments of factors of production and that these differences determine their comparative advantage in producing certain goods. For example, if a country has a relatively abundant supply of labor, it will have a comparative advantage in producing labor-intensive goods, such as clothing or shoes. Conversely, if a country has a relatively abundant supply of capital, it will have a comparative advantage in producing capital-intensive goods, such as machinery or computers.

According to the Heckscher-Ohlin theory, trade occurs because countries with different factor endowments can benefit from exchanging goods that they can produce more efficiently. For example, a country with abundant capital and scarce labor may find it cheaper to import labor-intensive goods from a country with abundant labor and scarce capital, rather than producing these goods itself. This trade can lead to increased welfare for all countries involved, as each country can specialize in producing the goods that make the most efficient use of its factor endowments.

The Heckscher-Ohlin theory has been influential in the field of international trade and has helped economists to better understand the patterns of trade observed between countries. However, the theory has also been subject to criticism, as it assumes that factors of production are immobile between countries, and does not take into account other factors, such as technology or economies of scale, that may also affect trade patterns.

The core premises of the Heckscher-Ohlin model are:

1. **Differences in Factor Endowments**: Countries have different endowments for factors of production, such as labor, capital, and land. Some countries may have abundant supplies of certain factors, while others may be relatively scarce in those same factors.
2. **Differences in Technology**: Countries have different levels of technological advancement, which affects their ability to produce goods efficiently.
3. **Factor Mobility**: Factors of production are immobile between countries, meaning that labor, capital, and land cannot be easily moved across national borders.
4. **Constant Returns to Scale**: The production of goods exhibits constant returns to scale, meaning that if a country doubles its inputs of labor and capital, it can double its output of goods.
5. **Perfect Competition**: Markets are perfectly competitive, meaning that there are many buyers and sellers, and no single entity has enough market power to influence prices.

Based on these premises, the Heckscher-Ohlin model predicts that countries will tend to specialize in the production of goods that make the most efficient use of their abundant factors of production, and will import goods that require the use of their relatively scarce factors. In other words, countries will trade based on their comparative advantage, which is determined by their factor endowments.

Remember

The theory suggests that a country should specialize in producing goods that make use of the factors of production that are abundant in the country, and that trade can lead to more efficient use of resources and increased welfare for all countries involved.

The Heckscher-Ohlin model has been influential in the field of international trade and has helped economists to better understand the patterns of trade observed between countries.

2.5.1. Heckscher-Ohlin Model in Trade

The Heckscher-Ohlin Model is a widely-used theoretical framework for studying the patterns and determinants of international trade between countries, particularly in terms of the relative abundance of different factors of production (such as capital and labor) and the types of goods produced by each country.

According to the Heckscher-Ohlin Model, countries will tend to specialize in and export goods that make intensive use of their abundant factors of production, while importing goods that require the use of their scarce factors. For example, a country with abundant oil reserves is likely to specialize in and export oil and petroleum products, while importing goods that require more labor or capital inputs. Similarly, a country with abundant agricultural land may specialize in and export agricultural products, while importing goods that require more capital or technology.

The Heckscher-Ohlin Model can be applied to a wide range of real-world trade patterns and has been used to explain many aspects of global trade, including the trade patterns of developed and developing countries, the effects of technological change on trade, and the impact of trade on income inequality within and between countries.

The model suggests that a country's relative abundance of different factors of production (such as natural resources, capital, and labor) will determine its pattern of trade and specialization, with countries tending to export goods that make intensive use of their abundant factors and import goods that require the use of their scarce factors.

In the case of OPEC countries, their abundance of oil resources means that they have a comparative advantage in producing and exporting oil-related products, while other countries may have a comparative advantage in producing and exporting other goods that require different factors of production. This can lead to mutually beneficial trade relationships, as countries can specialize in the production of goods in which they have a comparative advantage and trade with other countries for goods they cannot produce as efficiently.

The Heckscher-Ohlin Model highlights the potential benefits of international trade for promoting efficiency, specialization, and economic growth, and it can help explain why different countries specialize in the production and export of certain goods based on their factor endowments. However, it is worth noting that the model is a simplification of the complex reality of international trade, and there are many factors beyond factor endowments that can influence trade patterns and outcomes.

2.6. COUNTRY SIMILARITY THEORY

Country similarity theory is an economic theory that suggests that countries with similar economic, political, and cultural characteristics are more likely to engage in international trade with each other than with dissimilar countries. This theory is based on the idea that countries that share similarities are more likely to have similar preferences for goods and services, similar production capabilities, and similar institutional and regulatory frameworks, which can facilitate trade between them. The theory of country similarity is often used to explain the patterns of trade between developed countries, where countries with similar levels of economic development and institutional quality tend to trade more with each other than with developing countries. This is because developed countries often have similar preferences for high-quality goods and services, similar levels of technological sophistication and production capabilities, and similar institutional and regulatory frameworks that can facilitate trade.

Staffan Linder, a Swedish economist, first proposed the theory of country similarity in his 1961 article "An Essay on Trade and Transformation." Linder suggested that countries with similar levels of economic development and consumer preferences are more likely to engage in international trade with each other. Example: Japan exports Toyota cars to Germany whereas Germany exports BMW cars to Japan.

Linder's theory focused on the concept of "intra-industry" trade, which refers to the exchange of similar products between countries, rather than the traditional model of inter-industry trade, where countries trade goods that are dissimilar. Linder argued that countries tend to start producing goods for their domestic markets first, and as their production capabilities and economies of scale increase, they begin to export those goods to other countries with similar preferences and demand patterns.

Linder's theory of country similarity has been influential in explaining the patterns of trade between developed countries, where intra-industry trade is more common than inter-industry trade. Linder suggested that countries with similar per capita incomes and consumer preferences are more likely to engage in intra-industry trade in manufactured goods. He argued that this type of trade is more common in industries where consumers place a high value on brand names and product reputation, such as in the automotive and electronics industries.

While Linder's theory has been influential in explaining the patterns of trade between developed countries, it has limitations in explaining the patterns of trade between developed and developing countries. In these cases, there may be significant differences in consumer preferences, production capabilities, and institutional frameworks that can influence trade patterns.

2.6.1. Economic Similarity of Developed Countries

The economic similarity of developed countries refers to the fact that countries with similar levels of economic development tend to have similar patterns of economic activity, similar production capabilities, and similar institutional and regulatory frameworks. This similarity can make it easier for developed countries to engage in trade with each other, as they may have similar preferences for goods and services, similar levels of technological sophistication, and similar regulatory environments.

One example of economic similarity among developed countries is their high levels of industrialization and technological innovation. Developed countries tend to have advanced manufacturing industries and high-tech sectors, which allows them to produce high-quality goods and services that are in demand worldwide. Additionally, developed countries often have similar institutional frameworks, such as well-developed legal and financial systems, which can facilitate international trade.

Another example of economic similarity among developed countries is their high standards of living and consumer preferences. Developed countries tend to have similar levels of income and consumer preferences, which can make it easier for them to trade similar goods and services with each other. For example, developed countries with high levels of income tend to demand high-quality, luxury goods, such as high-end fashion, automobiles, and electronics.

2.6.2. Similarity of Location

The similarity of location can be an important factor in determining trade patterns between countries. Neighboring countries often share common borders and transport links, which can reduce transportation costs and make trade more efficient.

For example, Finland's proximity to Russia makes it an ideal trading partner for Russia, as goods can be transported quickly and cheaply across the shared border. Finland is a major exporter of goods such as wood, paper, and machinery to Russia, while Russia exports oil, gas, and minerals to Finland. This trade relationship benefits both countries, as Finland gains access to Russia's vast market and natural resources, while Russia gains access to Finland's advanced technology and high-quality manufactured goods.

The importance of location in determining trade patterns is not limited to neighboring countries. Countries that are geographically close to major trade routes or ports can also have an advantage in trade, as they can more easily access global markets and transport goods over long distances. For example, countries such as Singapore and the United Arab Emirates (UAE) are major transshipment hubs for goods moving between Asia, Europe, and the Middle East, due to their strategic location at key points along major shipping routes.

2.6.3. Cultural Similarity

Cultural similarity can also be an important factor in determining trade patterns between countries. Countries that share similar cultural backgrounds, languages, and traditions may have a greater affinity for each other's products and may find it easier to communicate and establish business relationships.

One example of cultural similarity in trade is the exchange of goods and services among European countries. European countries share a long history of cultural, linguistic, and economic ties, which has helped to create a common market for goods and services. The European Union, for example, was created to promote economic integration and facilitate trade among European countries by removing trade barriers, harmonizing regulations, and promoting the free movement of goods, services, and people.

Cultural similarity can also be important in facilitating trade in niche markets, such as food and beverages, fashion, and entertainment. For example, Italian wine and cuisine are highly valued in many countries due to their cultural heritage and reputation for quality, while Japanese fashion and technology are sought after for their innovative and unique designs.

2.6.4. The similarity of Political and Economic Interests

The similarity of political and economic interests can also be an important factor in determining trade patterns between countries. Countries that share similar political and economic systems may have a greater affinity for each other's products and may be more willing to engage in trade agreements and partnerships.

For example, countries that have strong diplomatic ties and share common political interests may be more likely to enter into free trade agreements or preferential trade arrangements, which can provide preferential access to each other's markets and reduce trade barriers. The North American Free Trade Agreement (NAFTA), which established a free trade zone between the United States, Canada, and Mexico, is an example of a trade agreement that was motivated by both economic and political interests.

Similarly, countries that share similar economic interests, such as a focus on technology, innovation, or natural resources, may be more likely to engage in trade partnerships that leverage their respective strengths. For example, countries with advanced technology industries may seek to partner with countries with abundant natural resources to create mutually beneficial trade relationships.

2.7. PRODUCT LIFE CYCLE THEORY

Raymond Vernon proposed the product life cycle theory in the mid-1960s, which explains the international trade patterns for products at different stages of their life cycle. The theory suggests that new products are initially developed and produced in developed countries, such as the United States because these countries have the resources and capabilities to invest in research and development (R&D) and produce the initial product.

According to Vernon, as the product becomes more established and demand increases, production tends to move to other countries with lower labor costs and production costs, such as developing countries. This is because as demand for the product increases, competition increases, and firms are forced to reduce costs and increase efficiency to maintain their market share. As a result, firms often seek to produce in countries with lower labor costs and production costs.

The product life cycle theory also suggests that as the product reaches maturity and demand stabilizes or declines, production tends to shift back to developed countries where production costs may be higher but where there is still demand for the product due to the product's brand reputation or other non-price factors.

According to Vernon's product life cycle theory, early in the life cycle of a new product, demand for the product is typically limited to the home market, which in this case is the United States. As demand for the product starts to grow rapidly in the US, demand in other advanced countries, such as Great Britain, France, Germany, and Japan, is limited to high-income groups, and thus not sufficient enough to warrant local production.

Therefore, in the early stages of the product's life cycle, the US typically exports the product to other advanced countries. Over time, as demand for the product starts to grow in these countries, foreign producers may begin to produce the product for their own markets. At this point, US firms may also start setting up production facilities in these advanced countries where demand is growing, to take advantage of the market potential.

As production becomes more concentrated in lower-cost foreign locations and developing countries, the United States may switch from being an exporter of the product to an importer. This happens as the product becomes more standardized and competition from lower-cost producers intensifies. However, US firms may still retain some advantages in terms of process innovation and brand reputation, allowing them to continue to compete in the global marketplace. In this way, the product life cycle theory highlights the importance of understanding how global production and trade patterns can evolve over time in response to changes in technology, demand, and cost pressures.

2.7.1. Stages of Product Life Cycle

Raymond Vernon's Product Life Cycle theory consists of three stages:

- **Stage 1: The New Product:** The new product innovation requires significant investment in R&D, as well as highly skilled labor and capital. The product is non-standardized, and the production process is flexible and costly due to the need for skilled labor. The innovator in this stage enjoys monopoly power and high-profit margins, as the price elasticity of demand is low, and high-income consumers buy the product regardless of its cost.

- **Stage 2: The Maturing Product:** This stage is characterized by an increase in demand for the product as it becomes more widely known and accepted. The product is standardized, and economies of scale are achieved as production becomes more efficient. Production may begin to shift to countries with lower labor costs, but the innovating firm still maintains a significant market share and pricing power. However, competition may begin to emerge, and the innovator may start to face pressures to lower prices and increase efficiency.
- **Stage 3: The Standardized Product:** This stage sees the product become a commodity, with standardized production and low prices. Production is typically located in low-cost countries, and the innovator may have lost market share to competitors. The product may also face technological obsolescence as newer and better products enter the market. At this stage, the innovator may choose to discontinue production of the product or focus on innovation for new products.

2.7.2. Limitations of Product Life Cycle Theory

This theory has been criticized because of the following weaknesses:

1. **Applicable to Technology-Based Products**: Technology-based products have a high degree of innovation and require continuous improvement to stay ahead of competitors, which leads to changes in the production process. On the other hand, resource-based products such as minerals and services such as education or healthcare do not have the same degree of innovation and are not subject to the same changes in the production process. The value of resource-based products is derived from their availability and quality, and the value of services is derived from the skills and knowledge of the people providing them.
2. **Most New Products Are Not Developed and Introduced in the United States**: The global landscape of innovation and new product development has shifted in recent years, with countries such as Japan and various European nations emerging as major players in the development of new technologies and products. This is due in part to their investments in R&D, as well as their highly skilled workforces and supportive government policies. As a result, we now see a more diversified distribution of new product introductions across different regions of the world.

Indeed, while Vernon's theory may have accurately explained the pattern of international trade during the post-World War II era when the United States was the dominant economic power, its relevance in the modern world is limited. The globalization of production, advances in technology, changes in consumer preferences and market conditions, and the emergence of new economic powers such as China, India, and Brazil have all contributed to the diversification of product innovation and the globalization of production.

2.8. GLOBAL STRATEGIC RIVALRY THEORY

Paul Krugman and Kelvin Lancaster were the economists who developed the Global strategic rivalry theory in the 1980s. The theory focuses on multinational companies and their strategies to gain a competitive advantage over other similar global firms in their industry.

Did you get it?

The concept of a product having stages of life (and the need to manage them) arose as early as 1931.

The firms must develop unique features, improve their quality, and lower their costs to become more competitive. The theory also highlights the importance of economies of scale and scope and the role of government policies and regulations in shaping global competition.

In this theory, the rivalry among global firms is not only limited to the pricing and quality of the products, but it also includes the overall strategies and capabilities of the firms. The theory also suggests that firms can cooperate and collaborate with each other to gain a competitive advantage, but this collaboration should not harm the interests of the consumers and society at large.

The barriers to entry in global strategic rivalry theory are obstacles that a firm faces when entering the market and trying to gain a competitive advantage over other similar global firms in the industry. Some of the main barriers identified by the theory are:

1. **Research and Development**: Firms may invest heavily in R&D to gain an edge over their competitors. This can create a barrier for new entrants who may not have the resources to invest in R&D.
2. **Intellectual Property Rights**: Firms may also own valuable intellectual property, such as patents or trademarks, which can give them a competitive advantage. New entrants may find it difficult to compete if they do not have access to similar intellectual property.

3. **Economies of Scale:** Firms may achieve economies of scale, which can lead to lower costs and higher profits. New entrants may not be able to achieve the same level of economies of scale, making it difficult for them to compete.
4. **Unique Business Processes or Methods**: Firms may have developed unique business processes or methods that give them a competitive advantage. New entrants may not be able to replicate these processes or methods, making it difficult for them to compete.
5. **Extensive Experience in the Industry**: Firms that have been in the industry for a long time may have extensive experience and knowledge that gives them a competitive advantage. New entrants may not have the same level of experience or knowledge, making it difficult for them to compete.
6. **Control of Resources or Favorable Access to Raw Materials**: Firms that have control over resources or have favorable access to raw materials may have a competitive advantage over others in the industry. New entrants may find it difficult to access the same resources or raw materials, making it difficult for them to compete.

The theory suggests that government policies and actions can have a significant impact on a nation's competitiveness in certain industries. For example, government support for R&D, infrastructure development, and education and training can help create a more conducive environment for firms to innovate and improve their products and processes. Government policies that promote fair competition, protect intellectual property rights (IPR), and provide access to financing can also help firms overcome barriers to entry and gain a competitive advantage in the global market.

2.9. PORTER'S NATIONAL COMPETITIVE ADVANTAGE THEORY

Michael Porter developed a model known as the "Diamond Model" or "Porter's Diamond" in 1990 to explain the factors that give a country a competitive advantage in certain industries. This model is an extension of his earlier work on the competitive advantage at the firm level (Figure 2.4).

The Diamond Model consists of four interrelated factors that determine national competitive advantage:

1. Local market resources and capabilities;
2. Local market demand conditions;
3. Local suppliers and complementary industries; and
4. Local firm characteristics.

Figure 2.4. Porter's national competitive advantage theory.

1. **Local Market Resources and Capabilities (Factor Conditions):** Michael Porter, a renowned economist, expanded on the traditional factor proportions theory by introducing a new set of advanced factors that he believed could provide a nation with a sustainable competitive advantage in global markets. These advanced factors include skilled labor, and investments in education, technology, and infrastructure, and they are critical for enhancing a nation's productivity and efficiency, creating new products and services, and improving the quality of existing products and services.

   Porter argued that these advanced factors are not static but are created and improved over time through a process of continuous innovation, investment, and improvement. He also believed that advanced factors are interconnected and mutually reinforcing, creating a virtuous cycle of innovation and competitiveness. For example, investments in education and training can lead to the development of new technologies and the creation of new products, which, in turn, can drive infrastructure development and further investments in education and training.

2. **Local Market Demand Conditions:** Michael Porter's theory of competitive advantage also emphasizes the role of

local market demand conditions in driving innovation and competitiveness. He argued that companies operating in a sophisticated home market, where customers are demanding and discerning, are more likely to develop innovative products and services that can meet the high expectations of their customers. This, in turn, can create a sustainable competitive advantage in global markets.

For example, the US software industry is often cited as an example of the role of local market demand conditions in driving innovation. The US market for software is highly sophisticated and demanding, with consumers and businesses requiring high-quality, reliable, and user-friendly software products and services. This demand has forced US software companies to continuously innovate and improve their products, leading to the development of new technologies and software applications.

Furthermore, the presence of a sophisticated domestic market can also provide companies with valuable feedback on their products and services, helping them to refine and improve their offerings over time. This feedback loop can create a virtuous cycle of innovation, where companies continuously improve their products and services in response to customer needs and preferences, leading to a sustainable competitive advantage in global markets.

3. **Local Suppliers and Complementary Industries:** According to this theory, the presence of strong local suppliers and complementary industries can provide significant benefits to companies operating in a particular industry. These local suppliers and complementary industries can provide the inputs, services, and technologies required by the industry, thus enhancing its efficiency and productivity.

   Moreover, the clustering of industries in a particular geographic location can also provide additional benefits, such as access to specialized labor pools, shared infrastructure and facilities, and knowledge spillovers. This can create a competitive advantage for companies operating in that location, as they can tap into these local resources and knowledge to improve their products, processes, and technologies.

   For example, the automotive industry is often cited as an example of the benefits of local suppliers and complementary industries. Automakers rely heavily on a network of suppliers for components, materials, and

TIPS

1. Today, many developing countries have the capacity to produce high-tech products and engage in R&D, while some developed countries have shifted their focus to service-based industries.

2. Therefore, while the product life cycle theory remains an important contribution to the field of international trade, it must be applied with caution in the context of the complex and dynamic global economy of today.

services, and the efficiency and quality of these suppliers can significantly impact the automaker's competitiveness. Therefore, having a strong network of local suppliers can enhance the efficiency and productivity of the entire industry.

In addition, the clustering of the automotive industry in certain regions, such as Detroit, Michigan, has provided significant benefits to the industry. The concentration of automotive firms and suppliers in this region has created a critical mass of knowledge, skills, and resources that have driven innovation and competitiveness in the industry.

4. **Local Firm Characteristics:** This theory also emphasizes the role of local firm characteristics in determining competitiveness. These characteristics include firm strategy, industry structure, and industry rivalry.

Local firm strategy refers to the choices made by individual firms regarding the products or services they offer, the markets they serve, and the ways in which they compete. Local firms that adopt effective strategies, such as focusing on niche markets, developing innovative products or services, or leveraging their unique capabilities and resources, can gain a competitive advantage over their rivals.

Moreover, the industry structure, which includes the number and size of firms operating in a particular industry, can also impact competitiveness. For example, industries with a large number of small firms may be more competitive and innovative than those dominated by a few large firms.

Lastly, the level of rivalry between local firms can also impact competitiveness. A healthy level of competition can spur innovation and motivate firms to improve their products, processes, and technologies. However, excessive rivalry or collusion between firms can stifle innovation and harm the industry as a whole.

Michael Porter's theory of competitive advantage acknowledges that government policies and chance events can also impact the competitiveness of industries. Government policies such as investment in infrastructure, education, and R&D can create an environment conducive to competitiveness and innovation. Moreover, government policies such as tariffs, subsidies, and regulations can also impact the competitive landscape of industries.

Chance events, such as technological breakthroughs or changes in consumer preferences, can also significantly impact the competitiveness of industries. For example, the advent of the internet and digital technologies has disrupted many industries and created new opportunities for firms to gain a competitive advantage.

However, as you noted, Porter's theory and other modern, firm-based theories of international trade are relatively new and have yet to be extensively tested. While they offer interesting insights into the factors that contribute to competitiveness, there is still much debate and research needed to fully understand the complexities of global trade patterns and the factors that drive them.

Thus, Porter's framework highlights the importance of considering multiple factors, including government policies and chance events, in understanding the competitiveness of industries and nations. By taking a holistic approach to competitiveness, policymakers and business leaders can create an environment that fosters innovation, productivity, and sustainable growth.

REVIEW QUESTIONS

1. What are the major theoretical frameworks used to explain international trade, and how do they differ?
2. How do the comparative advantage and factor endowment theories explain patterns of trade between countries?
3. What role do economies of scale and product differentiation play in international trade?
4. How do political economy theories view the role of government intervention in trade?
5. What are the strengths and weaknesses of the various international trade theories?

MULTIPLE CHOICE QUESTIONS

1. Which theory of international trade emphasizes that a country should specialize in producing and exporting goods that it can produce more efficiently than other countries?

a. Absolute advantage
b. Comparative advantage
c. Factor endowment theory
d. Product life cycle theory

2. Which theory of international trade argues that a country should export goods that require intensive use of its abundant factor(s) of production and import goods that require intensive use of its scarce factor(s) of production?

a. Absolute advantage
b. Comparative advantage
c. Factor endowment theory
d. Product life cycle theory

3. Which theory of international trade suggests that a country should specialize in producing and exporting goods that are at different stages of their life cycle, and import goods that are in other stages of the cycle?

a. Absolute advantage
b. Comparative advantage
c. Factor endowment theory
d. Product life cycle theory

4. According to the Heckshder-Ohlin theory, trade is determined by differences in countries' endowments of:

a. Capital and labor

b. Natural resources and technology
c. Skilled and unskilled labor
d. Manufactured goods and raw materials

5. Which theory of international trade emphasizes that a country's trade patterns are determined by the availability of factors of production, such as land, labor, and capital?

a. Absolute advantage
b. Comparative advantage
c. Factor endowment theory
d. Product life cycle theory

Answers to Multiple Choice Questions

1. (b); 2. (c); 3. (d); 4. (a); 5. (c)

REFERENCES

1. Cavusgil, S. T., Knight, G., & Riesenberger, J. R., (2018). *International Business: The New Realities* (5th edn., Vol. 1). Pearson Education, Inc.
2. Chadha, N. K., (2018). *International Business Management: A Managerial Perspective*. Vikas Publishing House.
3. Cherunilam, F., (2017). *International Business Management: Text and Cases*. Himalaya Publishing House.
4. Cullen, J. B., & Parboteeah, K. P., (2018). *International Business: Strategy and the Multinational Company* (2nd edn., Vol. 2). Routledge.
5. Daniels, J. D., Radebaugh, L. H., & Sullivan, D. P., (2018). *International Business: Environments and Operations*. Pearson Education.
6. Deresky, H., (2020). *International Management: Managing Across Borders and Cultures* (10th edn.). Pearson Education.
7. Hill, C. W. L., & Hult, G. T. M., (2019). *Global Business Today* (11th edn., Vol. 1). McGraw-Hill Education.
8. Hill, C. W. L., & Hult, G. T. M., (2021). *International Business: Competing in the Global Marketplace* (12th edn., Vol. 2). McGraw-Hill Education.
9. Kuthiala, B. K., & Kuthiala, D., (2017). *International Business Management: Theory and Practice*. Excel Books.
10. Luthans, F., & Doh, J. P., (2020). *International Management: Culture, Strategy, and Behavior* (10th edn., Vol. 2). McGraw-Hill Education.

11. Sharma, K., & Dubey, A., (2017). *International Business Management: Globalization and Beyond*. Pearson India.

12. Wild, J. J., Wild, K. L., & Han, J. C. Y., (2017). *International Business: The Challenges of Globalization* (9th edn., Vol. 1). Pearson Education, Inc.

CHAPTER 3

INTERNATIONAL BUSINESS ENVIRONMENT

UNIT INTRODUCTION

The growth of the international business has indeed been a significant trend in the past few decades. The globalization of markets has led to increased competition and greater opportunities for businesses to expand into new markets and reach a larger customer base.

The expansion of world product trade and the increase in globalization of financial markets have been particularly noteworthy. The growth of world product trade by more than six percent a year since 1950 has been a key driver of economic growth and development. It has enabled businesses to access new markets and take advantage of economies of scale, which in turn has led to increased productivity and innovation.

However, the most dramatic increase in globalization has been in financial markets, particularly in the foreign exchange markets. The volume of transactions in these markets has grown significantly in recent years, with billions of dollars being transacted each day. Many of these transactions are unrelated to trade or investment, and take place in markets outside the country whose currency is used, known as Euromarkets. In order to succeed in today's global business environment, companies must understand the various factors that can impact their operations and make informed decisions based on that understanding.

The environmental analysis involves examining both the internal and external factors that can affect a business, including economic, political, cultural, social, environmental and technological factors. By analyzing these factors, a company can identify opportunities for growth and expansion, as well as potential threats and challenges that may need to be addressed.

In addition to conducting an environmental analysis, a global company must also have a clear understanding of its mission, objectives, and goals. This will help guide its decision-making process and ensure that all strategies are aligned with its overall vision.

Once a company has a clear understanding of its environment and goals, it can begin to formulate strategies that will help it achieve its objectives. This may involve entering new markets, introducing new products or services, or implementing new marketing and distribution channels.

Learning Objectives

After completing this chapter, you should be able to understand:

- Meaning of international business environment
- Factors of the international business environment
- Cultural and social environment
- Technological environment
- Political environment
- Economic environment
- Legal environment

Key Terms

- Cultural Differences
- Economic Systems
- Exchange Rates
- Free Trade

- Globalization
- Intellectual Property Rights (IPRs)
- International Trade Agreements
- Legal Systems
- Non-tariff Barriers
- Political Risk
- Tariffs

3.1. MEANING OF INTERNATIONAL BUSINESS ENVIRONMENT

The business environment refers to the external and internal factors that influence the operations and strategies of a business, including its Multinational Corporations (MNCs) and transnational companies in the global marketplace.

The international business environment encompasses various factors, such as political, economic, legal, social, technological, environmental and cultural factors, that affect the operations of businesses operating in different countries. These factors create opportunities and threats for international businesses and can significantly impact their success in the global market.

Therefore, MNCs and transnational companies need to understand and adapt to the international business environment to develop effective business strategies, mitigate risks, and achieve their objectives in different countries and regions.

The following are definitions of the international business environment from various authors:

1. According to Daniels et al. (2020), the international business environment is "the totality of external and internal factors that influence the operations and strategies of a firm in a global context, including economic, political, legal, technological, and cultural factors."
2. According to Hill (2018), the international business environment is "the collection of factors, institutions, and forces that affect a firm's performance and strategies in the global market."
3. According to Rugman and Collinson (2018), the international business environment is "the external and internal factors that affect the strategies and operations of firms in a global context, including economic, political, legal, technological, and cultural factors, as well as the characteristics of the industry and competitive environment."
4. According to Cavusgil et al. (2017), the international business environment is "the set of external and internal factors that impact the decision-making process and operations of firms that operate across national borders."

Environmental analysis is the process of assessing and examining the external and internal factors that may impact a business's operations and strategies. The analysis involves identifying opportunities and threats in the business environment surrounding the organization, as well as assessing the strengths and weaknesses of within the organization itself. Here are some definitions of environmental analysis from various authors:

1. According to Kotler et al. (2017), environmental analysis is "the systematic examination of the external environment and the organization's internal resources and capabilities to identify key factors that could impact the organization's success."
2. According to Porter (1985), environmental analysis is "the ongoing process of scanning the external environment for changes in the competitive landscape and identifying potential opportunities and threats for the organization."
3. According to Johnson et al. (2017), environmental analysis is "a structured process of gathering and analyzing information about the external and internal environments to identify key trends, opportunities, and threats that could affect the organization's ability to achieve its objectives."
4. According to Grant (2016), environmental analysis is "the process of examining the organization's external environment to identify potential opportunities and threats and assessing the internal environment to determine the organization's strengths and weaknesses."

Environmental analysis is a critical tool for businesses to develop effective strategies, mitigate risks, and adapt to changes in the business environment. It helps organizations to stay competitive and achieve their goals in a dynamic and constantly evolving marketplace.

3.2. FACTORS OF THE INTERNATIONAL BUSINESS ENVIRONMENT

The international business environment refers to the external and internal factors that influence the operations and strategies of a business in the global marketplace. This is characterized by cultural, political, economic, legal, environmental and technological differences across countries and regions, which may impact the operations and profitability of businesses (Figure 3.1).

Business environmental factors are broadly divided into internal and external environmental factors, and external environmental factors are further classified into micro and macro factors. Here's a breakdown of the different environmental factors:

1. **Internal Environmental Factors**: These are factors that are within the control of the organization and can be influenced by its management.

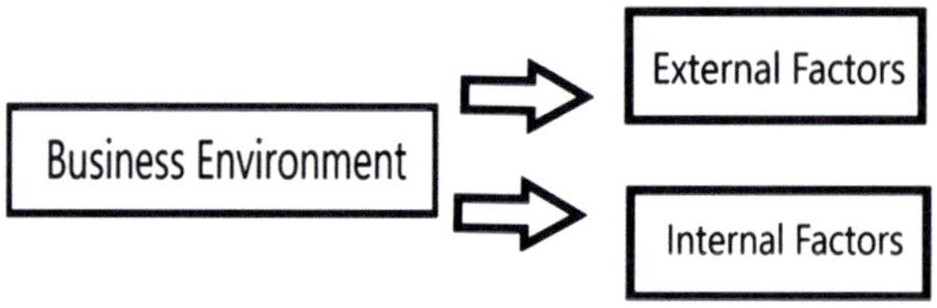

Figure 3.1. Business environmental factors.

They include:

- Human resource management
- Trade unions
- Organization structure
- Financial management
- Marketing management
- Production management
- Management/leadership style, etc.

2. **External Environmental Factors**: These are factors that are outside the control of the organization but can significantly impact its operations. They include:

- **Micro Environmental Factors:** These are factors that are closer to the organization and include competitors, customers, market intermediaries, suppliers of raw materials, bankers, other suppliers of finance and other shareholders of the business firm.
- **Macro Environmental Factors:** These are factors that are broader in scope and influence the organization's operations in the long term. They include social and cultural factors, technological factors, economic factors, political and governmental factors, international factors, and environmental factors.

Understanding and analyzing these internal and external factors is crucial for businesses to develop effective strategies, mitigate risks, and achieve their objectives in a constantly changing business environment.

3.3. CULTURAL AND SOCIAL ENVIRONMENT

Understanding cultural differences is essential when doing business abroad. A company must be aware of the differences in business practices, customs, and social norms that may vary from one country to another.

Cultural differences can affect all aspects of a business, from communication and marketing to negotiations and decision-making. For example, in some cultures, it may be considered rude to negotiate aggressively, while in others, it may be expected. Similarly, some cultures may place a greater emphasis on personal relationships and trust-building, while others may prioritize formal contracts and legal agreements.

By understanding the cultures of the groups of people they interact with, businesses can avoid misunderstandings, build trust, and establish successful partnerships. They can also tailor their marketing and communication strategies to appeal to local preferences and adapt their business practices to comply with local laws and regulations.

3.3.1. Values and Norms

Values are an important aspect of culture and provide a foundation for a society's norms and beliefs. They shape the attitudes and behaviors of individuals and are deeply ingrained in the collective consciousness of a society.

Values can differ greatly between cultures and may reflect a society's historical, religious, or political background. For example, individual freedom and democracy are highly valued in Western cultures, while collectivism and social harmony are emphasized in many Eastern cultures. Similarly, values such as honesty, loyalty, and respect for authority may be highly prized in some cultures, while others may place greater importance on family, community, or tradition.

Values are not just abstract concepts; they are imbued with strong emotional significance and can be a source of conflict and disagreement between individuals and groups. For example, differing views on the role of women or the importance of religion can lead to tension and conflict between cultures.

Values also play a significant role in shaping the political and economic systems of a society. For example, a society that values individual freedom and democracy may have a more open and liberal political system, while a society that values social harmony and collective responsibility may have a more centralized and authoritarian system of governance.

Values form an important part of the culture and shape the attitudes, behaviors, and beliefs of individuals and societies. Understanding the values of culture is essential for effective communication and collaboration between individuals and groups from different cultural backgrounds.

Mores, on the other hand, are norms that are considered to be of great moral significance. They are the essential customs and conventions of a society that reflect its core values and beliefs. Unlike folkways, violations of mores are considered to be serious offenses, and individuals who violate mores are often subject to social sanctions, including ostracism and punishment. For example, in many societies, stealing, lying, and killing are considered to be serious violations of mores.

It is important to note that the distinction between folkways and mores is not always clear-cut. What may be considered a folkway in one society may be considered a more in another. Additionally, the importance attached to different norms can change over time, as societies evolve and develop new values.

Norms play a crucial role in maintaining social order and cohesion. They provide a shared set of expectations and guidelines for behavior, and violations of norms can lead to social disapproval and ostracism. Understanding the different types of norms and their significance can help individuals navigate social interactions and avoid unintentionally offending others.

3.3.2. Culture, Society, and the Nation-State

Culture, society, and the nation-state are interconnected concepts in the study of cultural and social environments. Culture refers to the shared beliefs, values, customs, behaviors, and artifacts that characterize a group or society. It encompasses language, religion, art, music, literature, cuisine, and other aspects of human expression. Culture is transmitted from one generation to the next through socialization and can vary greatly between different groups and societies.

Society, on the other hand, refers to the people who live in a particular geographical area and share a common culture. Society is characterized by social organization, including patterns of social relationships, institutions, and power structures. It encompasses all aspects of social life, including politics, economics, education, and religion. Society is dynamic and constantly changing, influenced by various factors such as technology, migration, and globalization.

The nation-state is a political entity that includes a defined territory, a government, and a population that shares a common identity, including a common culture, language, and history. The nation-state is a modern concept that emerged in Europe in the 18th century and became the dominant form of political organization in the world. Nation-states are characterized by a centralized government, a national identity, and sovereignty over their territory. Nation-states are often based on the principle of citizenship, which grants legal and political rights to individuals who are members of the nation-state.

The relationship between culture, society, and the nation-state is complex and interdependent. Culture is often seen as the foundation of society, shaping its values, beliefs, and practices. In turn, society provides the context in which culture is expressed and transmitted. The nation-state, as a political entity, can play a significant role in shaping culture and society through policies and laws that promote certain values and practices. For example, a nation-state may promote a particular language or religion as part of its national identity.

At the same time, culture and society can also influence the nation-state. Social movements and cultural trends can challenge the authority of the nation-state and demand greater recognition of cultural diversity and individual rights. The nation-state may respond by either accommodating these demands or suppressing them.

3.3.3. Determinants of Culture in a Socio-Cultural Environment

The values and norms of a culture are not static and fixed. They are shaped by various factors, including the political and economic philosophy, social structure, religion, language, and education of a society. These factors interact and evolve over time, shaping the cultural practices and beliefs of a society. Understanding these factors is crucial to understanding the evolution and dynamics of a culture, and how it relates to other cultures and societies.

3.3.4. Social Structure

A society's social structure is a critical factor that shapes its culture. Social structure refers to the basic social organizations in society, including the patterns of relationships between individuals, families, groups, and institutions. Two important dimensions of social structure that help explain cultural differences are individualism-collectivism and social stratification. Individualism-collectivism refers to the degree to which the basic unit of social organization is the individual or the group. In individualistic societies, individual achievement and autonomy are highly valued, and personal goals often take precedence over group goals. In collectivistic societies, the group and its goals are more important than individual goals, and people are expected to be loyal to and cooperate with their group.

Social stratification refers to the degree to which a society is stratified into classes or castes. In highly stratified societies, there are significant differences in wealth, power, and status among different social groups, and social mobility between these groups is limited. In contrast, in more egalitarian societies, there is less stratification, and social mobility is more fluid. For example, Indian society is highly stratified into castes, and mobility between castes is relatively low. In contrast, American society is less stratified, and there is a higher degree of social mobility. These differences in social structure can help explain cultural differences between the two societies, including differences in values, norms, and social practices.

3.3.4.1. Individuals and Groups

A group is a collection of two or more individuals who share a sense of identity and interact with each other in structured ways based on common expectations. Human social life is essentially group life, and individuals participate in a range of groups such as family, work, and recreational groups.

However, societies differ in the degree to which they view groups as the primary means of social organization. In some societies, individual attributes, and accomplishments are considered more important than group membership. These societies tend to be individualistic, and the emphasis is on personal achievement, self-reliance, and autonomy. In contrast, in other societies, the group is viewed as the primary means of social organization. In these societies, group membership and loyalty are highly valued, and the individual's identity and achievements are often defined by their group affiliation. These societies tend to be collectivistic, emphasizing cooperation, conformity, and interdependence.

These cultural differences in the importance of the group versus the individual can influence many aspects of social life, including relationships, decision-making, and social norms. For example, in collectivistic societies, social harmony and conformity to group norms are highly valued, and decisions are often made based on group consensus rather than individual preferences. In individualistic societies, on the other hand, individual autonomy and personal choice are more highly valued, and decision-making is often more individualistic.

3.3.4.2. Social Stratification

All societies are stratified into social categories or strata based on characteristics such as family background, occupation, and income. These social strata are arranged hierarchically, and individuals are typically born into a particular stratum based on their parents' status.

Individuals born into the higher strata tend to have better life chances such as better education, better health, a better standard of living, and better work opportunities than those born into the lower strata. This social stratification can have a significant impact on an individual's social, economic, and political opportunities.

However, societies differ in two related ways in terms of social stratification that are of interest to business organizations. The first difference is the degree of mobility between social strata. Some societies have a high degree of social mobility, which means that individuals can move up or down the social hierarchy based on their achievements and talents. In contrast, other societies have a low degree of social mobility, which means that social status is largely determined by an individual's birth and family background (Figure 3.2).

Figure 3.2. Social stratification.

The second difference is the significance attached to social strata in business contexts. In some societies, social status and family background are important factors in business relationships and decision-making. For example, in societies with a high degree of collectivism, family ties, and personal relationships can play a significant role in business transactions. In contrast, in societies with a high degree of individualism, business decisions tend to be more focused on objective criteria such as performance and productivity.

3.3.4.3. Social Mobility

Social mobility refers to the extent to which individuals can move out of the social strata into which they are born. This can vary significantly from society to society, and the most rigid system of stratification is the caste system. In a caste system, an individual's social position is determined by the family into which they are born, and change in position is usually not possible during an individual's lifetime. Often, caste positions are associated with specific occupations that are passed down through the family to succeeding generations. India has a particularly well-known example of a caste system, with four main castes and several thousand sub-castes. Even though the caste system was officially abolished in 1949, it still has a significant impact on rural Indian society, with occupation and marital opportunities being partly related to caste.

In contrast, many societies have class systems, in which individuals are born into a particular social class based on family background, occupation, and income. However, social mobility within a class system varies from society to society. In some societies, such as the United States, there is a relatively high degree of social mobility, which means that individuals can move up or down the social ladder based on their achievements and talents. In other societies, such as the United Kingdom, social mobility is more limited, with individuals often remaining in the same social class as their parents.

Social mobility is a crucial factor in understanding the social stratification of different societies. While some societies have rigid caste systems that limit social mobility, others have more fluid class systems that allow individuals to move up or down the social ladder based on their abilities and achievements. Understanding these differences is crucial for businesses operating in different cultural contexts, as it can have significant implications for recruitment, hiring, and management practices.

3.3.4.4. Significance Attached to the Social Strata in Business Contexts

In Great Britain, class consciousness is significant for business organizations because it can affect the relationships between employees and customers, as well as the relationships between employees themselves. For example, an employee who comes from a working-class background may have difficulty relating to customers from upper-class backgrounds, and may also have difficulty fitting in with colleagues from upper-class backgrounds. This can create barriers to effective communication and cooperation within the organization. Additionally, class consciousness may affect the way that employees perceive opportunities for advancement within the organization. If an employee perceives that the organization is dominated by members of a certain social class, they may feel that their own opportunities for advancement are limited, which can lead to lower morale and decreased motivation. Therefore, understanding the degree of social stratification and mobility in a society is important for businesses operating in that society, as it can impact the dynamics of the workplace and the organization's success.

3.3.4.5. Religious and Ethical Systems

Religion and ethics play a significant role in shaping attitudes toward work and entrepreneurship in different societies. For example, the Protestant work ethic, which emphasizes hard work, thrift, and efficiency, has been associated with economic success in many countries, particularly in Western Europe and North America. Similarly, Confucian ethics, which stress hard work, education, and family values, have been credited with the success of many Asian economies. In contrast, some religions, such as Buddhism, emphasize the spiritual and ethical dimensions of life over material success, which may have implications for business practices in countries where Buddhism is dominant.

Religious ethics can also affect the costs of doing business in a country. For example, some religions have strict dietary or dress requirements that may affect the production, distribution, or marketing of certain products. Similarly, religious holidays may affect the timing and scheduling of business activities in different countries. In addition, some religious groups may have specific beliefs about the role of business in society, which may influence corporate social responsibility (CSR) and other ethical issues.

Religion and ethics play an important role in shaping cultural attitudes and values, which in turn affect business practices and operations. Understanding the role of religion and ethics in different societies is therefore critical for successful cross-cultural business operations.

3.3.5. Language

Language is a critical element of a culture and is often referred to as a defining characteristic of a society. It is a means of communication that facilitates the exchange of ideas, beliefs, and values among individuals within a society. Language can also serve as a tool for socialization, enabling individuals to learn and internalize the norms, values, and beliefs of their culture.

Different languages and dialects are spoken in different parts of the world, and they have a profound impact on the way people communicate and interact with one another. The language spoken in a country can have significant implications for business operations, as it can affect how easily companies can communicate with local customers and stakeholders.

Moreover, language also includes nonverbal communication such as body language, gestures, and facial expressions, which can vary significantly between cultures. Understanding and being aware of these nonverbal cues can be crucial for effective communication and building relationships in a cross-cultural business environment.

3.3.6. Education

Formal education plays a significant role in shaping individuals and societies. It is a means for individuals to acquire knowledge, skills, and attitudes that are essential for their personal and professional growth. Education is also a medium through which societies pass on their values, beliefs, and cultural norms to the next generation.

In addition to providing basic literacy and numeracy skills, formal education teaches social and civic responsibilities to children. It helps children learn how to respect authority, work collaboratively, and become responsible citizens. The grading system used in schools also teaches children the importance of personal achievement and occupation, which are essential in a competitive society.

From an international business perspective, education plays a crucial role in determining national competitive advantage. The availability of a skilled and educated workforce is a significant determinant of a country's economic success. The level of education in a country is also an indicator of the types of products that are likely to sell in that country and the type of promotional material that should be used.

3.3.7. Demand Conditions

The composition of home demand refers to the types of goods and services that are demanded by consumers within a particular country or region. This can include consumer goods such as clothing, electronics, and food, as well as services such as healthcare, education, and transportation. The composition of home demand can vary significantly from country to country, depending on factors such as income levels, cultural preferences, and the stage of economic development.

The size and pattern of growth of home demand refer to the overall size of the consumer market within a particular country or region, as well as the rate at which this market is expected to grow over time. The size of the consumer market is determined by factors such as population size, income levels, and the overall level of economic development. The pattern of growth, meanwhile, can be influenced by factors such as demographic shifts, changes in consumer preferences, and fluctuations in economic conditions.

Understanding the composition, size, and pattern of growth of home demand is important for businesses operating within a particular country or region. By analyzing these factors, businesses can identify growth opportunities and determine the types of products and services that are likely to be in the highest demand. Additionally, businesses can use this information to develop marketing strategies that are tailored to the specific needs and preferences of consumers within a particular market.

Other Indicators:

Quality of Life: Quality of life refers to the overall well-being and satisfaction of individuals and communities in various aspects of their lives. The factors mentioned in the question are key indicators of quality of life.

Life expectancy refers to the average length of time an individual is expected to live. A higher life expectancy indicates a better quality of life, as people are living longer and healthier lives.

Educational standards are also important indicators of quality of life. Access to education, the level of education achieved, and the quality of education received all play a role in shaping an individual's opportunities and overall well-being.

Individual purchasing power refers to the amount of money an individual has to spend on goods and services. A higher purchasing power generally means a higher standard of living and a better quality of life.

Health and sanitation are also critical factors in determining the quality of life. Access to healthcare, clean water, and adequate sanitation facilities is essential for maintaining good health and preventing diseases.

The treatment of women is also an important factor in the quality of life. Societies that value and respect women tend to have higher levels of gender equality and women's empowerment, which in turn can lead to greater social and economic opportunities for women, and overall improvements in quality of life.

3.3.8. Attitudes and Values

Attitudes and values are often influenced by religious beliefs and can impact how individuals perceive marketing activities and material gain.

For example, in Buddhist societies, where the emphasis is on spiritual well-being and detachment from material possessions, marketing activities that solely focus on the material gain may not be relevant. Similarly, in some African societies, where there is a preference for stability and aversion to risk-taking, entrepreneurialism may not be widely accepted.

Therefore, businesses need to research to understand the cultural values and attitudes of the target market before developing marketing strategies. This understanding helps to ensure that marketing efforts are culturally appropriate and effective. Additionally, in some cases, it may be more effective to relate products to traditional values rather than new ones, especially in societies where change may not be wanted or needed.

3.3.9. Socio-Cultural Factors and International Marketing

MNCs are large companies that operate in multiple countries around the world. In order to do so, they must navigate a variety of different factors, including political systems, economic conditions, geographical challenges, technological capabilities, and marketing environments.

All of these factors can vary greatly from country to country, making it challenging for MNCs to operate effectively and efficiently. Successful MNCs must be able to adapt to these different environments and find ways to thrive in each location. They may do so by customizing their products or services to meet local needs, developing strong relationships with local partners and governments, or leveraging their global resources and expertise to create competitive advantages.

Every host country has its own society and culture which is different in many important ways from almost every other society or culture. These differences can impact every aspect of the overseas business of an MNC, including marketing, finance, production, or personnel. The predominant attitudes, feelings, and opinions in the local environment can influence the success or failure of a local subsidiary or affiliate.

Differences in values and attitudes between the management and the parent offices, expatriate managers at the subsidiary or affiliate level, and local managers and employees can lead to serious operational and functional problems. Society and culture often mold general attitudes towards fundamentals of life such as time, money, productivity, and achievement, which can differ widely across countries and lead to situations of differing expectations between the management in the home office and local employees of subsidiaries and affiliates. Therefore, MNCS need to appreciate these differences and how they influence the business before attempting to set up an operation in a host country.

Moreover, each host country has its own society and culture which is different in many important ways from almost every other society or culture, although there are some commonalities. Though society and culture do not appear to be a part of marketing situations, they are actually key elements in showing how marketing activities will be conducted, what goods will be produced, and through what means they will be sold to establish industrial and management patterns and determining the success or failure of a local subsidiary or affiliate. Society and culture influence every aspect of the overseas business of an MNC and successful MNC operations – whether it is marketing, finance, production, or personnel – have to be acutely aware of the predominant attitudes, feelings, and opinions in the local environment. Differences in values and attitudes between the management and the parent offices and expatriate managers at the subsidiary or affiliate level and local managers and employees can lead to serious operational and functional problems, which arise not because there are individual problems, but because of the important differences between societies and cultures. Society and culture often mold general attitudes towards fundamentals of life such as time, money, productivity, and achievement, all of which can differ widely across countries and lead to situations of differing expectations between the management in the home office and local employees of subsidiaries and affiliates. While some socio-cultural differences are obvious, others are relatively subtle, though equally important. It is often difficult for an international manager to catch on to these subtle differences if he or she has not lived or worked in cultures other than that of the home country. MNCs have realized, sometimes through costly blunders that socio-cultural factors are vital ingredients that make up the overall business environment and that it is essential to appreciate these differences and how they influence the business before an attempt is made to set up an operation in a host country.

3.4. TECHNOLOGICAL ENVIRONMENT

Technology has indeed revolutionized the way we live our lives, and has had a significant impact on how we conduct business, communicate, and interact with each other. From traditional snail mail to modern e-mail, technology has transformed the way we communicate and has made the world a smaller place by removing the barriers of distance and time.

With the latest technological developments such as the Internet, video conferencing, and cell phones, people can now connect with others from different parts of the world without the need for physical travel. This has been a game-changer for international business, as it has made it easier to conduct business transactions, collaborate with others, and form global partnerships.

Thanks to technology, people can now work remotely and participate in virtual meetings, which saves time and money on travel expenses. The ability to work from anywhere and stay connected with others has also improved work-life balance and has given people more flexibility in their careers.

Technology has made the world a more connected place and has opened up new opportunities for businesses and individuals alike.

3.4.1. Benefits of Technology in Management Decision-Making

Running a business involves making numerous decisions, both simple and complex, daily. Every decision made by a business owner or manager can have a significant impact on the success of the company in the long term. Therefore, it is important to have the necessary tools to make informed decisions.

In today's world, technology plays an indispensable role in business operations and activities. It enables decision-makers to access information that is vital to their decision-making process, thus helping to speed up processes and increase efficiency. This is especially important in today's fast-paced business environment where time is of the essence.

Technology also allows for better collaboration among department heads and their teams. This is essential for executing decisions effectively and efficiently. By using technology, managers can update employees on how to carry out tasks that will benefit the company. This is particularly relevant when changes need to be implemented quickly or when staff members are working remotely.

Technology helps the manager to make decisions related to business in the following ways:

1. **Decision Support System:** Decision Support System (DSS) is a computer-based information system designed to support managers in making informed decisions. The DSS collects data from various sources, such as government reports, customer feedback, supplier information, global market trends, and competitor analysis, to provide managers with a comprehensive and up-to-date view of the business environment. This data is then analyzed using mathematical decision models that help the manager to evaluate different scenarios and options for decision-making.

   A DSS can assist managers in making complex decisions that involve multiple factors and variables. For example, a DSS can be used to analyze financial data, market trends, and customer feedback to determine the optimal pricing strategy for a new product. Alternatively, it can be used to forecast sales for a given period based on historical data and current market trends.

2. **Group Decision Support System:** A group decision support system (GDSS) is a system that combines hardware, software, and procedures to assist a group of people who are involved in making decisions during a meeting. The system enables the group to collaborate in real time by providing a shared platform where everyone can contribute ideas, discuss options, and make decisions together.

   The software in a GDSS typically includes features such as electronic voting, brainstorming tools, and collaborative writing tools. The hardware can consist of computers, projectors, and other audio-visual equipment, which allow participants to share information and present their ideas.
3. **Office Automation System:** An office automation system refers to the use of computers or computer networks to carry out a range of office operations. This includes tasks such as word processing, data entry, email communication, managing appointments and schedules, and managing documents and files. By automating these tasks, office automation systems can improve efficiency and productivity, reduce errors and improve data accuracy. As a result, office automation systems help organizations to streamline their day-to-day operations and achieve greater efficiency and effectiveness.
4. **Transaction Processing System:** A Transaction Processing System (TPS) is a type of computerized system designed to manage and track the processing of transactions, typically involving large volumes of data. This system is used to automate and facilitate the processing of business transactions, such as order processing, inventory management, and payroll processing.

   The TPS works by collecting transaction data from various sources, processing it in a standardized format, and then recording it in a database. This system is designed to be highly reliable and efficient, with built-in mechanisms to ensure the accuracy and consistency of the data being processed.

   The use of TPS provides several benefits, including improved data accuracy, faster processing times, reduced errors and redundancy, and increased productivity. By automating transaction processing, organizations can free up staff time to focus on more important tasks, reduce costs, and improve overall efficiency.
5. **Management Information System:** Management Information System (MIS) is a software toolset that helps managers collect, organize and evaluate information about a workgroup, department, or entire organization. The system provides managers with the information they need to make informed decisions and monitor the performance of their organization.
6. **Expert System:** An expert system is a type of computer program that

uses artificial intelligence to simulate the decision-making ability of a human expert. It is designed to perform specialized tasks and provide expert-level advice in a particular field or industry.

3.4.2. Effect of Technology on Strategy and Competition

Some of them are discussed as under:

1. **Creating Barriers to Entry:** The cutting-edge technology used by MNCs has created barriers for the new entrants into the industry. It also poses as a threat to domestic industries since this cutting-edge technology has increased the need to invest in research and development (R&D) in a limited resource market.
2. **Generating New Products:** Technology has always created new world products and modified new products; there is a greater need for business organizations to invest in large volumes in R&D to bring out new products. Some minor changes in features of the product with the same underlying technology have given rise to new products.
3. **Changing Relationships with Suppliers:** The relationships maintained by the suppliers have dramatically changed, shifting from traditional procurement processes to one that encompasses technology and is tagged now as e-procurement, e-supply chain management, and global integration. This has given rise to increases in quality and efficiency while lowering production time.
4. **Changing the Basis for Competition:** Technology is a make-or-break criteria when comparing against competition, with superior technology used by successful business firms resulting in improved quality of producing goods, improved efficiency by automation and mechanization, and adhering to Total Quality Management (TQM), to name a few.

3.4.3. Features of Technology

The following are the features of technology:

1. **Technology Brings Change**: Technology has a significant impact on various aspects of our lives, including cooking, transportation, and communication. It has also transformed the way businesses operate, from traditional barter systems to e-businesses, enabling greater efficiency and global reach.
2. **Technology Reduces Time**: Advancements in technology have significantly reduced the time required to conceive and implement new ideas, leading to faster innovation and development. Additionally, the internet has facilitated seamless communication and information

transfer across the world, transforming the world into a global village with no geographical barriers.

3. **Technology Reduces Distance**: The invention of advanced transportation systems, such as supersonic jets, has significantly reduced travel time, enabling people to travel across the world in a matter of hours instead of days. This has facilitated greater global connectivity and mobility, leading to increased trade, tourism, and cultural exchange.
4. **Technology Improves Quality of Life**: The quality of life for people has improved with the advancements in medical technology, leading to increased life expectancy rates and improved control over various diseases. This has also facilitated better healthcare and improved standards of living.

3.4.4. Diffusion of Technology

Diffusion of technology refers to the process by which new technology is spread and adopted by individuals or organizations. This process can be influenced by factors such as the perceived benefits and costs of the technology, the level of awareness and education of potential users, and social and cultural factors.

The technology will diffuse in the following ways:

1. **Joint Ventures:** When two companies, A and B, decide to jointly work on a venture, it means they collaborate and pool their resources to achieve a common goal. This collaboration could involve sharing technology, expertise, human resources, or any other relevant resources.

   For instance, Company A might have a technology that Company B needs to develop its product, while Company B might have the expertise or the workforce that Company A needs to implement that technology. Instead of each company working independently on its own, they can collaborate and work together to achieve their common goals.
2. **Licensing:** Companies in the domestic market can obtain a license from a multinational corporation (MNC) to produce and sell their products in the local market. This allows domestic companies to benefit from the MNC's established brand, technology, and market presence.
3. **Technological Transfer:** Technology can be transferred from one country to another through collaborations between companies or governments, such as a German collaboration or Japanese collaboration, where expertise and resources are shared to achieve common goals. Such collaborations allow countries to leverage each other's strengths and resources to promote economic growth and development.

3.4.5. Business Implications of Technology

The use of technology in business has several implications, such as:

- Companies can launch new products and services to their sales force without taking them out of the field, using digital tools like online training and virtual product demos.
- Companies can use technology to highlight product releases and introductions to employees, shareholders, and clients through virtual presentations and webinars.
- Companies can provide certification programs to geographically dispersed audiences through online learning platforms, which can save time and reduce travel costs.

3.5. POLITICAL ENVIRONMENT

The political environment of a country can have a significant impact on any business, regardless of its size or area of operation. This is because the policies and attitudes of the government towards business can affect how a company operates and grows. In international business, both the host and home governments are integral partners, and their policies and attitudes towards business reflect their ideas of how to best promote their national interests, based on their resources and political philosophies.

Governments have the power to control and restrict the activities of companies by either encouraging or offering support or by discouraging and banning or restricting their activities based on their policies and regulations. International law recognizes the right of nations to grant or withhold permission for businesses to operate within their political boundaries and to regulate the activities of their citizens when it comes to conducting business. Therefore, the political environment of different countries is a critical concern for international marketers, and they should examine the political features of the global markets they plan to enter to ensure compliance with relevant laws and regulations.

3.5.1. Sovereignty of Nations

From an international law perspective, a sovereign state is independent and free from external control and has the power to govern its own territory, select its own political, social, and economic systems, and enter into agreements with other nations. The extension of national laws beyond a country's borders is where much of the conflict in international business arises. Nations can give up some of their sovereign rights voluntarily to participate in common goals with other member nations, as seen in the examples of the European Union and the North American Free Trade Agreement (NAFTA) (Figure 3.3).

Figure 3.3. *North American free trade agreement.*

The ideal political climate for a multinational firm is a stable and friendly environment, but unfortunately, that is not always the case. Since foreign businesses are judged by standards that vary from nation to nation, it is crucial to assess the friendliness and stability of the government in each country as an ongoing business practice. This assessment will help the multinational firm to make informed decisions and to navigate the legal and regulatory framework of the foreign country.

- **Stability of Government Policies:** The stability or instability of the prevailing government policies is the most important political condition that concerns an international business. Continuity of set rules or codes of behavior, regardless of the party in power, is crucial for MNCs. A change in the government does not always mean a change in the level of political risks, and sometimes even the most stable governments can undergo radical changes in policies toward foreign business. As long as there is some long-term predictability and stability, MNCs can function under any type of government if permitted to operate within a country.
- **Political Parties:** To succeed in international business, marketers need to have knowledge of all major political parties and their philosophies within a country. This is

because a change in government or shift in prevailing attitudes can greatly impact trade policies. In countries where there are two strong political parties, it is important to understand the direction each party is likely to take on trade and related issues. It is also important to be aware of politically strong interest groups and factions within political parties, as they can cooperate to influence trade policies.

TIPS

Businesses need to consider the political environment when making strategic decisions and planning their operations.

3.5.2. Types of Political Systems

The following are the types of political systems:

Democracy: In a democratic system, people have the right to vote and choose their leaders through free and fair elections. The elected representatives are then responsible for making decisions and policies that benefit the people and the country as a whole. This system promotes participation, transparency, and accountability in the government. India is an example of a democratic country where the citizens have the right to vote and elect their representatives.

Dictatorship: Dictatorship also called authoritarianism is a form of government in which power is concentrated in the hands of a single leader and the small group of individuals surrounding him, leaving the majority of the citizens with little to no say in the political process. The leader or group in power often restricts civil liberties and suppresses political opposition. In terms of business and the economy, the leader may have a significant influence on policies, regulations, and trade agreements. Authoritarian governments typically have monarchs holding relatively absolute power over the country.

Political Risks of Global Business: Political risks of global business refer to the potential negative impact that political factors, such as government instability or policy changes, can have on a company's operations and profitability in international markets. Some of the political risks of global business are stated below:

- **Confiscation***:* Confiscation refers to the act of seizing a company's assets without any form of payment or compensation. This is considered the most severe political risk for businesses operating in foreign countries, as it can lead to significant financial losses and damage to the company's reputation. It is important for businesses to assess the political climate of a country before investing in order to mitigate the risk of confiscation.

- **Expropriation:** Expropriation refers to the action of a government to take over private property or assets, including foreign investments, for public use with reimbursement of fair compensation. It is a political risk that multinational companies may face in certain countries where there is a change in government policy or economic conditions. Unlike confiscation, expropriation involves compensation, but the amount of compensation may not always be fair or adequate, and the process may also involve lengthy legal disputes.
- **Domestication:** A domestication is a form of political risk where a host country takes steps to transfer foreign investments to national control and ownership through a series of government decrees. This often involves the requirement for foreign investors to share ownership and control of their business with local partners, or for the government to acquire a majority stake in the foreign investment. Domestication is often motivated by a change in the government's attitudes, policies, economic plans, and philosophies toward the role of foreign investment in the country.
- **Assessing Political Vulnerability:** Certain products, such as those related to defense, technology, or natural resources, are often more politically vulnerable and receive more government attention. This attention can result in positive actions, such as subsidies or contracts, or negative actions, such as restrictions or bans. It is difficult for marketers to predict whether their products will receive government attention or not, as it varies by country and is influenced by a range of factors including national security concerns, public health issues, and cultural sensitivities.
- **Politically Sensitive Products:** Products that have a significant impact on the environment, exchange rates, national and economic security, or the welfare of people are more likely to be politically sensitive. For example, products related to nuclear energy or genetically modified organisms may receive more government attention due to their potential impact on the environment and public health. Similarly, products that are considered essential to a country's economic development, such as oil or natural resources, may also be politically sensitive. On the other hand, products that are deemed non-essential may face less government scrutiny.
- **Good Corporate Citizenship***:* Being a corporate citizen means that a company takes into account the impact of its actions on society and the environment, and acts responsibly in all aspects of its operations. In this way, the company can build a positive reputation and relationships with governments, communities, and other stakeholders. This can help to reduce the company's political vulnerability by demonstrating its commitment to social responsibility and contributing to the overall well-

being of society. It can also help to mitigate negative political reactions and potential risks that may arise from the company's operations.

Strategies to Lessen Political Risks: MNCs can minimize political risks by using strategies like JVs, expanding their investment base, marketing and distribution, licensing, planned domestication, and political payoffs. These strategies help to establish good relationships with host countries and reduce political vulnerability. They are:

i. **Joint Ventures**: MNCs can form partnerships with local companies to gain knowledge of local markets, customs, and regulations. This can help to reduce political risks and increase acceptance by the host Country.
ii. **Expanding the Investment Base**: MNCs can reduce political risks by investing in a diversified range of products and services, and by expanding their operations in different geographic regions.
iii. **Marketing and Distribution**: MNCs can reduce political risks by developing marketing and distribution strategies that are sensitive to the host country's cultural, social, and political values.
iv. **Licensing:** MNCs can license their technology, patents, and trademarks to local firms, which can help to reduce political risks and increase acceptance by the host country.
v. **Planned Domestication**: MNCs can proactively transfer ownership and control of their operations to local partners or subsidiaries. This can help to reduce political risks and increase acceptance by the host country.

3.5.3. Government Encouragement of Global Business

Government encouragement of global business refers to policies and actions taken by governments to attract and support foreign investment and trade, such as tax incentives, subsidies, and favorable trade agreements.

3.5.3.1. Foreign Government Encouragement

Governments may provide incentives such as tax breaks, subsidies, and relaxed regulations to encourage foreign investment. Many countries are now adopting a proactive approach to foreign investment and are setting specific guidelines to encourage MNCs to invest in their country. These guidelines often include expectations that MNCs will create job opportunities for the local population, transfer technology, and knowledge to local firms, increase exports, and contribute to the growth and development of local industries. As a result, governments hope to accelerate their country's economic development and achieve their long-term economic goals.

3.5.3.2. National Government Encouragement

The US government encourages American firms to do business abroad by providing assistance that helps minimize politically motivated financial risks. MNCs face complex political environments and must consider foreign, domestic, and international politics. Developing countries view foreign firms and investments with distrust due to concerns over the potential exploitation of natural resources. The Dependency Theory explains why Latin American countries are reluctant to welcome MNCs. Similarly, parties with leftist and indigenous thinking in India are reluctant to encourage MNCs fearing the perpetuation of class conflicts and oppressive governments. However, MNCs should be allowed to operate in highly technological sectors where countries lack know-how and R&D.

Did you get it?

The North American Industry Classification System (NAICS) was developed by the NAFTA countries in 1997 as a business classification system that allows comparative analysis of business statistics across the three countries.

Developed countries, like the US, have concerns about FDIs due to potential threats to their national security and economy. However, foreign investments can add to the domestic capital stock and contribute to the country's standard of living. Despite the benefits, opposition to foreign investments can also be based on moral principles, such as protests against investing in South Africa during the apartheid era. Therefore, various factors influence a country's attitudes toward foreign investments, including economic, political, and social considerations.

The example of certain Arabian countries not participating in JVs in Israel due to their anti-Muslim policies highlights the influence of political factors on business decisions. It is important for companies to be aware of the political climate in different countries and how it may change over time. The example of the shift in the relationship between the US and China shows how political relationships can change, and companies must be flexible in responding to such changes.

The partition of India and Pakistan in 1947 led to a violent separation that resulted in the loss of millions of lives. Since then, India and Pakistan have had a troubled relationship with each other, and have engaged in three wars. The tension between the two countries has escalated to the point where they have threatened to use nuclear weapons in the event of an extreme emergency.

However, with the recent movement of Bus from Delhi to Lahore, there is a possibility of improved relations and potential economic benefits for businesses operating in both countries. The statement emphasizes the importance of monitoring and adapting to the changing political climate to minimize political risk and maximize economic opportunities.

In the case of India, the country had a highly regulated, closed economy that discouraged foreign investment until the government implemented reforms in 1991, which helped India become one of the world's most dynamic economies.

However, it also highlights the negative impact of political instability on foreign investment. When the political condition deteriorates, a favorable investment climate can disappear overnight. The example given is the United States' withdrawal of Chile's duty-free trade status due to its failure to take "steps to afford internationally recognized worker rights," which led to Chile being suspended from the Generalized System of Preferences (GSP). As a result, Chile joined Romania, Nicaragua, and Paraguay in being suspended from the GSP.

3.5.4. Factors Affecting Global Business

Some factors that can affect global business include political instability, economic conditions, exchange rates, cultural differences, and legal frameworks.

3.5.4.1. Political Risk Analysis

The political risks that international marketers face in their operations include confiscation, expropriation, nationalization, domestication, and creeping expropriation. These actions are more likely to be imposed on foreign investments, although local firms are not immune.

Confiscation refers to a government taking ownership of a property without compensation, such as when the Chinese government seized American property after the communist takeover in 1949. Expropriation, on the other hand, involves some form of compensation, although it may not necessarily be fair compensation. Companies whose property is being expropriated may agree to sell their operations due to explicit or implied coercion.

An example is Occidental Petroleum Company, which wanted the United States to review Venezuela's GSP eligibility after the country confiscated the company's assets without compensation.

Expropriation is used to describe the act of taking property or assets from their owners without their consent, typically by a government or other legal authority. Expropriation differs from confiscation in that there is some compensation, but arguably not at the level of compensation comfortable to the owners. Nationalization is the act of the government taking ownership and control of a business or industry. This action affects the whole industry, not just a single company, and the government operates the business being taken over. The motive behind nationalization can vary, but it is often due to poor economic performance or social pressures.

Domestication involves foreign companies relinquishing control and ownership either partially or completely to the nationals. Private entities are then allowed to operate the confiscated or expropriated properties. Domestication can be a voluntary act or forced due to poor economic performance or social pressures.

General instability risk refers to the uncertainty about the future viability of a host country's political system. Ownership/controlled risk is related to the possibility that the host government might take action to restrict an investor's ownership and control of a subsidiary. Operation risk relates to the uncertainty that a host government might constrain the investor's business operations in all areas, including production, marketing, and finance. Transfer risk applies to any future acts by a host government that might constrain the ability of a subsidiary to transfer payments, capital, or profits out of the host country back to the parent firm.

The 1970s saw a peak in expropriation activities, with 83 acts involving 28 countries in 1975, representing 14.4% of all such acts between 1960 and 1992. However, based on data from 1980 and 1992, expropriation is unlikely to occur in the future.

3.5.4.2. Indicators of Political Instability

To evaluate a potential marketing environment, a company must identify and assess relevant indicators of political instability. Sources of political instability include social unrest, the attitude of nationals, and the policies of the host government.

Social unrest refers to disorder caused by underlying conditions such as economic hardship, internal dissension, insurgency, and ideological, religious, racial, and cultural differences. For example, conflict among religious groups in Lebanon and India has caused severe disruptions to local businesses.

Human nature is characterized by both individualism and collectivism, which provide alternative ways of utilizing resources to meet society's needs. Competition is encouraged by individualism, while collectivism emphasizes cooperation. According to Alderson, "A cooperative society tends to be a closed society. The closure is essential if the group is in some sense to act as one." China, although seeking to modernize its economy, does not fully embrace an open economy, which may lead to dissension among various groups. To maintain its own survival, a cooperative society may obstruct the dissemination of new ideas and neutralize external threats, as China has learned from the Soviet Union's experience.

A liberated political climate may prompt long-suppressed national minority groups to call for cultural and territorial independence, which could escalate conflicts. Three types of conflicts may arise: domestic disputes that remain within the country's boundaries, internal disputes that involve interested parties outside the country, and disputes between neighboring countries. For example, the civil war between Serbs and Croats in Yugoslavia and the centuries-old ethnic animosity between Christian Armenia and Muslim Azerbaijan both drew in outside parties.

3.5.4.3. Attitudes of Nationals

To assess the marketing environment of a potential host country, it is important to consider the attitudes of both its citizens and government towards foreign businesses and individuals. Host nationals may have concerns about the intentions of foreign enterprises and may be wary of perceived exploitation or colonialism. These attitudes may be influenced by local socialist or nationalist philosophies, which could be at odds with the policies of the company's home country government. Additionally, citizens' hostility towards foreign entities may persist even if governments change. An example of this is the decision of a handful of US firms to exit El Salvador in the 1980s due to persistent hostility towards foreign businesses.

3.5.4.4. Policies of the Host Government

The attitude of the host government towards foreign enterprises can be subject to change depending on leadership and time, which can result in either positive or negative effects for businesses. Government policies can impact business operations both internally and externally. Internal policies regulate operations within the home country, while external policies regulate activities in other countries. External policies can create complex issues for firms doing business in countries that conflict with each other. For instance, restrictions on exports between Chile and Argentina, due to the boundary dispute, disrupted the marketing plans of automobile manufacturers such as General Motors, Peugeot, and Renault. Similarly, India and Pakistan have restricted their export-import due to the Kashmir boundary dispute. Unfriendly rhetoric before an election does not always translate to action, as seen in the case of Ronald Reagan, who advocated for free trade before his election in 1984 but became more of a protectionist during the campaign. Companies should not take drastic actions during such situations but rather endure through the election. Enron Corporation's experience with the $2.8 billion Dhabol project in India serves as an example of how companies should consider public sentiment and avoid secrecy and lack of competition in their dealings. In this case, Enron's disregard for public perception and the opposition coalition led to the suspension of the project.

3.6. ECONOMIC ENVIRONMENT

International marketers have access to a wealth of data that provides insights into the economic environment of different countries. National accounts data, such as gross national product, gross domestic product, consumption, investment, government expenditures, and price levels, are available for each country. Demographic data, such as population size, age distribution, and population growth rates, are also available globally.

In addition, there is a vast amount of economic data available through sources such as The Statistical Year Book of the United Nations. This includes information on agriculture, mining, manufacturing, construction, energy production and consumption, internal and external trade, transportation, wages and prices, health, housing, education, and communication. These data are readily available for high-income countries, but less developed countries may have limited economic data beyond basic national accounts and demographic information (Figure 3.4).

Figure 3.4. An illustration of economic environment.

Despite the abundance of data, international marketers still face challenges in utilizing this information effectively. The challenge is not one of data availability, but rather how to extract meaningful insights and apply them to specific business contexts. Therefore, it is important for marketers to carefully analyze and interpret the data in order to make informed decisions about their international marketing strategies.

The economic environment of various countries has a direct impact on international business operations. This interaction between the international economic environment and global business is characterized by major changes such as the flow of capital across the globe, which has become more important than the flow of goods or products. Additionally, the establishment of production facilities in various countries has become increasingly common. Another major change is the technological revolution, which has linked the relationship between the size of production and the level of employment. Lastly, the macroeconomic factors of individual nations do not have significant control over the global economies, indicating that global economic factors are now more important in shaping the international business landscape.

3.6.1. Economic System

The economic system refers to the way a society organizes its resources to produce goods and services. It is an essential factor that influences the economic development of a country, which in turn affects international business. An economic system comprises institutions such as government agencies, financial institutions, and markets that are established to meet the needs and wants of individuals and society as a whole (Figure 3.5).

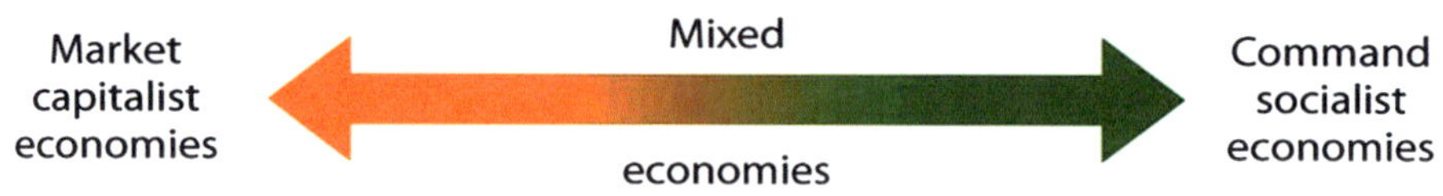

Figure 3.5. *Economic system.*

The type of economic system a country has, whether it is a free-market, socialist, or mixed economy, affects how resources are allocated, what goods and services are produced, and how they are distributed among the people. This, in turn, has a significant impact on the international business community, as businesses must adapt to the unique economic systems and regulations of different countries in order to be successful.

There are three types of economic systems:

1. **Capitalistic Economic System:** This system is characterized by economic democracy and customer choice. It is based on the belief in individualism and private ownership of production and distribution facilities. In a capitalistic system, the means of production and distribution are owned and controlled by private individuals or companies, rather than the state or government. The system operates through the mechanism of market forces and competition, where producers and consumers interact through the buying and selling of goods and services. A good example of a country following this system is the United States.
2. **Communistic Economic System:** Under this system all property and the means of production are owned and controlled by the state, with no private ownership or property rights to income. This system operates on the principle of collective ownership and centralized planning, to achieve social and economic equality. However, the major limitation of this system is the lack of individual freedom of choice, as the state controls all economic activity. Additionally, the system has often failed to achieve significant economic growth and development, as the absence of market forces and incentives can lead to inefficiencies and misallocation of resources. Examples of countries that have adopted their own version of communist economic systems include China and Cuba.
3. **Mixed Economic System:** It is a combination of both the capitalist and communist economic systems. In this system, both the government and private individuals own and control the factors of production and distribution. The aim is to balance economic growth with social welfare by providing benefits to the public on an equitable basis. While the government plays a significant role in regulating the economy, there is also space for private enterprise and market competition. This system emphasizes full employment and just rewards for workers' efforts. India one country using this mixed economic system.

3.6.2. Countries' Classification Based on Income

Countries can be classified into different income groups based on their gross national income (GNI) per capita, which is the total amount of money earned by a country's residents and businesses divided by its population. The World Bank currently classifies countries into the following income groups:

- Low-income countries: Countries with a GNI per capita of $1,085 or less.
- Lower-middle-income countries: Countries with a GNI per capita between $1,086 and $4,225.

- Upper-middle-income countries: Countries with a GNI per capita between $4,256 and $13,205.
- High-income countries: Countries with a GNI per capita of more than $13,205.
- **Low-Income Countries:** Low-Income Countries, also known as Least Developed Countries (LDCs), are nations that have a low level of economic development and are characterized by high poverty rates, low literacy rates, inadequate infrastructure, and a low standard of living. These countries often have high birth rates, political instability and unrest, limited access to education and healthcare, and underutilization of natural resources. Additionally, these countries are heavily dependent on foreign aid and have the limited export capacity, resulting in a large trade deficit and an excessive dependency on imports. Thus, LDCs face significant challenges in achieving economic growth and improving the standard of living for their citizens.
- **Lower Middle-Income Countries:** Lower Middle-Income Countries (LMICs) are countries that have an intermediate level of economic development. They are also known as developing countries. These countries have a range of characteristics, such as an early stage of industrialization, expansion of consumer markets, and availability of cheap and motivated human resources. These countries are often considered locations for the production of standardized products or exporting, such as clothing for exports. Some of the challenges that these countries face include limited infrastructure, political instability, and inadequate access to education and healthcare. However, LMICs have the potential for growth and development and can offer opportunities for international business.
- **Upper Middle-Income Countries:** These countries are classified as industrializing countries. These countries have already gone through the initial stages of economic development, and have a more diverse economy than Lower Middle Income or Low-Income countries. The characteristics of these countries include less dependency on agriculture, high export rates, increasing levels of literacy and formal education, rapid economic development, occupational mobility of people from agriculture to industry, and increased wage rates. Examples of Upper Middle-Income Countries include China, Brazil, and Malaysia.
- **High-Income Countries:** These countries are commonly referred to as developed countries. They are characterized by a high standard of living, high levels of education and technology, advanced infrastructure and services, and a diversified economy. The economy of these countries is mainly based on service sectors, such as finance, technology, and education, and manufacturing sectors, such as automotive and electronics. These countries have a well-established legal and political

system and a stable economy. The focus is on sustainable development and building an information society, where information and communication technology plays a significant role in economic growth and development. Examples of such countries include the United States, Japan, Germany, and Australia.

3.6.3. Impact of Economic Environment on International Business

The economic environment can have a significant impact on international business by affecting factors such as market demand, supply chain costs, foreign investment regulations, and currency exchange rates. It can influence the success or failure of a business's international operations.

1. **Economic Growth**: Business plays a crucial role in the economic development of a country by identifying people's needs and wants and supplying them with goods and services. The high economic growth rate of countries creates opportunities for international businesses to expand their market shares, and managers of MNCs rely on economic growth rate projections to make decisions on market entry or resource allocation.
2. **Inflation**: The inflation rate of a country is a crucial factor that can impact the profitability and market share of an international business firm. High inflation rates lead to higher prices of goods and services, which in turn affects the purchasing power of consumers. This can lead to reduced demand for products and services offered by international business firm. Additionally, inflation can affect interest rates and exchange rates, which can further impact the operations and profitability of the firm.
3. **Balance of Payments**: The balance of payments position of a country is an important factor that affects international business as it reflects the country's ability to pay for its imports and the attractiveness of the country for foreign investments. A favorable balance of payments position can lead to a stable exchange rate and an increase in foreign investments, while an unfavorable balance of payments position can lead to a decrease in foreign investments and depreciation of the domestic currency. MNCs should monitor the balance of payments position of the countries they operate in to make informed decisions about investment and expansion.
4. **Economic Transition**: Liberalization refers to the removal of government restrictions and regulations on trade and investment. This has provided MNCs with significant opportunities to enter new markets, either by locating their manufacturing facilities or expanding their existing operations. As a result, MNCs have become the immediate and greatest

beneficiaries of liberalization, privatization, and globalization of world economies.

3.7. LEGAL ENVIRONMENT

The legal environment refers to the complex set of laws, regulations, and government policies that affect businesses. In the United States, this environment is influenced by a wide range of issues, including international trade, taxes, employment laws, technology, and social concerns.

3.7.1. Origins of International Law

As international trade and commerce have grown over time, various treaties, agreements, and organizations have emerged to establish guidelines and regulations for business transactions between countries. However, there is still no single comprehensive system of laws or regulations governing international business transactions. Instead, the legal environment is a complex patchwork of laws and policies from all countries involved in international commerce. These laws and policies cover a wide range of issues, including trade agreements, intellectual property rights, labor standards, environmental regulations, and more.

The lex mercatoria, also known as the law merchant, was a set of legal principles that governed commercial transactions during the Middle Ages in Europe. These principles provided a framework for international trade and were based on customs and codes of conduct. The codes were created to encourage and protect international transactions. Today, the international commerce codes in use in many countries, including Europe and the United States, are based on these old codes.

3.7.2. Sources of International Law

International commercial law refers to the body of legal principles and rules that govern international business transactions and relationships between countries. These laws are derived from a variety of sources, including the laws of individual countries, trade agreements between or among countries, and rules and regulations issued by international organizations.

The laws of individual countries play a significant role in shaping international commercial law. These laws include both domestic laws that apply within a country's borders and laws that regulate the conduct of that country's businesses abroad. For example, a country's laws may regulate how its citizens conduct business in foreign countries, or they may impose sanctions or trade restrictions on certain countries or industries.

Trade agreements between or among countries are another important source of international commercial law. These agreements typically establish rules for trade between the participating countries and may address issues such as tariffs, intellectual property rights (IPRs), and investment protection. Examples of such agreements include the NAFTA, the Trans-Pacific Partnership (TPP), and the World Trade Organization (WTO) agreements.

International organizations such as the United Nations and the European Union also play a role in shaping international commercial law. These organizations issue rules and regulations that apply to member countries and their businesses. For example, the UN Convention on Contracts for the International Sale of Goods (CISG) provides a standardized set of rules governing international sales contracts. Despite the existence of these various sources of international commercial law, there is no universally accepted regulatory agency or system of courts for enforcing these laws. Instead, international business disputes may be resolved through the International Court of Justice (ICJ), international arbitration, or the courts of an individual country. However, the decisions of these tribunals are only enforceable if the countries involved agree to be bound by them.

3.7.3. International Trade Agreements

International trade agreements are legally binding agreements between two or more countries that establish rules for trade and investment between them. These agreements aim to increase economic cooperation and reduce barriers to trade, thereby promoting growth and development.

One of the main benefits of trade agreements is that they help to improve economic relations between countries. By establishing clear rules for trade and investment, these agreements provide greater certainty and predictability for businesses and investors, which can encourage greater cross-border activity. They can also help to reduce trade barriers, such as tariffs and quotas, which can make it easier and cheaper for businesses to sell their goods and services abroad.

Another important feature of trade agreements is that they often cover a wide range of commercial issues beyond just tariffs and quotas. For example, many trade agreements include provisions on IPRs, investment protection, and dispute settlement mechanisms. This can help to create a more level playing field for businesses operating in different countries and provide greater legal protections for their investments and intellectual property.

Two important trade agreements for the United States are the NAFTA and the WTO.

3.7.3.1. NAFTA

The NAFTA is a treaty that was ratified by the legislatures in Canada, Mexico, and the United States and went into effect in 1994. Its primary purpose is to reduce or eliminate tariffs and trade barriers among these nations, thereby promoting economic growth and development. Under NAFTA, some tariffs were eliminated immediately, while others are being phased out through the year 2009.

NAFTA has had a significant impact on several industries, including agriculture, automobiles, pharmaceuticals, and textiles. By reducing trade barriers and tariffs, NAFTA has made it easier and cheaper for businesses in these industries to trade goods and services across borders, which has increased competition and lowered prices for consumers.

One of the unique features of NAFTA is that it includes a variety of issues that are not typically found in trade agreements. For example, NAFTA includes provisions for the protection of intellectual property and the environment, as well as the creation of special panels to resolve disputes involving unfair trade practices, investment restrictions, and environmental issues. These provisions reflect a broader recognition that trade policies can have significant impacts beyond just economic growth and development.

Looking ahead, NAFTA has the potential to expand beyond its current membership to include other countries in North and South America. If this were to happen, it would create the largest free trade area in the world, covering 850 million people with over $18 trillion in annual purchasing power. However, any expansion of NAFTA would likely face significant political and economic challenges, as different countries have different interests and priorities when it comes to trade policies.

3.7.3.2. WTO

The General Agreement on Tariffs and Trade (GATT) was a treaty that operated from 1948 to 1994 with the primary objective of reducing trade barriers imposed by governments. GATT focused on trade restrictions such as import quotas and tariffs, and it published tariff schedules to which its signatories agreed. Tariff schedules were developed in multinational trade negotiations or "rounds." The most recent round, the Uruguay Round, involved 124 nations.

GATT was replaced by the WTO in 1995. One of the most significant developments of the Uruguay Round was the creation of the WTO, which has since overseen the trade agreement and has a dispute-resolution system using three-person arbitration panels. Unlike in the GATT, WTO members cannot veto decisions (unless they withdraw from the agreement).

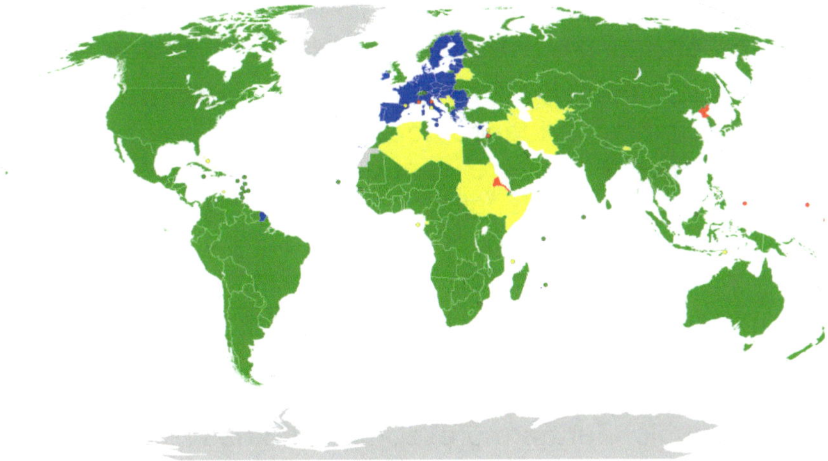

The latest round of negotiations under the WTO will eventually lower world tariffs by 40%. The US, Japan, members of the EU, and other industrialized nations have agreed to eliminate all tariffs in ten industries, including beer, construction equipment, distilled spirits, farm machinery, furniture, medical equipment, paper, pharmaceuticals, steel, and toys.

The WTO's primary objective is to promote free trade by reducing trade barriers, including tariffs and non-tariff barriers, such as quotas, regulations, and standards. By reducing trade barriers, the WTO aims to increase international trade, economic growth, and development. The WTO also works to provide technical assistance and training to developing countries to help them participate more effectively in the global trading system.

Remember

To be successful, businesses must carefully consider the legal environment when developing their strategic plans. Failure to do so can lead to costly legal problems and damage to a company's reputation.

3.7.4. International Dispute Resolution

Contract disputes can arise due to a variety of reasons such as breach of contract, disagreement over contract terms, or failure to perform contractual obligations. When disputes occur, parties involved in the contract may wish to enforce their rights and seek remedies available under the contract. Such disputes can often be resolved through negotiation or alternative dispute resolution mechanisms like mediation or arbitration. However, in some cases, parties may need to resort to litigation in order to enforce their rights and seek legal remedies.

a. **Litigation:** When parties in a contract dispute are unable to resolve their issues through negotiation or alternative dispute resolution mechanisms, they may resort to litigation in the court system of either country. However, litigation can be a complicated and challenging process, particularly when the dispute involves parties located in different countries.

One of the primary challenges in cross-border litigation is obtaining evidence, locating individuals, and accessing documents that are central to the dispute. This can be particularly challenging if the evidence or individuals are located in multiple countries, each with their own legal system and rules regarding evidence collection.

Another challenge of cross-border litigation is dealing with different judicial systems. Courts in different countries may have different legal standards, procedures, and remedies available. Furthermore, some countries legal systems may be influenced by political pressures or may not be as transparent as others.

In addition to these challenges, establishing jurisdiction can also be difficult in cross-border litigation. In the US, for instance, courts require proof of "minimum contact" with the country in order to have proper jurisdiction over a foreign defendant. This means that the plaintiff must show that the defendant had sufficient contact with the US such that it is fair to require them to appear in US courts to defend themselves.

b. **Arbitration:** Arbitration is a popular alternative dispute resolution mechanism for resolving international disagreements, as courts may not always be effective in resolving them. Many organizations, such as the UN Commission on International Trade Law, the International Chamber of Commerce (ICC), and the American Arbitration Association, have been created to standardize arbitral rules. In more than fifty countries, including the United States, the 1958 UN Convention on the Recognition and Enforcement of Foreign Arbitral Awards facilitates the enforcement of arbitral awards. U.S. federal district courts have the authority to hear motions to confirm or challenge a foreign arbitration award involving a U.S. business.

c. **International Court of Justice:** The International Court of Justice (ICJ) is a judicial body established by the United Nations to settle disputes between countries. The ICJ is headquartered in The Hague, Netherlands, and only countries have standing to go before the court. This means that individuals and businesses cannot initiate a lawsuit in the ICJ. Instead, countries must decide whether to pursue claims on behalf of their citizens.

Did you get it?

The WTO came into being in 1995. One of the youngest of the international organizations, the WTO is the successor to the General Agreement on Tariffs and Trade (GATT) established in the wake of the Second World War.

If the ICJ issues a decision that includes monetary judgments or injunctive relief, it may be referred to the United Nations Security Council for enforcement.

d. **Doctrine of Sovereign Immunity:** The doctrine of sovereign immunity can be applied in cases where a court would otherwise have jurisdiction over a foreign party. This doctrine is based on the traditional idea that a sovereign should not be subject to litigation in a foreign court.

The Foreign Sovereign Immunities Act (FSIA) of 1976 is a law in the United States that provides a uniform rule for determining sovereign immunity in legal actions in U.S. courts. The law aims to bring the U.S. into conformity with other countries in its application of the doctrine of sovereign immunity. The application of the doctrine can have severe consequences on parties when the suit involves a commercial transaction.

Remember

Businesses operating internationally must navigate a complex and constantly evolving legal landscape to ensure compliance and mitigate legal risks.

3.7.5. Types of Legal Systems

There are some types of legal system, such as:

a. **Common Law System:** A common law system is a legal system that is based on tradition, precedent, custom, and usage. In a common law system, courts play an important role in interpreting the law based on these characteristics. Precedent refers to past decisions of courts, which are considered binding on lower courts in future cases with similar facts. Custom and usage refer to the way things have been done in the past and are considered evidence of what the law is.

In a common law system, the law is developed through judicial decisions over time, rather than through written codes or statutes. This system contrasts with a civil law system, where the law is primarily based on written codes and legislation. Common law systems are used in countries such as the United Kingdom, the United States, Canada, Australia, and New Zealand, among others.

b. **Civil Law System or a Codified Legal System:** A civil law system is a legal system that is based on a detailed set of laws organized into a code, which serves as the foundation for doing business. More than 70 countries around the world use civil law as their legal system.

In a civil law system, legal disputes are resolved based

on how the law is applied to the facts of the case. This means that judges and legal authorities follow a strict set of laws and rules when making decisions. The focus is on finding the right application of the law to the specific case at hand.

In contrast, common law is a legal system where legal decisions are made based on the interpretation of past court decisions or precedents, rather than a detailed set of laws. This means that the focus is on how similar cases have been decided in the past, rather than a strict application of a specific law.

For example, in civil law countries, contracts are typically very detailed and specific, outlining the exact terms and conditions of the agreement. In a common law system, contracts may be less detailed and more focused on the intentions of the parties involved.

c. **Theocratic Law System:** A theocratic law system is a legal system that is based on religious precepts or principles. In this type of system, religious texts or teachings serve as the primary source of law and legal authority. Theocratic law systems can be found in countries where religion plays a central role in society and government.

Islamic law, also known as Sharia law, is an example of a theocratic law system. It is based on the teachings of the Quran and the Hadith and is used in several Muslim-majority countries. In Islamic law, judges interpret religious texts to make legal decisions, and the law covers a wide range of areas, including criminal law, family law, and economic law.

In contrast to theocratic law systems, secular legal systems are not based on religious principles, and instead rely on a combination of written laws, court decisions, and legal precedent. For example, the United States has a secular legal system that is based on the Constitution, federal and state laws, and court decisions.

Regarding the number of lawyers per capita, the United States has the highest number of lawyers of any country in the world, with 312 lawyers per 100,000 people. This is significantly higher than Japan, which has 101 lawyers per 100,000 people. This may be due to the fact that the United States has a large and complex legal system that requires a significant number of lawyers to operate effectively.

REVIEW QUESTIONS

1. What are the major factors that shape the international business environment?
2. How do cultural differences impact international business operations?
3. What are the key economic, political, and legal risks that companies face when operating in different countries?
4. What are the challenges and opportunities presented by emerging markets?
5. How do global trends such as globalization, digitalization, and sustainability impact international business?

MULTIPLE CHOICE QUESTIONS

1. Which of the following is NOT a component of the international business environment?

a. Economic factors
b. Legal factors
c. Political factors
d. Cultural factors
e. None of the above

2. Which of the following is an advantage of operating in a foreign market?

a. Access to new customers
b. Reduced political risk
c. Lower transportation costs
d. Familiarity with local culture
e. All of the above

3. Which of the following is a disadvantage of operating in a foreign market?

a. Increased political risk
b. Increased transportation costs
c. Reduced access to new technology
d. Familiarity with local culture
e. All of the above

4. Which of the following is an example of a non-tariff barrier to trade?

a. Import tariffs
b. Export subsidies
c. Quotas
d. Intellectual property laws
e. None of the above

5. Which of the following organizations is responsible for promoting free trade and reducing trade barriers?

a. World Trade Organization

b. International Monetary Fund

c. World Bank

d. United Nations

e. None of the above

Answers to Multiple Choice Questions

1. (e); 2. (a); 3. (a); 4. (d); 5. (a)

REFERENCES

1. Cavusgil, S. T., Knight, G., & Riesenberger, J. R., (2018). *International Business: The New Realities* (5th edn., Vol. 1). Pearson Education, Inc.
2. Chadha, N. K., (2018). *International Business Management: A Managerial Perspective*. Vikas Publishing House.
3. Cherunilam, F., (2017). *International Business Management: Text and Cases*. Himalaya Publishing House.
4. Cullen, J. B., & Parboteeah, K. P., (2018). *International Business: Strategy and the Multinational Company* (2nd edn., Vol. 2). Routledge.
5. Daniels, J. D., Radebaugh, L. H., & Sullivan, D. P., (2018). *International Business: Environments and Operations*. Pearson Education.
6. Deresky, H., (2020). *International Management: Managing Across Borders and Cultures* (10th edn.). Pearson Education.
7. Hill, C. W. L., & Hult, G. T. M., (2019). *Global Business Today* (11th edn., Vol. 1). McGraw-Hill Education.
8. Hill, C. W. L., & Hult, G. T. M., (2021). *International Business: Competing in the Global Marketplace* (12th edn., Vol. 2). McGraw-Hill Education.
9. Kuthiala, B. K., & Kuthiala, D., (2017). *International Business Management: Theory and Practice*. Excel Books.
10. Luthans, F., & Doh, J. P., (2020). *International Management: Culture, Strategy, and Behavior* (10th edn., Vol. 2). McGraw-Hill Education.
11. Sharma, K., & Dubey, A., (2017). *International Business Management: Globalization and Beyond*. Pearson India.
12. Wild, J. J., Wild, K. L., & Han, J. C. Y., (2017). *International Business: The Challenges of Globalization* (9th edn., Vol. 1). Pearson Education, Inc.

CHAPTER 4

ENTRY STRATEGIES IN INTERNATIONAL MARKETING

UNIT INTRODUCTION

When a company decides to expand its operations internationally, it must take into consideration its mission, objectives, and strategies. A company's mission ultimately lays out what it is doing today and what it represents. That company mission stems from the company's long-term vision of where it wants to be in a given timeline. Tying the company's mission and vision are the company values which guide the company's decisions and actions. The company needs to align its international operations so that it can achieve its long-term goals.

The objectives of a company are specific and measurable targets that it aims to achieve for the company to accomplish its goals. For example, a company might set a target for increasing its sales by a certain percentage within a certain period. These objectives help the company stay focused and motivated, and they provide a way to measure progress toward the vision.

The strategy is how the company plans to achieve its objectives. It involves making decisions about how to allocate resources, what products or services to offer, and how to reach customers. The company's strategy must be aligned with its mission and objectives, and it must be flexible enough to adapt to changing market conditions.

One of the key reasons for expanding internationally is to increase sales. By selling products or services in new markets, a company can reach more customers and generate more revenue. In fact, many of the world's largest companies generate almost half of their sales from outside their home countries. This demonstrates the importance of international expansion for companies that want to achieve significant growth.

Another reason for international expansion is to take advantage of different growth rates in different markets. By diversifying its entry methods into new markets, a company can offset lower growth rates in one market with higher growth rates in another. This can help the company maintain its overall growth rate and achieve its objectives.

International transactions are a fast way to improve a company's commercial and strategic position in a new market. By entering a new market, a company can gain access to new customers, suppliers, and partners. This can help the company improve its competitive advantage and achieve its objectives.

Market entry methods have become an essential element of corporate strategy. Companies use various methods, such as joint ventures (JVs), mergers and acquisitions (M&A), licensing, and franchising, to enter new markets. These methods are popular because they can be easily assimilated by the parties involved and they can help the company achieve its objectives quickly. Companies that align their international operations with their mission and objectives, and that use effective market entry methods; can achieve significant growth and competitive advantage. By taking advantage of different growth rates in different markets, companies can diversify their operations and maintain their overall growth rate. The various methods of selling products in international markets are discussed in this chapter.

Learning Objectives

After completing this chapter, you should be able to understand:

- Exporting, licensing, and franchising
- Contract manufacture

- Management contracts
- Joint ventures
- Counter Trade
- Strategic alliances
- Mergers & Acquisitions
- Turnkey Projects
- Factors influencing a firm's selection of entry strategy
- Factors considered before finalizing a joint venture agreement.

Key Terms

- Acquisition
- Exporting
- Foreign direct investment (FDI)
- Franchising
- Joint venture
- Licensing
- Strategic alliance
- Turnkey project

4.1. EXPORTING

Exporting is a method of entering foreign markets where businesses directly sell their goods or services to customers in another country. It is one of the most popular and lowest-risk methods of entering foreign markets as it doesn't require businesses to invest in production facilities in the foreign market. Instead, businesses produce their goods in their home market and sell them to customers overseas.

One of the advantages of exporting is that it can be cost-effective as businesses don't need to make large investments in setting up production facilities in a foreign market. They can use their existing production facilities and only incur additional costs related to transportation, packaging, and marketing. However, businesses need to be aware that rising transportation costs can increase the cost of exporting in the future, impacting their profitability (Figure 4.1).

Figure 4.1. Exporting.

The majority of costs associated with exporting come from marketing expenses. Businesses need to invest in marketing their products in the foreign market to attract customers and establish a market presence. This includes costs related to market research, advertising, and distribution. In addition, businesses need to work with importers, transport providers, and the government of the foreign country to ensure their products comply with local regulations and are delivered safely and efficiently.

- **Direct Export**: Direct export involves a business producing its products in its home market and selling them directly to customers overseas. This method is the most common and low-risk method of entering a foreign market. It is cost-effective since businesses do not need to invest in production facilities in their chosen country. However, rising transportation costs may increase the cost of exporting in the future.
- **Indirect Export**: In indirect export, a business sells its products to a third party which then sells them in the foreign market. This method is also low-risk, but it may result in reduced profits since the third party adds a markup.
- **Licensing**: Licensing involves granting an organization in the foreign market a license to produce the product or use the brand name in return for a royalty payment. It is a less risky method of entry since it does not require substantial investments.
- **Franchising**: Franchising is similar to licensing but involves a business putting together a package of successful ingredients that made them successful in their home market and franchising this package to overseas investors. The franchise holder may provide training and marketing services or products.
- **Contracting**: Contracting involves the manufacturer of a product contracting out the production of the product to another organization to produce the product on their behalf. This method is cost-effective since the business does not need to export to the foreign market.
- **Direct Investment**: Direct investment involves multinational organizations engaging in full-scale production and marketing abroad by directly investing in wholly-owned subsidiaries. This method allows firms to compete more aggressively abroad since they are literally "in" the marketplace. However, it requires a much larger investment and a complete understanding of business conditions and customs in a foreign country.
- **Joint Venture**: A JV is a partnership between a domestic and foreign firm, where both partners invest money, share ownership, and share control of the venture. This method requires a greater commitment from firms since it is riskier and less flexible. JVs may afford tax advantages in many countries and may also span multiple countries.

4.2. LICENSING

Licensing is a business arrangement where a company grants another company the right to access its intellectual property rights (IPRs) for a certain period of time and under specific conditions. This includes the use of its manufacturing process, brand name, copyright, trademark, patent, technology, and trade secrets.

4.2.1. Reasons for Licensing

There are two primary reasons for entering into a licensing agreement:

1. **International Expansion of a Brand Franchise**: A company may choose to license its products to a foreign company to expand its brand franchise globally.
2. **Need for Commercialization of New Technology**: A company may choose to license its technology to another company to help commercialize and market the product.

Did you get it?

In the UK, India, and in many common law countries, a joint-venture (or a company formed by a group of individuals) must file with the appropriate authority the memorandum of association, a statutory document which informs the outside public of its existence.

4.2.2. Advantages and Disadvantages of Licensing

Licensing offers several advantages and disadvantages for both the licensor and licensee.

Advantages for the Licensor:

- **Low Risk**: Licensing allows a company to enter the international market at little risk since it does not have to invest in new production facilities.
- **Increased Revenue**: By licensing its products, a company can generate additional revenue from licensing fees and royalties.
- **Increased Brand Recognition**: Licensing allows a company to expand its brand recognition to new markets.

Disadvantages for the Licensor:

- **Little control**: A licensor has little control over the licensee's production, distribution, and sales of the product.
- **Limited Profits**: If the licensee becomes successful, the licensor may have given up a significant portion of the profits.
- **Creation of Competition**: When the licensing agreement expires, the licensor may have created a competitor.

Advantages for the Licensee:

- **Access to New Technology**: A licensee gains access to a licensor's technology, which can help the licensee develop new products and enter new markets.
- **Lower Costs**: Licensing can be cost-effective as the licensee does not have to invest in new research and development.

- **Reduced Risk**: Licensing is less risky than investing in new production facilities in a foreign market.

Disadvantages for the Licensee:

- **Limited Control**: A licensee may have limited control over the product and how it is marketed.
- **Limited Profit Potential**: The licensee may have to pay a significant portion of its profits in licensing fees and royalties.
- **Dependency on the Licensor**: The licensee may become too dependent on the licensor's technology and may struggle to innovate on its own.

Licensing can be an effective method for companies to enter new markets and generate additional revenue.

4.3. TECHNOLOGY TRANSFER

Technology transfer refers to the process of sharing knowledge, expertise, or technologies from one entity to another. It can involve the transfer of information, machinery, equipment, or personnel, and it can occur within a single organization, between different organizations, or across international borders. Here, we will explore the different types of technology transfer and the factors that influence its success.

- **International Technology Transfer**: It involves the transfer of technology across national boundaries. This type of transfer often occurs between developed and developing countries, where the developing countries are seeking to acquire new technologies that can help them to improve their economic growth and development. International technology transfer can occur through various channels, such as licensing agreements, JVs, FDI, and the transfer of know-how.
- **Regional Technology Transfer**: It involves the transfer of technology within a particular region. This can occur between countries that are geographically close to each other, or between different regions within the same country. Regional technology transfer can be driven by factors such as the availability of resources, market demand, and government policies.
- **Cross-industry or Cross-sector Technology Transfer**: It refers to the transfer of technology from one industry or sector to another. This type of transfer can lead to the development of new products, processes, or services that can benefit multiple industries or sectors. For example, the development of computer technology has led to the creation of new products and services in a wide range of industries, such as healthcare, finance, and education.

- **Interfirm Technology Transfer**: It involves the transfer of technology from one company to another. This type of transfer can occur through various channels, such as licensing agreements, JVs, M&A, or the purchase of technology. Interfirm technology transfer can be driven by factors such as the need to access new markets, the desire to acquire new technologies, or the need to reduce costs.
- **Intra-firm Technology Transfer**: It involves the transfer of technology within a single organization. This can occur between different locations within the same organization or between different departments within the same facility. Intra-firm technology transfer can be driven by factors such as the need to improve efficiency, the desire to standardize processes, or the need to access new markets.
- **Pirating or Reverse-Engineering**: It refers to the unauthorized use, replication, or modification of technology by individuals or organizations without the permission of the owners of the technology. This is typically done in order to obtain access to technology at the expense of the property rights of the owners of the technology.

Pirating involves illegally obtaining copies of copyrighted software, music, movies, or other digital content without the permission of the copyright owner. This is usually done by downloading or sharing copyrighted content through peer-to-peer networks, torrents, or other illegal means. Pirating is a form of copyright infringement and is punishable by law.

Reverse engineering involves the process of analyzing a product or system in order to understand how it works, to create a copy or improve upon the original. This can be done legally, for example to create compatible software or hardware, or illegally, by copying or modifying the original without permission. Reverse engineering can be a useful tool for innovation and competition, but it can also infringe on the IPRs of the original owners of the technology.

Both pirating and reverse-engineering can harm the owners of technology by reducing their profits and undermining their ability to invest in research and development (R&D). They can also result in the creation of inferior or unsafe products that can harm consumers. It is important for individuals and organizations to respect the property rights of the owners of technology and obtain permission before using, copying, or modifying their products.

4.3.1. International Technology Transfer: Horizontal and Vertical Dimension

Technology transfer is the process of sharing technology, knowledge, and expertise between two or more parties, which could be countries, organizations, or individuals. It is a crucial aspect of global economic development and plays a vital role in advancing technological innovations. However, technology transfer has both horizontal and vertical dimensions, each with its own elements. The basic elements of technology transfer from both the horizontal and vertical perspectives are:

Horizontal Perspective: From the horizontal perspective, technology transfer involves three basic elements: the home country, the host country, and the transaction. The home country refers to the country that owns the technology being transferred, while the host country is the country that receives the technology. The transaction refers to the actual process of transferring the technology from the home country to the host country.

- **Home Country's Reactions to Technology Transfers**: The home country's reaction to technology transfer is often mixed. While they may want to export their technology, there are concerns about the impact on their economy. One of the major concerns is that the establishment of production facilities by MNCs in subsidiaries abroad reduces their export potential. Additionally, because some of the MNCs' imports come from their subsidiaries, the volume of imports of the home country tends to increase. This decrease in exports and increase in imports can adversely affect the balance of trade.

  Labor unions in the home country may also oppose technology transfer as they believe that the jobs generated from the new technology will benefit citizens of the host country. Moreover, technology transfer may affect the comparative advantages of the home country.
- **Host Country's Reactions to Technology Transfers**: The reactions of the host country to technology transfer are often more severe. The transfer of technology is a sensitive issue that often evokes strong reservations against it from the country's citizens. The criticisms against technology transfer are based on both economic and social factors.

  The economic implications of technology transfer include payment of fees, royalties, dividends, interest, and salaries to technicians and tax concessions resulting in a loss to the national exchequer. These payments are made to the transferring country and can prove to be very expensive for the host country. The technology supplier may also succeed in extracting payments through various other techniques such as overpricing and buying intermediates at high prices. Malpractices such as tie-up purchases, restrictions on exports, and charging excessive prices are also prevalent.

  The social and cultural implications of technology transfer are more severe than the economic significance. Along with the transfer of technology, there is a transmission of culture from the exporting countries. Workers who work in firms using imported technology get influenced and accustomed to the skills, concepts, policies, practices, thoughts, and beliefs. Additionally, there are social problems such as pollution, urbanization, congestion, depleted natural resources, and other evils that arise due to technology transfer.

- **Transaction**: The transaction element of technology transfer focuses on the nitty-gritty of the transfer. The issues in this element relate to the terms and conditions of technology transfer. It is important to negotiate the terms and conditions of technology transfer to ensure that both parties benefit from the transfer. The transaction element covers the legal, financial, and technical aspects of technology transfer, including licensing agreements, patent rights, know-how, trademarks, and other IPRs.

TIPS

Many times, the technology transferred by international businesses is not appropriate for developing countries. The technology developed is often the one most suitable for industrial countries and is appropriate to the resource endowment of developed nations. Such technology is not in the interest of developing countries.

Vertical Dimension: Issues Specific to the Nation State or Industry. The vertical dimension of technology transfer refers to issues specific to the nation-state or industry. This dimension is concerned with the factors that affect the ability of a country or industry to absorb and adapt foreign technology. The following are some of the issues that fall under the vertical dimension of technology transfer:

- **National Innovation System**: A country's national innovation system refers to the network of institutions, policies, and people involved in the development and diffusion of technology within the country. A strong national innovation system can help a country to absorb and adapt foreign technology, while a weak system can hinder technology transfer.
- **Intellectual Property Rights**: Intellectual property rights (IPR) play a crucial role in technology transfer. A country's IPR regime affects the ability of technology holders to protect their technology and the ability of potential users to access it. Strong IPR protection can encourage technology holders to transfer technology, while weak protection can discourage them from doing so.
- **Education and Training**: The education and training system in a country can affect its ability to absorb and adapt foreign technology. A well-educated workforce with relevant skills can facilitate the transfer and adaptation of technology, while a poorly educated workforce can hinder it.
- **Regulatory Environment**: The regulatory environment in a country can either facilitate or hinder technology transfer. Regulatory barriers such as import restrictions,

export controls, and licensing requirements can impede the flow of technology across borders.

- **Industry Structure**: The structure of an industry can also affect technology transfer. Industries that are dominated by a few large firms may be less receptive to foreign technology, while industries with many SMEs may be more receptive.
- **Culture and Language**: Culture and language can also play a role in technology transfer. Differences in culture and language can create barriers to the transfer and adaptation of foreign technology.

4.4. INTERNATIONAL SUBCONTRACTING

International subcontracting has gained importance in recent years due to the globalization of trade and the need for large manufacturing firms to cut down on costs. It is an extension of domestic subcontracting, which has been prevalent in highly industrialized countries such as the United States and Japan. In international subcontracting, a large manufacturing firm contracts with a smaller firm, often located in a different country, for the supply of parts, components, or services. The subcontractor can provide these services at a lower cost due to lower wages and overhead costs (Figure 4.2).

Figure 4.2. International subcontracting for business.

4.4.1. Advantages of Subcontracting

One of the major advantages of subcontracting is that it frees up time for contractors to focus on their core business activities. By outsourcing certain tasks to subcontractors, contractors can concentrate on their areas of expertise and deliver better results. Subcontracting is also less expensive than hiring full-time employees, as contractors only need to pay for the services provided by the subcontractor. Additionally, a contract is drawn up to guarantee the warranties of the services being provided, which ensures that the subcontractor is accountable for their work.

Subcontracting can also help contractors gain more knowledge and resources. By working with subcontractors, contractors can learn about new technologies, techniques, and ideas that they can apply to their own businesses. The subcontractor is responsible for bringing their own equipment, which saves the contractor from investing in expensive equipment. Payroll taxes and benefits will also decrease, as contractors only pay for the services provided by the subcontractor, and not for any additional benefits.

Legal liability is transferred to the subcontractor, which relieves contractors of any potential legal issues. If any issues arise with the subcontractor's work, the subcontractor is responsible for addressing them, and the contractor is not held liable.

4.4.2. Disadvantages of Subcontracting

One of the major disadvantages of subcontracting is the lack of staff development. Subcontractors are not employees, and contractors do not invest in their training or development. This can result in a lack of loyalty and commitment from subcontractors, as they are free to work with other contractors.

Contractors will also use more time researching potential subcontractors, which can take away from their core business activities. In addition, contractors will lose control over the timeliness and quality of work, as they rely on the subcontractor to deliver on time and to a certain quality standard. Poor performance quality can result in negative consequences for the contractor's reputation and business.

4.5. FRANCHISING

Franchising is a business model that involves the establishment, granting or use of a franchise. A franchise is authorization granted by a company to sell or distribute its goods or services in a certain area. The franchisor is the company or person who grants franchises, while the franchisee is the holder of a franchise (Figure 4.3).

Figure 4.3. International franchising.

4.5.1. Types of Franchising

There are several types of franchising, including product distribution franchising, business format franchising, and management franchising. Product distribution franchising involves the franchisor providing the franchisee with the right to sell its products but not the right to use its trademark or business processes. Business format franchising, on the other hand, grants the franchisee the right to use the franchisor's trademark, products, and business processes. Management franchising involves the franchisor providing the franchisee with management services such as training, recruiting, and financial management.

4.5.2. Advantages of Franchising

1. **Faster Expansion**: One of the primary advantages of franchising is that it can facilitate faster expansion for a business. This is because franchisees provide the labor and their sales provide the growth. Since the franchisee invests in the business, they have a vested interest in its success and are likely to work hard to achieve it.
2. **Motivated Franchisees**: Another advantage of franchising is that franchisees are responsible for their company's success. Therefore, they are more motivated to succeed than employees who work for a fixed wage. This motivation can translate into increased sales, profits, and growth for the franchisor.

3. **Talented Franchisees**: may be more talented at growing the business and turning a profit than employees would be. This is because franchisees have a direct stake in the success of the business and are likely to use their skills and experience to grow the franchise.
4. **Low Capital Investment**: The franchisor puts relatively little money into new locations, as this comes from the franchisee. This means that the franchisor can expand the business without having to invest large amounts of capital.
5. **Consistent Operations**: Franchisees must operate according to the franchisor's system and guidelines. This ensures that operations are consistent across the business, leading to improved efficiency and higher quality levels.

4.5.2.1. Advantages of Franchising for the Franchisor Expansion

Franchising allows the franchisor to expand its business rapidly without having to invest significant amounts of capital. The franchisee provides the initial capital for the new location, and the franchisor earns royalties from sales without having to bear the associated costs.

- **Motivated Franchisees:** Franchisees have a vested interest in the success of their business as they have invested their own money in it. They are therefore more motivated than employees, which can lead to increased sales and profitability.
- **Consistency:** Franchisees must adhere to the franchisor's operating procedures and standards, resulting in a consistent customer experience across all locations.
- **Risk Sharing:** The franchisor shares the risk with the franchisee. The franchisee assumes the initial financial risk associated with the new location, and the franchisor's financial risk is limited to the ongoing royalties it receives.

4.5.2.2. Advantages of Franchising for the Franchisee

- **Proven Business Model:** Franchisees benefit from an established business model that has been proven to be successful.
- **Brand Recognition:** Franchisees benefit from the franchisor's established brand and marketing support, which can lead to increased sales.
- **Training and Support:** Franchisees receive training and support from the franchisor, which can lead to increased efficiency and profitability.
- **Reduced Risk:** Franchisees benefit from the franchisor's experience and expertise, reducing the risk associated with starting a new business.

4.5.3. Disadvantages of Franchising

1. **Limited Control:** Franchisees cannot be managed as closely as employees, and they may have different goals and priorities than the franchisor. This can make it difficult for the franchisor to maintain control over the business.
2. **Recruitment Challenges**: Franchise recruitment can be slower and less efficient than employee recruitment. This is because the franchisor needs to find franchisees who are not only interested in the business but also have the necessary skills and experience to run it successfully.
3. **Potential for Conflict**: Franchisors earn royalties from sales, while franchisees earn money from profits. Achieving growth in both areas is not always straightforward, potentially causing conflict between the franchisor and franchisee.
4. **Upfront Investment**: The upfront investment of time and money required to establish a franchise can be substantial. A pilot operation may need to be tested before the franchise can be launched, and this can be both time-consuming and expensive.
5. **Risk to Reputation**: Selecting the wrong franchisee can ruin the reputation of the whole franchise. Franchisees may not work together like employees, which can cause reputational damage if one franchisee acts unethically or fails to deliver the required standards.
6. **Confidentiality Risks**: Sharing confidential information with franchisees is risky if they are not fully committed to the business. This can include trade secrets, customer data, and other sensitive information that could be used against the franchisor if it falls into the wrong hands.

Franchising can be a powerful way for a business to expand rapidly, but it comes with its own set of advantages and disadvantages. Franchisors must carefully consider the risks and benefits of franchising before embarking on this strategy. By weighing up the pros and cons, businesses can make an informed decision about whether franchising is right for them.

4.5.3.1. Disadvantages of Franchising for the Franchisor

- **Loss of Control:** Franchisees operate independently, which can lead to the franchisor losing control over the quality of the product or service being offered. Franchisees may also have different goals from the franchisor, which can lead to conflicts.
- **Slow Recruitment:** Recruiting the right franchisee can be a slow and inefficient process, delaying the expansion of the business.
- **Upfront Investment:** The franchisor must invest significant amounts of time and money in creating a pilot operation and developing a

franchise program. This investment may not be recouped if the franchise program is unsuccessful.

- This is risky if the franchisee is not fully committed to the business.

4.5.3.2. Disadvantages of Franchising for the Franchisee

- **Limited Control:** Franchisees must operate within the franchisor's operating procedures and standards, limiting their control over the business.
- **Upfront Investment:** Franchisees must invest significant amounts of money in the initial franchise fee and ongoing royalty payments. This can be a barrier to entry for some potential franchisees.
- **Royalty Payments:** Franchisees must pay ongoing royalties to the franchisor, reducing their profitability.

The table 4.1 shows more advantages and disadvantages of Franchising for the franchisor:

Table 4.1. Advantages and Disadvantages of Franchising for the Franchisor

Advantages	Disadvantages
Expansion can be faster because franchisees provide the labor and their sales provide the growth.	Franchisees cannot be managed as closely as employees, and they may have different goals than the franchisor.
Franchisees are responsible for their company's success, so they are more motivated.	Franchise recruitment can be slower and less efficient than employee recruitment.
Franchisees may be more talented at growing the business and turning a profit than employees would be.	Franchisors earn royalties from sales, while franchisees earn money from profits. Achieving growth in both isn't always possible, potentially causing conflict.
The franchisor puts relatively little money into new locations, as this comes from the franchisee.	Franchisees don't always work together like employees might, thus losing any potential collective benefit.
Successful locations can return high royalties.	The upfront investment (time and money) required can be huge – a pilot operation may need to be tested.
Consistent operations across the business generally mean improved efficiency and higher quality levels.	Selecting one wrong franchisee can ruin the reputation of the whole franchise.

Franchisees should be fully committed due to the investment they put in.	Sharing confidential information with franchisees is risky if they are not fully committed to the business.

It's important to note that these advantages and disadvantages may vary depending on the specific circumstances of the franchisor and franchisee, as well as the industry in which they operate.

4.6. JOINT VENTURES

Joint Venture (JV) is a strategic alliance between two or more organizations or parties, where they come together to pool resources and expertise to achieve a common goal. This business arrangement is common among organizations seeking to expand their operations or gain access to new markets. JVs are often used to combine the resources and expertise of different organizations to increase efficiency and reduce costs.

4.6.1. Advantages of Joint Ventures

1. **Sharing of Risks and Costs**: JVs offer an opportunity for organizations to share risks and costs associated with new ventures. This allows companies to undertake larger projects than they would be able to on their own, with a lower risk profile.
2. **Access to New Markets**: JVs provide access to new markets that may not be available to a company on its own. This is particularly useful when entering markets where local knowledge and expertise are essential, and regulatory barriers may be significant.
3. **Shared Expertise and Technology**: JVs enable organizations to combine their expertise and technology, creating a pool of resources that can drive innovation and growth. This helps companies to stay competitive in their respective industries.
4. **Diversification of Business**: JVs enable organizations to diversify their businesses, which can help to mitigate risks associated with market volatility. For instance, an organization operating in a particular industry can use a JV to expand its operations into a related industry.
5. **Access to Capital**: JVs can help organizations access capital that may not be available to them on their own. This can be particularly useful when seeking to undertake large-scale projects that require significant funding.

4.6.2. Disadvantages of Joint Ventures

1. **Potential for Conflict**: JVs can create conflicts between parties due to differences in objectives, management styles, or decision-making

processes. This can lead to disagreements on how to manage the business, which can negatively affect the success of the JV.

2. **Sharing of Profits**: JVs require the sharing of profits between parties, which may not always be equitable. This can lead to tensions between parties, particularly if one party feels that it is contributing more than the other.
3. **Dependence on Partners**: JVs rely on the participation of all parties for their success. If one partner is unable or unwilling to contribute, it can negatively impact the venture.
4. **Complexity:** JVs can be complex to set up and manage, particularly when multiple parties are involved. This can lead to delays in decision-making and a lack of agility, which can negatively affect the success of the venture.
5. **Legal and Regulatory Issues**: JVs are subject to legal and regulatory requirements that can vary from one jurisdiction to another. This can create additional complexity and costs, which can negatively affect the success of the venture.

4.7. COUNTER TRADE

Countertrade is a type of international trade in which the seller agrees to provide goods or services to a buyer and promises to buy goods or services from the same buyer in return. It is a complex and diverse set of transactions that can involve different forms of exchange, including the use of currency and bartering. Countertrade is used by businesses to expand operations in markets where competition is intense, and currency-based exchange is not possible. It can also be used to stimulate home industries, where raw materials are in short supply, or to encourage reciprocal trade.

4.7.1. Forms of Counter Trade

Countertrade can take many forms, including barter, clearinghouse arrangement, switch trading, and buy-back transactions.

1. **Barter:** Barter is a direct exchange of goods or services without the use of currency. It requires a double coincidence of wants, which means that both the buyer and the seller must want what the other is offering. Barter trade can take various formats. Simple barter is the least complex and oldest form of bilateral, non-monetarized trade. It is also called "straight," "classical," or "pure" barter.
2. **Clearinghouse Arrangement:** A clearinghouse arrangement is a type of barter in which two traders agree to buy a certain amount of goods or

services from each other. They set up accounts with each other that are debited and credited as needed. At the maturity of the arrangement, the parties settle up in cash or merchandise. Clearinghouse arrangements are often used in countertrade to reduce the risk of non-delivery of goods or services.

3. **Switch Trading:** Switch trading is a practice in which one company sells to another its obligation to make a purchase in a given country. In switch trading, a third party purchases one country's clearing agreement balance for hard currency. This type of countertrade can be used to facilitate transactions in markets where currency exchange is not possible or is difficult.
4. **Buy-Back Transactions:** A buy-back transaction is a type of countertrade that involves a technology transfer via the sale of a manufacturing plant. In this type of transaction, a seller agrees to sell a manufacturing plant to a buyer in exchange for a commitment to purchase a specified quantity of the plant's output at a predetermined price. The seller usually provides financing to the buyer to facilitate the purchase of the plant. Once the buyer has repaid the financing, they become the owner of the plant.

4.7.2. Advantages of Counter Trade

1. Helps to Overcome Foreign Exchange Difficulties: Countertrade helps to overcome difficulties associated with the foreign exchange by providing an alternative means of payment. This is particularly useful in developing countries where there is a shortage of foreign currency.
2. Provides Access to New Markets: Countertrade provides businesses with access to new markets that would otherwise be difficult to enter due to currency exchange difficulties or intense competition.
3. Provides a Means of Trade without Currency: Countertrade provides a means of trade without the use of currency, which can be advantageous for businesses that have difficulty obtaining foreign currency.
4. Helps to Promote Reciprocal Trade: Countertrade can help to promote reciprocal trade by encouraging trading partners to buy goods or services from each other.

4.7.3. Disadvantages of Counter Trade

Countertrade transactions can be risky because there is a risk of non-delivery of goods or services by either party. Countertrade, like any other business strategy, has its own set of drawbacks that need to be considered before entering into such an agreement.

Some of the disadvantages of counter-trade are as follows.

1. **Difficulties in Pricing and Valuation**: One of the biggest challenges in countertrade is determining the value of the goods or services being exchanged. It is often difficult to determine a fair price for the goods being traded, which can lead to disputes and disagreements between the parties involved.
2. **Lack of Transparency**: Countertrade can lack transparency and accountability, which can create problems in terms of compliance with regulations and laws. It is important to ensure that all aspects of the transaction are clearly defined, including the terms of the agreement, the obligations of the parties involved, and any legal requirements.
3. **Limited Market Access**: Countertrade may limit market access to certain countries or regions. It can also limit the ability of companies to access global markets, which can be a significant disadvantage for firms looking to expand their reach.

Remember

In a simple barter, the parties exchange goods or services without the involvement of money.

4. **Risk of Non-payment**: Countertrade can create a risk of non-payment, as the goods or services being exchanged may not always have a clear market value or may be difficult to sell. This can be particularly problematic in countries where the legal system is weak or corrupt, as it can be difficult to enforce contracts and recover debts.
5. **Exchange Rate Risk**: Exchange rate risk is a significant concern in countertrade. Because goods and services are being exchanged without the use of currency, it can be difficult to determine a fair exchange rate. This can create uncertainty and volatility in the market, which can be difficult to manage.
6. **Limited Control Over Goods and Services**: In some cases, counter trade may involve the transfer of sensitive technology or intellectual property. This can create a risk of loss of control over the goods and services being exchanged, which can be a significant disadvantage for firms looking to protect their intellectual property.
7. **Increased Complexity**: Countertrade can be a complex and time-consuming process. It may involve a number of different parties, including brokers, clearinghouses, and other intermediaries. This can make it difficult to manage and track transactions, which can create additional costs and complexity.

4.8. TURNKEY PROJECTS

A turnkey project is a type of international business where a firm fully designs, constructs, and equips a production or service facility. The project is handed over to the purchaser upon completion, in a state that is ready to use without requiring any further adjustments or upgrades. This type of project is often carried out as an agreement between a business in a developed country and one in a developing country, where the former provides advanced technology, know-how, and economies of scale to the latter.

4.8.1. Advantages of Turnkey Projects

A turnkey project has several advantages over a design and construct project that involves multiple contractors working on a single project. One of the main benefits is having a single point of contact for the plethora of sub-contracts that go into the construction of a single contract. The purchaser is much more comfortable since he can hand over the complete execution to the vendor. Additionally, turnkey vendors are experts in their field, which enables them to provide a high level of quality at lower 0costs due to the economies of scale they experience.

4.8.2. Disadvantages of Turnkey Projects

One major disadvantage of turnkey projects is that the vendor has no specific interest in the project apart from its completion. The vendor will not be present when the plant is operationalized on a day-to-day basis, and because of a lack of long-term interest, the vendor may be casual during the construction phase. This could result in overlooking small slip-ups here and there, which could impact the performance of the plant once it is handed over to the purchaser. Additionally, since the project is handled by the vendor from start to finish, the purchaser is not made a part of the process. This means that they will not have an acquaintance with how their own plant works once the control is handed over to them.

4.9. MERGERS AND ACQUISITION

M&A is a corporate strategy that involves the consolidation of two or more companies with the aim of creating a more valuable entity. This is achieved by combining the strengths of the companies and eliminating their weaknesses. M&A is an important aspect of the business world that is aimed at wealth maximization for companies. Following are the types of M&A (Figure 4.4).

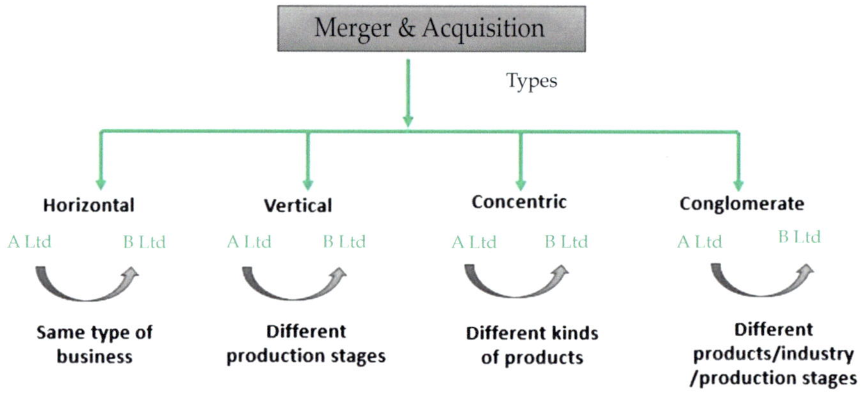

Figure 4.4. Types of mergers and acquisition.

4.9.1. Types of Merger

Mergers can be classified into different categories based on the nature of the business and the companies involved. The four most common types of mergers are horizontal, vertical, co-generic, and conglomerate.

- **Horizontal Merger:** A horizontal merger is a type of merger that takes place between two companies in the same industry segment. The companies involved in the merger have similar products or services, and the merger is aimed at improving their overall performance. This type of merger helps to reduce competition in the industry segment and provides the merged company with an advantage over its competitors. The merged company is able to improve its performance, increase its capital base, and enhance its profits.
- **Vertical Merger:** A vertical merger is a type of merger that occurs between two or more companies in the same industry but in different fields. In this type of merger, the companies involved decide to combine all their operations and production processes under one roof. This type of merger helps to reduce the costs of production, improve the quality of products and services, and increase efficiency.
- **Co-Generic Merger:** A co-generic merger is a type of merger that takes place between two or more companies that are related in terms of production processes, business markets, or required technologies. This type of merger allows companies to expand their product lines, acquire components required for daily operations, and diversify around a common set of resources and strategic

requirements. Co-generic mergers offer significant opportunities for businesses to enhance their operations and improve their profitability.

- **Conglomerate Merger:** A conglomerate merger is a type of merger that occurs between two or more companies belonging to different industrial sectors. The companies involved in this type of merger have no relationship in terms of their business or product lines. The operations of the merged companies may overlap with each other, and the merger is aimed at unifying businesses from different verticals under one flagship enterprise or firm.

4.9.2. Advantages of Mergers and Acquisitions

M&A can provide several benefits to companies, including:

- **Improved Performance**: M&A can improve the performance of companies by combining their strengths and minimizing weaknesses. This can result in increased revenues, improved profitability, and greater market share.
- **Access to New Markets**: M&A can help companies to access new markets that they may not have been able to enter on their own.
- **Cost Savings**: M&A can result in cost savings through economies of scale, improved efficiency, and elimination of redundancies.
- **Increased Market Power**: M&A can give companies increased market power by reducing the number of competitors in the industry segment.

4.9.3. Disadvantages of Mergers and Acquisitions

M&A can also have several disadvantages, including:

- **Cultural Differences**: Companies involved in M&A may have different cultures, which can lead to conflicts and difficulties in integrating the operations of the merged companies.
- **Integration Challenges**: Merging companies can face challenges in integrating their operations, systems, and processes. This can lead to inefficiencies and disruptions in the business.
- **High Costs**: M&A can be expensive, especially when legal, accounting, and consulting fees are factored in.
- **Regulatory Hurdles**: M&A may be subject to regulatory approval, which can be time-consuming and costly.

4.9.4. Process of Merger and Acquisition

The merger and acquisition (M&A) process is an important aspect of corporate restructuring. It involves the consolidation of two or more companies to form a single entity with the objective of creating more value than they would have achieved as individual entities. This process can be complex and challenging, and one wrong move can have significant consequences. The process of merger and acquisition includes the following steps.

- **Business Valuation:** The first step in the M&A process is business valuation. This step involves a thorough examination and evaluation of the target company's present and future market value. The acquiring company conducts extensive research on the target company's history, including its capital gains, organizational structure, market share, distribution channel, corporate culture, and specific business strengths. This information is essential in determining whether the target company is a good fit for the acquiring company.
- **Proposal Phase:** Once the acquiring company has completed the business valuation process and has determined that the target company is a good fit, it will send a proposal for the merger or acquisition. The proposal will include all the details of the deal, including the strategies, amount, and commitments. The proposal is often sent through a non-binding offer document.
- **Planning Exit:** When a company decides to sell its operations, it has to undergo the stage of exit planning. This stage involves making firm decisions about when and how to exit in an organized and profitable manner. The management has to evaluate all financial and other business issues and decide whether to pursue a full sale or a partial sale. They also need to evaluate various options for reinvestment.
- **Structuring Business Deal:** After finalizing the merger and the exit plans, the new entity or the takeover company has to take initiatives for marketing and create innovative strategies to enhance the business and its credibility. The entire phase emphasizes the structuring of the business deal. In this phase, the acquiring company and the target company negotiate the terms of the deal, including the price and the method of payment.
- **Stage of Integration:** The next stage of the M&A process is the integration stage. This stage involves the merging of the two companies operations, systems, and employees. It includes the entire process of preparing the document, signing the agreement, and negotiating the deal. This stage also defines the parameters of the future relationship between the two companies.
- **Operating the Venture:** After signing the agreement and entering into the venture, it is equally important to operate the venture. This operation is attributed to meet the said and pre-defined expectations of all the companies involved in the process. A transaction after the

deal includes all the essential measures and activities that work to fulfill the requirements and desires of the companies involved.

4.10. FACTORS INFLUENCING A FIRM'S SELECTION OF ENTRY STRATEGY

When expanding into international markets, firms must carefully consider various factors before selecting an appropriate entry strategy. Following are the internal and external factors that influence a firm's selection of entry strategy.

4.10.1. External Factors

1. **Market Size:** The market size of the target market is a crucial factor in selecting an entry mode. Large markets justify long-term commitment and higher levels of investment, such as wholly-owned subsidiaries or equity participation.
2. **Market Growth:** Firms invest more resources in markets with high growth potential for long-term growth.
3. **Government Regulations:** The legislative framework of the overseas market plays a significant role in the selection of a market entry mode. Governments of certain countries have made it mandatory for foreign firms to have a local partner.
4. **Level of Competition:** The presence of competitors and their level of involvement in the overseas market is a crucial factor in deciding on an entry mode.
5. **Physical Infrastructure:** The level of development of physical infrastructure such as roads, railways, telecommunications, financial institutions, and marketing channels is a pre-condition for a company to commit more resources to an overseas market.
6. **Level of Risk:** From the point of view of entry mode selection, a firm should evaluate the following risks: political, economic, and operational risks.
7. **Production and Shipping Costs:** Markets with substantial shipping costs may increase logistics costs for firms, while lower production costs may incentivize manufacturing operations in foreign countries.

4.10.2. Internal Factors

1. **Company Objectives:** Companies with limited aspirations in domestic markets generally enter foreign markets as a result of a reactive approach to international marketing opportunities.

2. **Availability of Company Resources:** Venturing into international markets needs the substantial commitment of financial and human resources, so the choice of an entry mode depends upon the financial strength of a firm.
3. **Level of Commitment:** In view of the market potential, the willingness of the company to commit resources in a particular market also determines the entry mode choice.
4. **International Experience:** A company well-exposed to the dynamics of the international marketing environment would be at ease when making a decision regarding entering into international markets with a highly intensive mode of entry such as JVs and wholly-owned subsidiaries.
5. **Flexibility:** Companies should also keep in mind exit barriers when entering international markets.

   Understanding these factors and their impact on the entry mode choice can help firms make better decisions when entering international markets.

4.10.3. Factors Considered Before Finalizing a Joint Venture Agreement

JV agreements can be a powerful way for companies to expand their market reach, share risks, and access new technologies and resources. However, they can also be complex and challenging, and require careful consideration before finalizing. Here, we will discuss the key factors that companies should consider before signing a JV agreement.

4.10.4. Know Your Partner

Before entering into a JV agreement, it is crucial for both parties to thoroughly research and evaluate each other. Companies should investigate their potential partner's financial health, market reputation, management style, and operational capabilities. This will help to identify potential risks and ensure that the partnership is built on a solid foundation.

4.10.5. Know Your Partner's National Culture

In addition to assessing the partner's business capabilities, companies should also consider the cultural differences between the two organizations. Cultural differences can have a significant impact on how business is conducted, including communication styles, decision-making processes, and management practices. Understanding and respecting these differences is essential for building a strong and productive partnership.

4.10.6. Decide on the Respective Roles in Detail at the Start

Before signing the JV agreement, both parties should have a clear understanding of their respective roles and responsibilities. This includes defining the scope of the JV, the roles of each partner, and the expected outcomes. It is important to address potential conflicts and challenges at the outset to minimize misunderstandings later on.

4.10.7. Discuss Contingencies Before the Agreement is Signed

It is important to discuss potential contingencies and scenarios that may arise during the course of the partnership, such as changes in market conditions or unexpected financial setbacks. Both parties should have a plan in place for how to handle these situations, including a clear exit strategy if necessary.

4.10.8. Create a Detailed Joint Venture Agreement

The JV agreement should be comprehensive and clearly outline the terms and conditions of the partnership. This includes details such as the duration of the agreement, ownership structure, financing arrangements, decision-making processes, and dispute-resolution procedures. It is important to ensure that the agreement is legally binding and enforceable in all relevant jurisdictions.

4.10.9. Clear Performance Indicators

To ensure that the JV is on track to meet its goals, clear performance indicators should be established from the outset. This includes metrics such as revenue growth, market share, customer satisfaction, and operational efficiency. Regular monitoring and reporting of these indicators can help both parties stay aligned and make necessary adjustments as needed.

4.10.10. Establish an Open Dialogue

Effective communication is critical to the success of a JV. Both parties should establish a regular and open dialogue to discuss progress, challenges, and potential areas for improvement. This includes regular meetings and reporting, as well as a system for resolving disputes and addressing concerns.

4.10.11. Keep Good Records

Finally, it is important to keep detailed records of all aspects of the JV, including financial transactions, decision-making processes, and communication. This can help to minimize misunderstandings and provide a clear record of the partnership's progress over time.

REVIEW QUESTIONS

1. What are the different entry strategies available for companies looking to expand their business internationally? Write the advantages and disadvantages of each.
2. How do cultural differences between countries impact the choice of entry strategy for international marketing? Explain.
3. What factors should companies consider when choosing a target market for international expansion?
4. How do political and legal factors in different countries affect the choice of entry strategy for international marketing?
5. What are the key success factors for companies implementing an international entry strategy?

MULTIPLE CHOICE QUESTIONS

1. Which of the following entry strategies allows a company to gain full control over its foreign operations?

a. Exporting
b. Joint venture
c. Licensing
d. Wholly owned subsidiary

2. Which of the following entry strategies is most suitable for a company that wants to enter a new market quickly and with low investment?

a. Exporting
b. Joint venture
c. Franchising
d. Licensing

3. Which of the following entry strategies is most suitable for a company that wants to share risks and costs with a local partner?

a. Exporting
b. Joint venture
c. Licensing
d. Direct investment

4. Which of the following entry strategies involves granting a foreign company the right to use a company's intellectual property for a fee or royalty?

a. Exporting
b. Joint venture
c. Licensing

d. Franchising

5. Which of the following entry strategies is most suitable for a company that wants to leverage the brand recognition and management expertise of a local partner?

a. Direct investment

b. Exporting

c. Franchising

d. Licensing

Answers to Multiple Choice Questions

1. (d); 2. (a); 3. (b); 4. (c); 5. (c)

REFERENCES

1. Cavusgil, S. T., Knight, G., & Riesenberger, J. R., (2018). *International Business: The New Realities* (5th edn., Vol. 1). Pearson Education, Inc.
2. Chadha, N. K., (2018). *International Business Management: A Managerial Perspective*. Vikas Publishing House.
3. Cherunilam, F., (2017). *International Business Management: Text and Cases*. Himalaya Publishing House.
4. Cullen, J. B., & Parboteeah, K. P., (2018). *International Business: Strategy and the Multinational Company* (2nd edn., Vol. 2). Routledge.
5. Daniels, J. D., Radebaugh, L. H., & Sullivan, D. P., (2018). *International Business: Environments and Operations*. Pearson Education.
6. Deresky, H., (2020). *International Management: Managing Across Borders and Cultures* (10th edn.). Pearson Education.
7. Hill, C. W. L., & Hult, G. T. M., (2019). *Global Business Today* (11th edn., Vol. 1). McGraw-Hill Education.
8. Hill, C. W. L., & Hult, G. T. M., (2021). *International Business: Competing in the Global Marketplace* (12th edn., Vol. 2). McGraw-Hill Education.
9. Kuthiala, B. K., & Kuthiala, D., (2017). *International Business Management: Theory and Practice*. Excel Books.
10. Luthans, F., & Doh, J. P., (2020). *International Management: Culture, Strategy, and Behavior* (10th edn., Vol. 2). McGraw-Hill Education.
11. Sharma, K., & Dubey, A., (2017). *International Business Management: Globalization and Beyond*. Pearson India.
12. Wild, J. J., Wild, K. L., & Han, J. C. Y., (2017). *International Business: The Challenges of Globalization* (9th edn., Vol. 1). Pearson Education, Inc.

CHAPTER 5

FOREIGN DIRECT INVESTMENT

UNIT INTRODUCTION

In the 1990s, cross-border capital flows increased significantly, and an increasing share of flows was directed toward developing countries in the form of foreign direct investment (FDI). While FDI flows declined sharply during the global financial crisis of 2007–2008, they rebounded more quickly than other components of global capital flows to developing countries and remain high at roughly 10% of gross fixed capital formation. The increasing participation of developing and emerging market economies in FDI inflows reflects both push and pull factors.

On the push side, declining transportation costs, significant differences in factor prices, and slowing growth rates in developed countries drove an increasing number of firms to establish operations abroad. On the pull side, many governments, seeing FDI as key to bringing the capital, technology, and know-how needed to move their economies from traditional activities to higher-end manufacturing and services, not only liberalized flows but actively competed for FDI with a variety of preferential incentives and policies.

The effect of FDI on development in the host economies can be assessed by looking at its impact on economic development. In the broadest sense, FDI can affect economic development by increasing the availability of factors of production, specifically capital. However, FDI can be more than just capital. Foreign-owned firms can have a positive impact on the local economy and on the productivity levels of domestic firms, which is perhaps of even greater importance.

Improvements in local productivity due to the presence of foreign companies may arise from several channels. On the macro side, FDI could spawn new economic sectors, push an economy's technological frontier, and diversify exports. On the micro side, through knowledge spillovers and linkages between foreign and domestic firms, FDI could foster technology transfer, improve managerial and employee skills, and boost investment incentives and productivity in upstream and downstream sectors. Intensifying competition resulting from foreign entry could incentivize local firms to upgrade their productivity, drive out unproductive domestic firms, and reallocate factors of production to more productive firms and uses.

The benefits of FDI to developing countries are well-established, and empirical studies have confirmed the positive effects of FDI on economic growth, employment, and productivity. However, the impact of FDI on development can vary depending on the host country's policies and institutions. FDI can also have negative effects, such as exacerbating income inequality and environmental degradation. Therefore, host countries need to adopt appropriate policies to maximize the positive effects of FDI while minimizing its negative impacts.

FDI has become an increasingly important component of global capital flows, particularly toward developing countries. FDI can have a significant impact on economic development by increasing the availability of capital and improving the productivity levels of domestic firms.

Learning Objectives

After completing this chapter, you should be able to:

- Define Foreign Direct Investment (FDI) and explain its various forms and types.
- Understand the factors that attract FDI and the benefits and challenges associated with it.
- Analyze the impact of FDI on host countries' economic development.
- Understand the FDI strategies of multinational corporations (MNCs)

Key Terms

- Backward vertical FDI
- Forward vertical FDI
- Greenfield investment
- Home country
- Horizontal FDI
- Host country
- Multinational corporation (MNC)
- Outward FDI
- Technology transfer
- Vertical FDI

5.1. OVERVIEW OF FOREIGN DIRECT INVESTMENT

Foreign Direct Investment (FDI) refers to a company's investment in facilities to produce and/or market goods and services in a foreign country. It is a crucial component of globalization and has become an integral part of the world economy. By investing in foreign countries, multinational enterprises (MNEs) seek to expand their market presence, increase their profits, and enhance their competitiveness. FDI takes on two main forms: Greenfield investment or brownfield investment (acquisition method).

Greenfield investment involves the establishment of a new operation in a foreign country. This approach allows MNEs to create new jobs, transfer technology, and benefit from lower production costs. Greenfield investments can also stimulate economic growth and development in the host country. However, this approach requires a significant amount of capital and can be risky due to uncertainties in the foreign market.

The acquisition method involves purchasing or merging with an existing firm in a foreign country. This approach allows MNEs to quickly enter a foreign market and acquire existing assets and customer bases. Acquisitions can also provide access to local distribution channels, supply chains, and skilled labor. However, this approach can be challenging due to cultural differences, legal issues, and integration problems.

There are different types of foreign investment depending on the level of equity stake acquired by the foreign firm. A minority stake refers to a foreign interest of 10% to 49% of the company's share capital and voting rights. This approach allows the foreign firm to have some control over the company's operations but not enough to make significant decisions. A majority stake refers to a foreign interest of 50% to 99%, which gives the foreign firm control over the company's operations. Finally, a full outright stake refers to a foreign interest of 100%, which means that the foreign firm owns the company outright.

It is important to distinguish FDI from foreign portfolio investment (FPI). FPI involves investment in foreign financial instruments such as government bonds and foreign stocks. Unlike FDI, FPI does not involve taking an equity stake in a foreign business entity. FPI provides great opportunities for individuals and businesses to build a diversified portfolio of international investments in financial assets, which can lower risk.

FDI can have positive and negative impacts on the host country. On the positive side, FDI can bring new technology, management expertise, and job opportunities. FDI can also stimulate competition, increase productivity, and promote economic growth. On the negative side, FDI can lead to the exploitation of natural resources, labor, and intellectual property. FDI can also have negative effects on the environment, cultural heritage, and social welfare.

5.1.1. Understanding Foreign Direct Investment (FDI)

Foreign Direct Investment (FDI) refers to the investment made by a company or individual in a foreign country, where the investor retains control over the investment. FDI can be in the form of starting a subsidiary, acquiring a stake in an existing firm, or entering into a joint venture (JV) with a local partner. The primary aim of FDI is to gain access to new markets, resources, and talent, and to take advantage of favorable business conditions in a foreign country (Figure 5.1).

Figure 5.1. Foreign direct investment (FDI).

5.1.2. Factors Affecting FDI Decisions

FDI decisions are influenced by a range of factors that impact the long-term profitability and sustainability of the investment. The following are the key factors that impact FDI decisions:

1. **Political Stability:** Political stability is a crucial factor that influences FDI decisions. Investors look for countries that have stable political systems, a transparent legal framework, and a low risk of political unrest. The presence of a stable government and policies that support foreign investment create an environment that is conducive to long-term investments. Political instability, on the other hand, can create uncertainty, increase risk, and reduce investor confidence.
2. **Government Policy:** Government policy is another critical factor that influences FDI decisions. The policies of the host country's government can either encourage or discourage foreign investment. Policies that

support foreign investment can include tax incentives, and subsidies, and streamline bureaucratic processes. In contrast, policies that hinder foreign investment can include high taxes, trade restrictions, and excessive regulation.

3. **State of Economic Development:** The state of economic development of a country is another key factor that influences FDI decisions. Countries with strong economic growth, a stable currency, and a skilled workforce tend to be attractive destinations for foreign investment. Such countries often have a strong industrial base and a favorable business environment that can support the growth of foreign firms. In contrast, countries with weak economic growth, high inflation, and a weak currency are likely to be less attractive to foreign investors.
4. **Industrial Prospects:** Industrial prospects refer to the potential for growth and development in a particular sector or industry. Investors tend to look for sectors that are likely to experience significant growth in the future. Sectors that are characterized by innovation, high productivity, and high value-added activities are particularly attractive to investors. In contrast, sectors that are characterized by low productivity, low profitability, and low growth prospects are less attractive.

5.2. THE GROWING IMPORTANCE OF FDI IN THE GLOBAL ECONOMY

FDI is the investment made by an entity or individual in one country into a business enterprise located in another country. FDI can take various forms, such as mergers and acquisitions (M&A), JVs, and Greenfield investments. In recent years, the world has witnessed a marked increase in the flow and stock of FDI, which has become a significant driver of economic growth and development.

5.2.1. The Growth of FDI

The flow of FDI refers to the amount of investment undertaken over a given time period, usually a year, while the stock of FDI refers to the total accumulation of foreign-owned assets at a particular time. In the past two decades, the world economy has seen a dramatic increase in both the flow and stock of FDI. The average outflow of FDI has increased from about $25 billion in 1975 to a record of $1.3 trillion in 2000. During the last quarter, the flow of FDI accelerated faster than the growth in world trade. For example, between 1990 and 2000, the flow of FDI for all countries increased about five-fold, while world trade grew by some 82% and world outflow by 23%. By 2000, the global stock of FDI exceeded $5.7 trillion. In total, 63,000 parent companies had 6, 90,000 affiliates in foreign markets that effectively produced an estimated $14 trillion in global sales, nearly twice the value of global exports.

5.2.2. Reasons for the Growth of FDI

FDI has been growing more rapidly than world trade and world output for several reasons. One of the significant reasons is the fear of protectionist pressure despite the general decline in trade barriers. For example, much of the Japanese automobile companies' investments in the United States during the 1980s and early 1990s were driven toward the reduction of exports from Japan, thereby removing trade tensions between nations.

Another reason for the growth of FDI is the dramatic political and economic changes that have been occurring in many of the world's developing nations. The general shift towards democratic political institutions and market economies has encouraged FDI. Economic growth, economic deregulation, privatization programs that are open to foreign investors, and the removal of many restrictions on FDI have made Asia, Eastern Europe, and Latin America more attractive to foreign investors.

The increase in the number of bilateral investment treaties designed to protect and promote investment between two countries has also contributed to the decrease in facilitating FDI. These treaties have facilitated FDI by providing a framework of investment rules and by offering legal protection to investors.

The globalization of the world economy is also having a significant impact on the volume of FDI. Globalization has led to the increased mobility of goods, services, and capital across borders. As a result, many firms believe it is essential to have production facilities close to their major customers. This is creating pressures for greater FDI.

5.3. TYPES OF FDI

There are several types of FDI, such as:

5.3.1. Horizontal FDI

Horizontal FDI is an expensive and risky venture, which requires the firm to bear the costs of establishing production facilities or acquiring a foreign enterprise in a new cultural environment. However, firms prefer FDI over exporting or licensing due to the factors that alter the relative attractiveness of exporting, licensing, and FDI, which include transportation costs, market imperfections, following competitors, strategic behavior, and location advantages.

1. **Transportation Costs:** Transportation costs are the costs of moving goods from one location to another, which can be significant for products that have a low value-to-weight ratio and can be produced in almost any location, such as cement or soft drinks. For such products, the attractiveness of exporting decreases relative to either FDI or licensing when transportation costs are added to production costs. In contrast, products with a high value-to-weight ratio, such as electronic components, personal computers, medical equipment, and computer software, have little impact on the relative attractiveness of exporting, licensing, and FDI as transportation costs are normally a very minor component of total landed cost.
2. **Market Imperfections:** Market imperfections refer to the factors that prevent markets from functioning perfectly. Market imperfections arise when there are impediments to the sale of know-how or when there are impediments to the free flow of products between nations. Impediments to the free flow of products between nations, such as government-imposed tariffs or quotas on imported goods, decrease the probability of exporting relative to FDI and licensing. On the other hand, impediments to the sale of know-how increase the profitability of FDI relative to licensing. Thus, the market imperfections explanation predicts that FDI will be preferred whenever there are impediments that make both exporting and the sale of know-how difficult and/or expensive.
3. **Following Competitors:** Following competitors refers to the tendency of firms to engage in FDI to keep up with their competitors who are also investing abroad. Firms may engage in FDI to match their competitors' investments, to pre-empt their competitors, or to counter their competitors' advantages. Following competitors is particularly relevant in industries where there are strong interdependencies among the major players, such as oligopolistic industries, where what one firm does can have an immediate impact on the major competitors, forcing a response in kind.
4. **Strategic Behavior:** The strategic behavior theory explains FDI flows as a reflection of strategic rivalry between firms in the global marketplace. Strategic behavior theory suggests that FDI is motivated by the desire of firms to gain a strategic advantage over their competitors. Firms may engage in FDI to gain access to resources, markets, and technology that they cannot acquire through other means. Firms may also engage in FDI to pre-empt their competitors, protect their market position, or increase their bargaining power.
5. **Location Advantages:** Location advantages refer to the advantages that a firm gains from locating its operations in a particular country. Location advantages can include access to natural resources, access to a skilled labor force, access to a large market, or access to a

favorable regulatory environment. Location advantages can make FDI more attractive than exporting or licensing. For example, a firm may engage in FDI to access a particular market or to take advantage of favorable tax policies in a particular country.

5.3.2. Vertical FDI

FDI is a strategic decision that firms make to establish production facilities in foreign countries to take advantage of various benefits. One form of FDI is vertical FDI, which can be backward or forward. Backward vertical FDI occurs when a firm invests in an industry abroad to obtain inputs for its domestic production processes, while forward vertical FDI involves investing in an industry abroad to sell the outputs of a firm's domestic production processes.

- **Backward Vertical FDI:** Historically, most backward vertical FDI has been in extractive industries, such as oil extraction, bauxite mining, tin mining, and copper mining. Firms like Royal Dutch/Shell, British Petroleum (BP), RTZ, and Consolidated Gold Field are classic examples of such vertically integrated multinationals. The objective of backward vertical FDI is to provide inputs into a firm's downstream operations, such as oil refining, aluminum smelting and fabrication, and tin smelting and fabrication.
- **Forward Vertical FDI***:* Forward vertical FDI is less common than backward vertical FDI. An example of forward vertical FDI is when Volkswagen entered the US market, it acquired a large number of dealers rather than distributing its cars through independent US dealers. The reason for this was to have control over the distribution of its cars, ensuring better market penetration and higher profits.
- **Different Theories of Vertical FDI:** Vertical FDI is a type of FDI in which a firm establishes or acquires production facilities in a foreign country to control the source of raw materials or to sell its products directly in a foreign market. The strategic behavior argument and the market imperfections approach are two theories that explain why firms engage in vertical FDI.

i. **Strategic Behavior Argument:** The strategic behavior argument suggests that firms engage in vertical FDI to gain control over the source of raw materials, raise entry barriers, and prevent new competitors from entering the industry. There are two ways in which this theory can be applied:

   - **Building Entry Barriers:** A firm can vertically integrate backward to gain control over the source of raw material, thereby raising entry barriers and shutting new competitors out of the industry. If the raw material is found abroad, such strategic behavior involves vertical FDI. For example, a firm that extracts raw materials from a foreign country and uses them to manufacture products in its home country can prevent other firms from entering the market by controlling the supply of raw materials.

- **Circumventing Established Barriers:** Another way in which strategic behavior can explain vertical FDI is by circumventing the barriers established by firms already doing business in a country. For instance, Volkswagen established its dealer network when it entered the North American auto market to circumvent the barriers established by its competitors.

ii. **Market Imperfections Approach:** The market imperfections approach offers two explanations for vertical FDI, both of which are based on the idea that market imperfections prevent the sale of know-how and specialized assets through the market mechanism:

- **Impediments to the Sale of Know-how:** The first explanation for vertical FDI under the market imperfections approach is that there are impediments to the sale of know-how through the market mechanism. For example, a firm may have the knowledge and ability to extract raw materials in another country, but there may be no efficient producer in that country that can supply raw materials to the firm. Oil refining companies such as BP and Royal Dutch/Shell pursued backward vertical FDI to supply their British and Dutch oil refining facilities with crude oil in the early decades of the 20th century when neither Great Britain nor the Netherlands had domestic oil supplies.
- **Investments in Specialized Assets:** The second explanation for vertical FDI under the market imperfections approach is that investments in specialized assets expose the investing firm to hazards that can be reduced only through vertical FDI. A specialized asset is an asset designed to perform a specific task and whose value is significantly reduced in its next-best use. For example, an aluminum refinery is designed to refine bauxite ore and produce aluminum. Bauxite ores vary in context and chemical composition from deposit to deposit, and each type of ore requires a different type of refinery. Running one type of bauxite through a refinery designed for another type increases production costs by 20 to 100%. Thus, the value of an investment in an aluminum refinery depends on the availability of the desired kind of bauxite ore.

5.3.3. Implications for Business Practice

The theories of horizontal and vertical FDI have implications for business practice. The location-specific advantages argument associated with John Dunning helps explain the direction of FDI, both concerning horizontal and vertical FDI. The most useful theory for explaining FDI from a business perspective is the market imperfections approach. About horizontal FDI, this approach identifies how the relative rates of return associated with horizontal FDI, exporting, and licensing vary with circumstances. The theory suggests that exporting is preferable to licensing and horizontal FDI is more costly and risky as long as transport costs are minor and tariff barriers are trivial. However, as transport costs and/or tariff barriers increase, exporting becomes unprofitable,

Did you Know?

Before Stephen Hymer's landmark work on FDI in 1960, no theory existed on matters specifically talking about FDI. However, there were theories that dealt generally with foreign investments.

5.4. IMPLICATIONS OF FDI FOR FIRMS OPERATING IN DIFFERENT INDUSTRIES

The implications of FDI are significant for firms operating in different industries. Licensing may not be a suitable option for firms in high-technology industries, global oligopolies, or industries with intense cost pressures. These firms require tight control over their foreign operations and have difficulty codifying their managerial or marketing knowledge. On the other hand, licensing is more common and profitable in fragmented, low-technology industries where globally dispersed manufacturing is not an option, and the knowledge to be transferred is relatively easy to codify.

Franchising is a form of licensing that is commonly used in the service industry, such as the fast food industry. McDonald's has successfully expanded globally using a franchising strategy, where it licenses its brand name to foreign firms in return for a percentage of its profits. Franchising allows McDonald's to economize the costs and risks associated with opening foreign markets and protect its brand name using a contract. McDonald's know-how in running a fast-food restaurant is amenable to being specified in a written contract, making it a suitable industry for franchising.

Product life-cycle theory and Knickerbocker's theory of horizontal FDI are descriptive rather than analytical and do not identify the factors that influence the relative profitability of FDI, licensing, and exporting. Vertical FDI may be a way of building barriers to entry into an industry, while investments in specialized assets and market imperfections in the market for know-how increase the relative attractiveness of vertical FDI.

In short, the implications of FDI for Different Types of Firms and Industries. Firms for which licensing is not a good option:

1. High-technology industries

- Protection of firm-specific expertise is crucial
- Licensing is hazardous

2. Global oligopolies

- Competitive interdependence requires tight control over foreign operations
- Ability to launch coordinated attacks against global competitors

3. Industries with intense cost pressures

- Tight control over foreign operations is needed to disperse manufacturing to locations with favorable factor costs

Firms for which licensing is a good option:

- Fragmented, low-technology industries
- Globally dispersed manufacturing is not feasible
- Knowledge to be transferred is relatively easy to codify

Example of an industry where licensing is successful:

- Fast food industry
- McDonald's has expanded globally through Franchising
- Franchising is the service industry version of licensing

McDonald's Franchising Strategy

- License brand name to a foreign firm in return for a percentage of the franchisee's profits
- Franchisee must fulfill specific conditions outlined in the Franchising contract
- McDonald's know-how can be specified in a written contract

Product Life-Cycle Theory and Knickerbocker's Theory

- Descriptive rather than analytical
- Poor job of identifying factors that influence the relative profitability of FDI, licensing, and exporting

Vertical FDI

- Market imperfections approach and strategic behavior approach have useful implications for business practice
- Vertical FDI may build barriers to entry into an industry
- Investments in specialized assets and imperfections in the market for know-how increase the relative attractiveness of vertical FDI

5.5. REASONS FOR FDI

Reasons why Multinational Corporations (MNCs) are welcome to invest in foreign countries:

1. Bridging the gap between available domestic resources and the desired level of resources

- FDI can fill the gap between available domestic resources and the desired level of savings, foreign exchange, government revenue, and human capital skills necessary for growth and development targets.
- MNCs generate foreign exchange earnings from exports, which can alleviate the trade deficit or gap in the balance of payments current account.
- Taxation of MNCs' profits and participation in their local operations can mobilize public financial resources for development projects.

2. Bridging the gap in management, entrepreneurship, and technology

- MNCs provide financial resources, factories, managerial experience, entrepreneurial abilities, and technological skills that can be transferred to local counterparts employing training programs and "learning by doing."
- MNCs educate local managers about international marketing practices, locate alternative sources of supply, diversify market outlets, and establish contacts with foreign banks.
- MNCs bring sophisticated technological knowledge about production processes and modern machinery and equipment to capital-starved developing countries, which can leak out to the broader economy when engineers and managers leave to start their enterprises.

3. Promotion of domestic investment

- Factories set up by MNCs act as a nucleus of growth and give birth to several other enterprises, which supply inputs to the parent company.
- Every dollar of FDI can increase domestic investment by 80% of the amount of FDI.

4. Promotion of healthy competition in host countries

- FDI can generate healthy competition in recipient countries, creating new enterprises and increasing the number of players in the market.
- Intense competition enhances consumer choice, brings down prices, and boosts economic welfare.
- Increased competition stimulates capital investments by firms in plant, equipment, and R&D, resulting in increased productivity, innovation, and economic growth.

5. Taking advantage of locational advantage

- Locational advantages, such as natural resources and a low-cost, highly skilled labor force, can attract FDI.
- Firms must undertake FDI to exploit such endowments.
- The availability of a highly skilled labor force at low wage rates, guaranteed power supply, cheap land, and proximity to the seaport attracted Hyundai's car manufacturing plant to Chennai, India.

TIPS

1. FDI often depends on a country's political attempts to reduce security risks.

2. Chinese state-owned petroleum companies have been investing abroad to minimize dependence on foreign companies for oil supplies and hold down prices on the petroleum they receive.

3. FDI can have political motives, such as reducing dependence on foreign countries for essential resources.

5.6. BENEFITS OF FDI

FDI can bring in resources such as capital and technology, create employment opportunities, improve the balance of payments, and stimulate competition and economic growth in the host country.

5.6.1. Benefits of Foreign Direct Investment (FDI) to Host Countries

FDI has several benefits for the host country, which are discussed below:

1. **Resource-Transfer Effects:** FDI can bring capital, technology, and management expertise to a host country that may not be readily available. This can lead to economic growth and development. MNEs have access to financial resources that host-country firms may not have, making it easier for them to invest in new technology and management practices.
2. **Employment Effects:** FDI can create both direct and indirect employment opportunities for host-country citizens. Direct employment is created when a foreign MNE employs local workers, while indirect employment is created when local suppliers and other support industries benefit from the investment. This can have a significant impact on the host country's economy, as indirect employment effects are often larger than direct employment effects.
3. **Balance-of-Payments Effect:** FDI can have a positive impact on a host country's balance of payments. The initial capital inflow from the MNE can benefit the host country's capital account. If the FDI substitutes for imports of goods or services, it can improve the host country's current account. Additionally, if the MNE uses a foreign

subsidiary to export goods and services to other countries, it can further benefit the host country's balance of payments position.

4. **Effect on Competition and Economic Growth:** FDI can increase the number of players in a market and stimulate competition, leading to lower prices and increased economic welfare for consumers. Increased competition also stimulates firms to invest in plant, equipment, and R&D to gain an edge over their rivals, leading to increased productivity growth, innovation, and greater economic growth. This effect may be particularly important for services, where exporting is often not an option and the service has to be produced where it is delivered.

5.6.2. Home Country Effects: Benefits and Costs of FDI

FDI has both benefits and costs for the home (or source) country. It is crucial to understand these benefits and costs to determine whether FDI is in the national interest or not.

Benefits of FDI to the Home Country:

FDI can bring benefits to the home country in three ways:

1. **Current Account Benefits**: The inward flow of foreign earnings can improve the current account of the home country's balance of payments. If the foreign subsidiary creates demands for the home country's exports of capital equipment, intermediate goods, complementary products, and so on, it can further improve the current account.
2. **Employment Effects**: Positive employment effects arise when the foreign subsidiary creates demand for home country exports of capital equipment, intermediate goods, complementary products, and so on.
3. **Learning Valuable Skills**: Exposure to foreign markets can enable the home country's Multinational Enterprises (MNE) to learn valuable skills such as superior management techniques and product and process technologies. These skills can be transferred back to the home country, leading to economic growth.

Costs of FDI to the Home Country:

Despite the benefits, there are costs associated with FDI that the home country must consider:

1. **Balance of Payments Concerns**: The home country's current account may deteriorate if the foreign investment aims to serve the home market from low-cost production locations. Additionally, if FDI is a substitute

for direct exports, it can negatively impact the current account.

2. **Employment Effects:** Outward FDI can lead to job losses in the home country. This is because foreign subsidiaries may substitute imports for domestically produced goods, leading to reduced demand for home country-produced goods and services.

The benefits and costs of FDI to the home country are complex and depend on various factors. Governments must consider these factors before deciding to allow or restrict FDI. By balancing the costs and benefits, policymakers can make informed decisions that promote the national interest.

5.7. FOREIGN DIRECT INVESTMENT – GLOBAL TRENDS

In 2022, the regulation of FDI has been a significant topic of discussion, and it is expected to remain a key issue for cross-border M&A in 2023. Although FDI restrictions are increasing globally, they vary significantly across jurisdictions. As a result, it will be challenging for dealmakers to navigate the rapidly evolving legal and regulatory FDI landscape, as well as other customary investment barriers such as merger control and regulated sectors. Dealmakers and investors must consider the application of any such investment restrictions during the planning phase, which necessitates early due diligence, careful transaction structuring, and pre-emptive engagement with advisers and the government. Despite these regulatory and legal challenges, investors can successfully navigate them with careful transaction management and deal structuring, or risk having a transaction blocked from closing or unwound after closing (Figure 5.2).

Figure 5.2. Global trends of FDI.

5.7.1. Global Overview

On a global level, there is a noticeable inclination towards greater regulation of FDI, as governments attempt to find a balance between open economic policies and protecting national defense and public security interests through protectionist measures.

- **United States:** The Committee on Foreign Investment in the United States (CFIUS) has experienced an expansion in its authority and an increase in its funding. This is evident in the CFIUS 2021 annual report, which showed a significant surge in the declaration and notice filings by almost 40% in 2021 compared to 2020.
- **Europe:** The European Union (EU) has established a common framework for the screening of FDI, which aims to protect its critical assets and technology while ensuring an open and welcoming environment for foreign investment. The FDI Screening Regulation came into force in 2019, and 18 member states have now adopted their screening mechanisms, while others are in the process of doing so.

  However, while the regulation establishes common rules and procedures for cooperation and information exchange among member states, the actual screening of FDI remains a national competence. This means that FDI regulations vary widely across Europe, and investors must carefully analyze the specific rules of each member state in which they intend to invest.
- **UK:** The United Kingdom, which is no longer a member of the EU after Brexit, implemented its own FDI regime in 2022. The National Security and Investment Act gives the UK government the power to intervene in M&A transactions that raise national security concerns. The regime covers 17 key sectors, including artificial intelligence, energy, and transport.
- **ASIA**: China has been actively reforming its FDI regime, seeking to attract foreign investment while maintaining control over critical sectors and safeguarding national security. In 2020, the PRC Foreign Investment Law came into effect, replacing three existing laws governing foreign investment in China. The new law aims to create a more level playing field for foreign investors and to provide better protection for their interests.

  However, while the law removes some of the restrictions on foreign investment, it also includes new provisions that give the Chinese government more power to scrutinize and control foreign investment in certain sectors. The law requires foreign investors to undergo a national security review if they intend to invest in areas related to national security or sensitive sectors such as technology, media, and telecommunications.

Hong Kong, a Special Administrative Region of China, has traditionally been a popular destination for foreign investment due to its open and business-friendly environment. However, the adoption of the Hong Kong National Security Law in 2020 has raised concerns among investors about the impact on the rule of law and the business environment. At this stage, the impact appears to be more political than economic, but investors should closely monitor developments.

Other jurisdictions in Asia have also introduced new regulatory restrictions and licensing regimes in certain sectors. For example, Indonesia has implemented a new licensing regime for foreign investors in the digital economy sector, while Malaysia has introduced new rules requiring foreign investors to obtain approval for any investments in strategic sectors such as healthcare, telecommunications, and transportation.

- **United Arab Emirates:** The United Arab Emirates (UAE) is a regional hub for foreign investment, with its business-friendly environment, strategic location, and liberal FDI policies. In recent years, the UAE federal government and the governments of the seven emirates that comprise the UAE have introduced various measures to further liberalize their FDI regimes.

  Non-UAE nationals may now own 100% of a UAE limited liability onshore company, subject to sector-specific FDI restrictions. However, foreign investors must comply with licensing and regulatory requirements in certain sectors, such as financial services, healthcare, and telecommunications.

  The UAE has also established several free zones that offer incentives and benefits to foreign investors, including 100% foreign ownership, exemption from corporate and personal income taxes, and simplified administrative procedures. These free zones are subject to their specific regulatory frameworks and are a popular choice for foreign investors seeking to set up operations in the UAE.

5.7.2. United States

The United States is still among the leading countries in receiving FDI from all over the world. According to the US Bureau of Economic Analysis, FDI inflows to the US rose by over $500 billion to around $5 trillion between 2020 and 2021, mainly due to European investments. As a result, the CFIUS, which is responsible for reviewing foreign investment transactions, experienced an almost 40% increase in notification and declaration filings in 2021.

Although some transactions necessitate mandatory filings with CFIUS, submitting a voluntary notification is recommended even if there is no obligation. CFIUS regulations allow parties to submit a brief "declaration" instead of the traditional voluntary notice, which is typically reviewed within 30 days. If CFIUS detects national security issues, it will follow up with a 45-day investigation and may impose various mitigation measures. These measures include protocols for sensitive information transfer or sharing, ensuring certain operations are solely located in the US, and divesting all or part of the US business. Failure to comply with CFIUS can result in civil penalties up to the transaction's value and, in some cases, a halt to pending transactions or the unwinding of completed ones.

To address the evolving national security risks in the US, CFIUS's authority and involvement in reviewing foreign investment have expanded over the last few years. The Foreign Investment Risk Review Modernization Act of 2018 and the US Department of Treasury's regulations in 2020 modernized and broadened CFIUS's authority over specific foreign investments in "TID US businesses," which are businesses engaged in critical technologies, critical infrastructure, sensitive personal data of US citizens, and certain real estate transactions.

On September 15, 2022, US President Joe Biden issued an executive order to provide CFIUS with guidance in conducting national security reviews. While the executive order does not expand or modify the regulatory requirements of CFIUS, it does provide additional information on whether to file voluntarily, including more information about whether a transaction may be subject to post-closing review. As CFIUS's involvement continues to expand, we expect an increase in the number of voluntary CFIUS filings and post-closing inquiries in 2023.

5.7.3. France

France has been actively reforming its FDI regime since its introduction in 2005. The most recent reform in 2019 consolidated previous amendments and introduced new modifications in response to the Covid-19 pandemic and the EU screening mechanism. Despite the changes, France remains a popular destination for FDI, attracting 1,600 FDI transactions in 2021, with Germany, the US, and the UK being the top investors.

The 2019 reform abolished the former distinction between EU and non-EU foreign investors and required investors to disclose any interest held by or financial support received from a non-EU state. It also harmonized the list of qualifying transactions and lowered the threshold to 10% for listed companies during the pandemic. The FDI regulation in France does not set any economic or financial conditions, but the size of the target is taken into account when reviewing filings.

The reform also clarified the list of sensitive sectors in which investment by a foreign investor would require prior approval. The list covers activities related to defense and national security, infrastructure, biotechnology, vital economic sectors, and research and development (R&D) in critical sectors. The government may require commitments from the investor, but outright refusals are rare.

Decisions on FDI filings are not made public, but both the investor and the target can submit a preliminary inquiry. The government does not consider itself bound by its own precedent decisions, particularly in defining the sectors covered by the regulations.

5.7.4. Germany

In recent years, Germany has introduced significant amendments to its foreign trade laws, which have introduced new requirements and restrictions on foreign investors. Under the new rules, if a foreign investor acquires 10% or more of the voting rights in a German company, the government may determine the acquisition to represent a threat to public order and security and restrict or prohibit the acquisition if necessary.

The key question under the new, broader screening standard is whether an acquisition or investment leads to an "expected impairment of public order or security." This represents a significant change from the previous requirement of a "genuine threat" before any intervention. This change is likely to result in greater scrutiny of FDI transactions, and the government will also consider whether the transaction affects other EU member states or EU programs and projects, adding further complexity and uncertainty to the review process. During the screening period, any acquisition subject to reporting requirements will be provisionally invalid until otherwise approved.

Germany has also implemented the EU-screening directive 2019/452, which establishes a new information and cooperation mechanism between EU member states for the examination of FDI. This directive aims to further strengthen the ability of member states to safeguard their essential security interests while ensuring that the EU remains open to foreign investment.

Several specific areas have attracted FDI restrictions, including healthcare, artificial intelligence, and robotics, biotechnology, and quantum technology. In healthcare, the government has introduced stricter regulations on companies that develop or produce goods essential for the long-term maintenance of a functioning healthcare system. Manufacturers of vaccines, antibiotics, medical protective equipment, and medical goods for the treatment of highly infectious diseases have been added to the list of protected companies. Foreign non-EU or EFTA investors are required to notify the government of certain transactions and are prohibited from proceeding with the transaction until the clearance is obtained.

These changes have led to greater uncertainty and complexity for foreign investors seeking to invest in Germany. It is therefore important for investors to carefully consider the regulatory framework and requirements before embarking on any transaction. In addition, it may be helpful for investors to seek the advice of legal and financial experts to navigate the complex regulatory landscape and ensure compliance with all relevant laws and regulations.

5.7.5. United Kingdom

The United Kingdom has historically been a top destination for FDI globally and has had a more hands-off approach to policing FDI compared to other countries. However, this has changed with the introduction of the National Security and Investment Act 2021, which allows the UK government to review and intervene in M&A transactions that raise national security concerns, even on an extraterritorial basis.

The Act establishes a framework for scrutinizing FDI similar to the CFIUS and closer to the regimes adopted in Europe. The Act applies to transactions that give an acquirer control over UK entities or control over foreign entities that carry on activities in the UK or supply goods or services to persons in the UK, even if that entity holds no assets in the UK. The government has powers to block, impose conditions on, delay the closing of, or unwind transactions in 17 key sectors, including communications, defense, data infrastructure, energy, transport, artificial intelligence, computing hardware, and robotics.

The Act contemplates a hybrid system of mandatory and voluntary notifications. The former applies when a transaction occurs to any of the 17 key sectors, and the latter applies when parties observe any defined "trigger event" that may be of interest from a national security perspective, even if it falls outside of the mandatory notification regime. This hybrid system is supplemented with a "call-in" ability that allows the government to review any transaction, including certain qualifying asset deals, that have been completed but not been notified to the authorities.

Non-compliance with the Act may result in fines of up to 5% of worldwide turnover or £10 million (whichever is greater) and imprisonment of up to five years. The lack of safe harbors and the possibility of having completed transactions being unwound or found to be legally void mean that a greater number of transactions are now susceptible to intervention or pre-emptive and voluntary notification.

The Act is a significant departure from the UK's previous approach to FDI, and it places a greater burden on investors to ensure that their transactions comply with the Act. The Act's introduction reflects a growing global trend towards greater scrutiny of FDI transactions on national security grounds, and it brings the UK in line with other countries such as the US and Australia. The National Security and Investment Act 2021 is an important development in the UK's approach to FDI, and it establishes a framework for scrutinizing transactions that raise national security concerns. The Act introduces a hybrid system of mandatory and voluntary notifications, along with a "call-in" ability that allows the government to review completed transactions that have not been notified to the authorities. Non-compliance with the Act may result in fines or imprisonment, which means that investors need to be aware of the Act's requirements and ensure their transactions are in compliance.

5.7.6. Mainland China

FDI in mainland China is regulated by the PRC Foreign Investment Law and its implementation rules, which came into effect on 1 January 2020. The law prohibits foreign investment in certain industries, while in regulated industries, foreign investors must meet certain criteria such as restrictions on ownership ratio and the composition of the management team. The Chinese government has been reviewing the list of industries on an annual basis, reducing its size, and indicating a willingness to open up the market for foreign investment.

The PRC government has also adopted a national security review regime for FDI. The Measures on National Security Review on Foreign Investment came into effect on 18 January 2021. This regime identifies several areas where foreign investment would be subject to national security review. These include military facilities or related businesses, agriculture, infrastructure, energy and resources, the manufacture of certain equipment, and cultural products and services.

The national security review process aims to safeguard China's national security interests by reviewing foreign investments that may impact national security. Under the review process, a foreign investor or Chinese enterprise with foreign investment must file an application for national security review when it is investing in a restricted industry or when the investment could impact national security.

If a transaction is subject to national security review, the review process is conducted by an interagency committee led by the National Development and Reform Commission (NDRC) and the Ministry of Commerce (MOFCOM). The committee will consider factors such as the nature of the investment, the impact on national security, and the investor's background, before deciding on whether to approve or reject the investment. The review process can take up to 60 days, with an extension of up to 60 additional days if necessary.

It is important to note that the national security review regime is not limited to FDI transactions in China. It also applies to transactions outside of China that could impact China's national security. This extraterritorial application of the national security review regime means that foreign investors must be cautious when investing in companies that have operations or supply chains that may impact China's national security.

The PRC Foreign Investment Law and its implementation rules, along with the national security review regime, aim to balance China's need for foreign investment with its national security interests.

5.7.7. Hong Kong

Hong Kong, as a Special Administrative Region of China, maintains a separate legal system from mainland China. As one of the most open economies in the world, Hong Kong has generally welcomed foreign investment into any sector, except for a 49% voting control restriction on local broadcasting companies and residency requirements on their directors. Foreign investors are usually given the same treatment as domestic investors, and there are no statutory laws that specifically regulate FDI in Hong Kong. Furthermore, there are no foreign exchange control restrictions in Hong Kong, meaning that profits and capital can be freely remitted in and out of the territory. Although a national security law was implemented in Hong Kong on 30 June 2020, it does not directly restrict foreign investment. However, the law requires all institutions, organizations, and individuals in Hong Kong to comply with various laws and regulations that pertain to the maintenance of national security. The Chinese government is expected to continue to strengthen the ties between Hong Kong and mainland China politically and economically. This presents both challenges and opportunities for foreign investors who plan to invest or continue to invest in the Greater China area. Hong Kong is expected to continue to serve as an intermediary jurisdiction for investors looking to enter the mainland China market. Hong Kong's legal system, with its strong rule of law and independence from mainland China, is a key factor that has made it an attractive destination for foreign investment. The territory's open and transparent business environment, low tax rates, and strategic location have also contributed to its appeal. Foreign investors looking to invest in Hong Kong should be aware of the territory's legal and regulatory framework, including its tax laws, corporate governance rules, and intellectual property laws. Therefore, Hong Kong's business-friendly environment and access to the Chinese market make it an attractive destination for foreign investors. While the current political and economic environment may

Remember

China continues to open up its market to foreign investments. Foreign investors must navigate these regulatory frameworks to ensure compliance and mitigate potential risks.

pose some challenges, the territory's strong legal system and open economy provide a solid foundation for foreign investment.

5.7.8. Singapore

Singapore's approach to FDI is sector-specific, with no overarching legislation governing FDI. The government focuses on promoting Singapore as an attractive global FDI hub, offering incentives such as tax breaks and grants to international companies that establish their regional headquarters or production facilities in the city-state. The government also grants permanent residence status to foreign individuals who intend to drive their businesses and investment growth from Singapore.

However, certain structural barriers to entry exist in sectors such as financial services, professional services, media, telecommunications, and real estate transactions. The government maintains control over FDI in these sectors through legislative restrictions and licensing regimes that apply qualitative and quantitative criteria. Each investment application is assessed on a case-by-case basis, to encourage cooperation and commercial partnerships with local companies. Singapore also engages in FDI outflows to other Southeast Asian, South Asian, and North Asian markets. The Regional Comprehensive Economic Partnership, a free trade agreement involving all Association of Southeast Asian Nations member countries, China, Japan, South Korea, Australia, and New Zealand, is expected to accelerate trade and investment in the region. Singapore is likely to remain a key regional hub for foreign investors seeking an entry point to deploy their capital across the region.

In terms of attracting FDI, Singapore's key strengths include its strategic location, efficient transport and logistics infrastructure, well-educated workforce, and business-friendly environment. The city-state also boasts a strong intellectual property regime, which protects and encourages innovation and technological advancement. So, Singapore remains committed to its long-standing economic development policy of promoting itself as an attractive global FDI hub in the longer term. By offering incentives, maintaining control over certain key sectors, and engaging in FDI outflows, the government aims to promote cooperation and commercial partnerships with local companies while encouraging foreign investors to establish a presence in the city-state.

5.7.9. UAE

The UAE has undergone significant changes in recent years to liberalize its foreign investment regime. Historically, the country placed restrictions on foreign ownership, limiting non-UAE persons from owning more than 49% of any UAE company. However, this has changed with the establishment of nearly fifty free economic zones, such as the Dubai International Financial Centre and the Abu Dhabi Global Market, which allow 100% foreign ownership. In 2020, the UAE federal government further opened up the market by allowing non-UAE nationals to own 100% of a UAE limited liability "onshore" company, subject to the business activity falling within a prescribed list of activities issued by the relevant Emirate's economic department.

However, certain exceptions to foreign ownership still exist in the form of the "strategic impact" list, which includes sectors such as security and defense, banking, foreign exchange, financing, insurance, telecommunications, Hajj and Umrah services, Holy Quran memorization centers, and services associated with fisheries. Non-UAE investors seeking to conduct activities falling within this list must apply to the relevant authorities in the relevant Emirate, which will determine, on a case-by-case basis, the required percentage of Emirati ownership and any other restrictions, such as board composition.

Despite these limitations, the UAE continues to promote foreign investment and offers incentives to attract international businesses. For instance, the country offers various tax exemptions and free zones for companies that establish a presence in the UAE, as well as streamlined administrative procedures for obtaining licenses and permits. The UAE's strategic location and proximity to fast-growing markets in Asia and Africa also make it an attractive destination for foreign investors. As the UAE continues to liberalize its foreign investment regime, it is likely to see an increase in foreign investment, particularly in sectors that were previously restricted. The country's strategic location, favorable tax and regulatory environment, and commitment to attracting foreign investment will likely continue to make it an attractive destination for international businesses.

The global trend towards greater protectionism is leading to increased government intervention in areas of strategic value and sensitivity. This means that FDI restrictions are likely to continue to be relevant regardless of political and economic tensions. Compliance with FDI restrictions tends to fall on the investor, which means that when planning a transaction, issues such as control, board rights, director appointments, shareholder voting rights, and reserved matters will need to be addressed. Deal structure and timetable will be affected, as well as how a target company is controlled. The use of commitments, such as safeguarding IPRs or divestments of certain assets, will continue to be important. In certain jurisdictions, regulators may provide some level of comfort before a transaction closes. An organized transaction team will be important, particularly for projects with cross-border elements that require coordination across FDI and other investment restrictions in multiple jurisdictions. The transaction documents will need to reflect risk allocation, conditions to closing, impact on execution risk, and the timetable and process for fulfilling regulatory requirements, given the severe sanctions for breach.

REVIEW QUESTIONS

1. What is Foreign Direct Investment (FDI)? Define in different terms.
2. What are the key factors that influence a country's attractiveness as a destination for foreign direct investment?
3. How can a country improve its FDI inflows?
4. What are the potential benefits and drawbacks of foreign direct investment for the host country's economy?
5. How does foreign direct investment affect the competitiveness of local firms and industries?
6. What are the emerging trends and challenges in foreign direct investment?

MULTIPLE CHOICE QUESTIONS

1. Which of the following is not a reason why countries encourage foreign direct investment?
   a. To gain access to new technology
   b. To create jobs and increase employment
   c. To increase competition and improve productivity
   d. To limit foreign influence on domestic economy

2. Which of the following is not a method for companies to engage in foreign direct investment?
   a. Acquiring a foreign company
   b. Starting a new subsidiary in a foreign country
   c. Investing in the stock market of a foreign country
   d. Investing in a foreign real estate market

3. Which of the following is not a benefit of foreign direct investment for the host country?
   a. Increased access to financing
   b. Increased technology transfer
   c. Increased competition for domestic companies
   d. Increased protectionism

4. Which of the following is not a potential risk for companies engaging in foreign direct investment?
   a. Political instability in the host country
   b. Changes in government regulations or policies
   c. Currency exchange rate fluctuations

d. Access to cheap labor in the host country

5. Which of the following is not a type of foreign direct investment?

a. Horizontal FDI

b. Vertical FDI

c. Conglomerate FDI

d. None of the above

Answers to Multiple Choice Questions

1. (d); 2. (c); 3. (d); 4. (d); 5. (d)

REFERENCES

1. Cavusgil, S. T., Knight, G., & Riesenberger, J. R., (2018). *International Business: The New Realities* (5th edn., Vol. 1). Pearson Education, Inc.
2. Chadha, N. K., (2018). *International Business Management: A Managerial Perspective*. Vikas Publishing House.
3. Cherunilam, F., (2017). *International Business Management: Text and Cases*. Himalaya Publishing House.
4. Cullen, J. B., & Parboteeah, K. P., (2018). *International Business: Strategy and the Multinational Company* (2nd edn., Vol. 2). Routledge.
5. Daniels, J. D., Radebaugh, L. H., & Sullivan, D. P., (2018). *International Business: Environments and Operations*. Pearson Education.
6. Deresky, H., (2020). *International Management: Managing Across Borders and Cultures* (10th edn.). Pearson Education.
7. Hill, C. W. L., & Hult, G. T. M., (2019). *Global Business Today* (11th edn., Vol. 1). McGraw-Hill Education.
8. Hill, C. W. L., & Hult, G. T. M., (2021). *International Business: Competing in the Global Marketplace* (12th edn., Vol. 2). McGraw-Hill Education.
9. Kuthiala, B. K., & Kuthiala, D., (2017). *International Business Management: Theory and Practice*. Excel Books.
10. Luthans, F., & Doh, J. P., (2020). *International Management: Culture, Strategy, and Behavior* (10th edn., Vol. 2). McGraw-Hill Education.
11. Sharma, K., & Dubey, A., (2017). *International Business Management: Globalization and Beyond*. Pearson India.
12. Wild, J. J., Wild, K. L., & Han, J. C. Y., (2017). *International Business: The Challenges of Globalization* (9th edn., Vol. 1). Pearson Education, Inc.

CHAPTER 6

MNCs IN INTERNATIONAL BUSINESS

UNIT INTRODUCTION

A multinational company (MNC) is a business entity that produces and markets its goods or services in multiple countries. To establish the capacity to operate in various locations, an MNC must acquire managerial control over operating entities in different countries and establish subsidiaries with the necessary assets. This sets the MNC apart from a domestic or unemotional company (UNC), which operates solely within its home country.

MNCs are motivated by various factors, such as profits, raw materials, markets, or diversification. Some cater to individual consumers, while others target government procurement, the industrial sector, or the military. They may operate in different market environments, from competitive to oligopolistic or monopolistic. MNCs are highly differentiated, with each possessing unique characteristics and ranking as complex organizations.

International businesses vary in size and the extent to which they cross national boundaries. MNCs are a special type of global business organization that engages in production or service activities through its affiliates in several countries, maintains control over those affiliates' policies, and manages from a global perspective. Top managers allocate resources and coordinate activities to take the best possible advantage of favorable business conditions throughout the world.

Learning Objectives

After completing this chapter, you should be able to:

- Understand the concept of multinational corporations (MNCs) and their role in international business.
- Identify the factors that influence the decision of MNCs to invest in foreign countries.
- Analyze the impact of MNCs on the host and home country's economy.
- Evaluate the challenges faced by MNCs in managing their global operations.
- Develop a framework for managing MNCs' operations in different international contexts.

Key Terms

- Corporate social responsibility (CSR)
- Cultural differences
- Exporting
- Franchising
- Globalization
- Home country
- Host country
- Intellectual property
- Joint venture
- Licensing
- Taxation
- Transfer pricing

6.1. DIFFERENT TERMS USED TO DESCRIBE COMPANIES OPERATING ACROSS NATIONAL BORDERS

In today's globalized economy, businesses are no longer restricted by national borders. The emergence of global markets has given rise to companies that operate in multiple countries and have complex ties with their home and host nations. These companies have been described in various terms, leading to a debate about the most appropriate name for them. Here, we will explore the unique terms used to describe companies that operate across national borders.

6.1.1. Transnational Corporation (TNC)

One of the most widely used terms to describe companies operating across national borders is TNC. The United Nations has created a research center for the study of TNCs, and it is the preferred term by some experts. The term 'transcend' implies that these companies go beyond national boundaries and operate across different countries. Therefore, TNCs are companies that have a global presence and operate in multiple countries (Figure 6.1).

Figure 6.1. Transnational corporation.

- **Defining Transnational Corporations (TNCs):** A TNC can be defined as a business enterprise that operates in more than one country and has a decentralized management structure that coordinates operations across national borders. TNCs are often called MNCs or global corporations, but the term 'transnational' is increasingly used to describe these companies.

- **Characteristics of TNCs:** TNCs are characterized by their size, global reach, and decentralized management structure. They typically have a large number of employees, generate substantial revenue, and have a significant presence in multiple countries. TNCs often operate in industries such as technology, telecommunications, pharmaceuticals, and finance.

  TNCs are also known for their ability to leverage global networks of suppliers, customers, and partners. They use these networks to source inputs, sell products and services, and coordinate operations across national borders. In addition, TNCs often invest heavily in R&D, enabling them to develop new products and services and maintain a competitive edge in the global marketplace.
- **Benefits and Challenges of TNCs:** TNCs offer a range of benefits to both host countries and home countries. They bring jobs, technology, and investment to host countries, contributing to economic growth and development. TNCs also help to transfer knowledge and skills, which can help to improve the competitiveness of local industries.

  However, TNCs also pose challenges, particularly their impact on the environment, labor standards, and human rights. TNCs are often accused of exploiting natural resources, exploiting workers, and engaging in unethical practices such as bribery and corruption.
- **Regulation of TNCs:** The regulation of TNCs is a complex issue, with different countries adopting different approaches. Some countries, such as the United States, have relatively relaxed regulations on TNCs, while others, such as China, have more stringent regulations.

  One of the main challenges in regulating TNCs is the difficulty of enforcing regulations across national borders. TNCs often have subsidiaries in multiple countries, and it can be difficult to ensure that all of these subsidiaries comply with regulations.

6.1.2. Multinational Corporation (MNC)

Multinational Corporation (MNC) is another popular term used to describe companies that operate across national borders. The term is commonly used in textbooks and the business press. Unlike TNCs, MNCs are primarily focused on expanding their operations by entering new markets in different countries. MNCs are known for their ability to adapt to local markets, cultures, and regulations while maintaining their corporate identity. They have subsidiaries in different countries, which are often managed as independent entities.

Definition and Characteristics of MNCs:

MNCs are defined as companies that operate in two or more countries with subsidiaries or affiliates located in different regions of the world. These subsidiaries are established to conduct business operations such as manufacturing, sales, distribution, R&D, and other activities. MNCs are known for their ability to operate in diverse environments, adapt to local cultures and regulations, and leverage their global resources to gain a competitive advantage.

MNCs are typically large corporations that operate in multiple industries, such as automotive, pharmaceuticals, consumer goods, technology, and finance. Some of the most prominent examples of MNCs include Walmart, Toyota, Coca-Cola, General Electric, and Nestle. These companies have a significant presence in many countries and regions, with subsidiaries and affiliates that are managed as independent entities.

MNCs typically have a centralized corporate headquarters that manages the company's global operations. The headquarters may be located in one of the countries where the company operates or in a separate location. The corporate headquarters sets the overall strategy for the company and guides its subsidiaries and affiliates.

MNCs have a global perspective and are driven by the need to expand their operations and enter new markets. They invest heavily in R&D, marketing, and distribution to gain a competitive advantage. MNCs also have a significant impact on the economies of the countries where they operate, as they create jobs, pay taxes, and contribute to the local economy.

Advantages of MNCs:

1. **Access to a Global Market**: MNCs can easily access a global market, which allows them to reach more customers and sell more products.
2. **Economies of Scale:** MNCs can take advantage of economies of scale by producing large quantities of products at a lower cost per unit. This can help them to increase their profits and compete more effectively with smaller businesses.
3. **Access to Resources**: MNCs can access a wide range of resources, including raw materials, labor, and technology, from different countries. This can help them to reduce costs, improve product quality, and develop new products.

Did you Know?

TNCs are among the world's biggest economic institutions. A rough estimate suggests that the 300 largest TNCs own or control at least one-quarter of the entire world's productive assets, worth about US$5 trillion.

4. **Technology Transfer**: MNCs can transfer technology and knowledge across different countries, which can help to improve the quality of products and services in those countries.
5. **Job Creation:** MNCs can create jobs in different countries, which can help to boost the local economy and reduce unemployment.

Disadvantages of MNCs:

1. **The Exploitation of Resources**: MNCs may exploit resources and labor in developing countries, where regulations are weaker, to reduce costs and increase profits.
2. **Monopolistic Power**: MNCs may have monopolistic power in some markets, which can lead to market distortion and reduce competition.
3. **Environmental Degradation**: MNCs may contribute to environmental degradation in developing countries by not following environmental regulations and standards.
4. **Loss of Cultural Diversity**: MNCs may promote a homogenized global culture by promoting their products and services worldwide, which can lead to the loss of cultural diversity.
5. **Tax Evasion:** MNCs may use tax havens to avoid paying taxes in the countries where they operate, which can reduce government revenue and harm the local economy.

6.1.3. Multinational Enterprise (MNE)

Multinational Enterprise (MNE) is another term used to describe companies operating across national borders. The term was coined because some of the international giants are state-owned enterprises rather than corporations. MNEs typically have a global reach and operate in multiple countries. They engage in cross-border transactions, including exports and imports, foreign direct investment (FDI), and licensing agreements.

MNEs play a significant role in the global economy, driving economic growth, creating employment opportunities, and enhancing technological advancement. These companies typically have large capital resources, which they use to invest in various countries, expand their operations, and tap into new markets. In this way, MNEs are also able to diversify their revenue streams and reduce their exposure to risks associated with operating in a single market.

The rise of MNEs has been facilitated by globalization, which has made it easier for companies to expand their operations across borders. Advances in technology, transportation, and communication have also played a significant role, enabling companies to access new markets, collaborate with partners and suppliers, and manage their operations from remote locations.

MNEs operate in various industries, including manufacturing, services, and technology. They typically have a significant presence in emerging markets, where the growth potential is high, and labor costs are relatively low. However, MNEs also face challenges in operating in these markets, including political instability, corruption, and legal and regulatory barriers.

One of the key advantages of MNEs is their ability to leverage their global presence and scale to gain a competitive advantage. By operating in multiple countries, they can access a larger pool of resources, including talent, raw materials, and capital. This enables them to optimize their operations and achieve economies of scale, reducing their costs and enhancing their profitability.

MNEs also play a critical role in promoting innovation and technology transfer across borders. By investing in R&D, MNEs can develop new products, services, and processes that can benefit consumers and businesses globally. Moreover, MNEs can also transfer technology and know-how to developing countries, helping them to build their own capacities and promote economic development.

However, MNEs also face criticism for their impact on local communities and the environment. Critics argue that MNEs often prioritize their own interests over those of local communities, leading to environmental degradation, exploitation of labor, and social unrest. MNEs are also accused of engaging in tax avoidance, which deprives countries of much-needed revenue and exacerbates inequality.

To address these concerns, some countries have introduced regulations aimed at promoting responsible business practices by MNEs. For instance, the United Nations Guiding Principles on Business and Human Rights, adopted in 2011, set out a framework for companies to respect human rights and avoid adverse impacts on local communities. Similarly, some countries have introduced regulations aimed at promoting transparency and preventing tax avoidance by MNEs.

6.1.4. Global Corporation

A Global Corporation is a company that operates its business as if the entire world were a single entity. They sell the same products and services in the same way everywhere, regardless of the location. The term Global Corporation gained popularity in the 1990s and was used to describe a small number of companies that did business in dozens, or even more than 100 nations. The term is often applied to companies doing business in several areas of the world, such as Europe, Latin America, Asia-Pacific, and North America (Figure 6.2).

Figure 6.2. Global corporation.

Unique Features of Global Corporations: Global Corporations differ from MNCs in several ways. The following are the unique features of Global Corporations:

- **Standardized Products and Services**: A Global Corporation sell standardized products and services worldwide. For example, a company like Sony sells the same product, such as a "Walkman," throughout the world, with components made or designed in different countries. This strategy allows them to benefit from economies of scale and lower production costs.
- **Single Strategy**: A Global Corporation operates as if the entire world is a single market. They follow a single strategy to sell their products and services in every location. This approach simplifies the decision-making process and allows them to achieve greater efficiency in operations.
- **Centralized Management**: A Global Corporation has a centralized management, which means that decisions are made at the corporate headquarters rather than at the local level. This approach enables them to maintain consistency in their operations and implement a standardized strategy across all locations.
- **Global Branding**: A Global Corporation has a global brand that is recognizable and trusted in all locations. For example, Coca-Cola and McDonald's are recognized and trusted brands worldwide. Global branding enables companies to benefit from economies of scale in marketing and advertising, and to achieve greater customer loyalty.

Advantages of Global Corporations: Global Corporations have several advantages, which include:

- **Economies of Scale**: Global Corporations benefit from economies of scale in production, marketing, and distribution. They can leverage their size and resources to achieve greater efficiency and lower costs than their competitors.
- **Brand Recognition**: A Global Corporation has a global brand that is recognized and trusted in all locations. This enables them to enter new markets more easily and to achieve greater customer loyalty.
- **Access to Resources**: A Global Corporation has access to resources such as raw materials, talent, and technology from all over the world. This enables them to develop innovative products and services and to remain competitive.

Limitations of Global Corporations: Global Corporations also have limitations, which include:

- **Lack of Adaptability**: A Global Corporation's standardized strategy may not be suitable for every location. They may find it challenging to adapt to the local culture, language, and regulations, which can limit their success in some markets.
- **Dependency on Global Economy**: A Global Corporation is highly dependent on the global economy. Changes in the global economy can have a significant impact on their operations and profitability.
- **Risk of Political and Social Instability**: A Global Corporation operates in multiple countries, which may have different political and social environments. This can expose them to the risk of political and social instability, which can impact their operations and profitability.

6.2. TYPES OF MNCS

6.2.1. Equity-Based MNCs

Equity-based MNCs are multinational enterprises (MNEs) that achieve managerial control through ownership of equity in affiliated enterprises in different host economies. This ownership structure provides the basis for the integration of these entities internationally by the headquarters firm.

There are four main types of equity-based MNCs:

1. **Resource-Based Companies**: These MNCs produce raw materials, such as metallic ores, oil, rubber, and tropical plantation crops like bananas, coffee, and dates. Many of these companies have roots in the colonial era and are among the oldest MNCs.

2. **Public Utility Companies**: These MNCs operate in sectors that are either natural monopolies or serve a monopolistic market, such as the national airline of the host nation. Examples include military arsenals and other government-controlled utilities.
3. **Manufacturing Companies**: These MNCs were the largest growth sector of multinational business from the 1950s to the 1970s. Host countries were instrumental in attracting manufacturing MNCs, often through foreign investment incentive programs that offered tax privileges, protection against import competition, relaxation of foreign exchange restrictions, and government loan guarantees.
4. **Service Industry MNCs**: The largest components of this category are banks, carriers, retail stores (such as F. W. Woolworth, Sears, and Takashimaya), and firms that sell similar management services. The multinationalization of industrial companies has led to the multinationalization of service industry firms.

While equity-based MNCs have been the traditional means of achieving multinationalization, direct foreign investment is no longer the only way for a firm to become multinational. Other methods include licensing agreements, franchising, and joint ventures (JVs).

Licensing agreements involve granting the right to use a trademark or patent in exchange for a fee or royalty. Franchising involves granting the right to use a business model, including a brand and operational processes, in exchange for a fee or percentage of sales. JVs involve two or more firms creating a separate entity to pursue a specific business opportunity.

Each method of multinationalization has its advantages and disadvantages. Equity-based MNCs offer the most control over operations but can be expensive and risky. Licensing agreements and franchising offer lower risk, but less control. JVs offer shared risk and control but can be complicated to manage.

Finally, equity-based MNCs are a traditional means of achieving multinationalization. While they still dominate the landscape of multinational business, other methods such as licensing agreements, franchising, and JVs are becoming increasingly popular. Each method has its own set of advantages and disadvantages, and firms must carefully consider their goals and resources before choosing a method of multinationalization.

6.2.2. Technology-Based MNCs

Technology-based MNCs, also known as no-equity MNCs, represent a new generation of MNEs that rely on technology and management expertise rather than ownership of operating assets. These companies have emerged in recent years as an alternative to traditional equity-based MNCs. The hotel, mining, and construction industries have pioneered this new generation of MNCs, and other industries are expected to follow suit.

The rise of technology-based MNCs can be attributed to several factors, including advances in communication and information technology, globalization, and changing consumer preferences. These companies can leverage technology to manage and control operations across borders without having to invest heavily in physical assets. This allows them to operate more efficiently and flexibly, and to respond quickly to changing market conditions.

One example of a technology-based MNC is Airbnb, a company that provides a platform for individuals to rent out their homes or apartments to travelers. Airbnb does not own any of the properties listed on its platform, but instead relies on technology to manage and control the booking process. The company has been able to expand rapidly across borders and is now present in more than 220 countries.

Another example is Uber, a company that provides a platform for individuals to offer ride-sharing services to passengers. Like Airbnb, Uber does not own any physical assets but relies on technology to manage and control the ride-sharing process. The company has faced regulatory challenges in some markets, but has been able to expand rapidly and now operates in more than 700 cities worldwide.

The emergence of technology-based MNCs has also led to changes in the way traditional industries operate. For example, the mining industry has traditionally been dominated by large, equity-based MNCs that invest heavily in physical assets. However, new technology-based MNCs are now emerging that rely on remote sensing, data analytics, and other advanced technologies to locate and extract minerals. These companies can operate more efficiently and with lower capital costs and are increasingly competing with traditional mining companies.

The construction industry is another sector that is being transformed by technology-based MNCs. Companies such as Katerra and Mighty Buildings are using technology to streamline the construction process, including design, planning, and fabrication. These companies can deliver projects faster and with higher quality than traditional construction companies and can operate across borders without having to invest in physical assets. Technology-based MNCs represent a new generation of MNEs that rely on technology and management expertise rather than ownership of operating assets. These companies are able to operate more efficiently and flexibly and are increasingly competing with traditional equity-based MNCs. The rise of technology-based MNCs is expected to continue in the coming years, as advances in communication and information technology continue to reshape the global economy.

6.2.3. Management Contracts

Management contracts are a form of agreement between two parties, where one party, typically a multinational corporation (MNC), takes over the management of a business or operation owned by the other party, often a local firm or government entity. The MNC then manages the business using its expertise, technology, and systems, while the owner retains ownership of the assets and shares in the profits.

Management contracts have been used in various industries, but the hotel industry has been a pioneer in this model. Under a hotel management contract, the MNC takes over the day-to-day operation of the hotel, including marketing, sales, and management of staff. The owner of the hotel, often a local firm or government entity, retains ownership of the hotel property and receives a share of the profits from the hotel's operation. The MNC, in turn, earns a fee for its management services and can leverage its global network and expertise to improve the hotel's performance.

The management contract model has also been used in the mining industry, where the MNC takes over the management of a mining operation, using its expertise and technology to improve productivity and reduce costs. The owner of the mine retains ownership of the mining property and shares in the profits. The management contract model has been particularly useful for developing countries that lack the expertise and resources to manage their mining operations effectively (Figure 6.3).

Figure 6.3. Illustration of management contracts.

The management contract model has also been applied to other service industries, such as healthcare and education. In these industries, the MNC provides management expertise and technology to improve the quality and efficiency of the services, while the owner of the operation retains ownership and receives a share of the profits. For example, an MNC could take over the management of a hospital, providing expertise in areas such as healthcare administration, technology, and training of staff.

The management contract model has also been used in the manufacturing industry, particularly in developing countries, where the host government provides incentives to attract foreign investment. Under this model, the MNC takes over the management of a manufacturing operation, using its expertise and technology to improve productivity and reduce costs. The owner of the manufacturing operation retains ownership of the assets and shares in the profits.

The management contract model has also been used in the high-tech industry, where the MNC provides management expertise and technology to improve the efficiency and quality of operations. For example, an MNC could take over the management of a R&D center, providing expertise in areas such as project management, intellectual property rights (IPRs), and technology transfer.

Management contracts offer several advantages over the traditional equity-based model of MNCs. First, they allow MNCs to leverage their expertise, technology, and systems to improve the performance of existing operations without having to invest in new assets. Second, they offer a way for local firms or government entities to tap into the global network and expertise of MNCs without having to give up ownership of their assets. Third, they can provide a way for developing countries to attract foreign investment and expertise without having to give up ownership of their assets.

However, management contracts also have some drawbacks. First, they can create a dependency on the MNC for management expertise, which can make it difficult for local firms or government entities to develop their own capabilities. Second, they can create a potential conflict of interest between the MNC and the owner of the operation, particularly if the MNC prioritizes short-term profits over long-term sustainability. Third, they can limit the ability of the MNC to invest in new assets and expand its operations.

6.2.4. Production-Sharing Arrangements

Production-sharing arrangements (PSAs) are a type of contractual agreement in which an MNC and a host government share the output of a specific venture. This model is often used in resource-based businesses, such as mining and crude oil production. Under a PSA, the MNC is not only permitted to extract resources but also must meet certain obligations for the development of indigenous supplier industries, training of engineers and managers, and keeping up with industry developments. The PSA model typically involves a sharing of output rather than profits. For example, if the PSA provides for a 40:60 output sharing of a mining property, the MNC would keep 40% of the tonnage extracted and turn over the remaining 60% to the owners. Alternatively, the MNC may market the remaining 60% on the owner's behalf.

The PSA model is often used in developing countries where governments lack the resources or expertise to develop natural resources on their own. By partnering with MNCs, host countries can access the technological expertise and investment capital required to develop resource-based industries. In turn, MNCs gain access to lucrative markets and resources that would be otherwise unavailable to them.

TIPS

1. PSAs can also be a source of tension between MNCs and host governments, especially if the terms of the agreement are perceived as unfair, or if there is a lack of transparency in the negotiation process.

2. Host governments may feel that they are not receiving a fair share of the output generated by the venture, while MNCs may feel that they are being unfairly burdened with obligations for local development and training.

PSAs can take many forms, depending on the specifics of the venture and the preferences of the parties involved. Some PSAs are structured as JVs, in which the MNC and the host government jointly own the assets and share the output. In other cases, the MNC may have full ownership of the assets but is required to share a portion of the output with the host government.

PSAs can be advantageous for both parties when they are structured in a way that is fair and equitable. For the host country, PSAs can provide a means of developing natural resources without bearing the full risk and cost of the investment. Additionally, PSAs can generate revenue for the government through taxes and royalties on the output generated by the venture. For MNCs, PSAs can provide access to lucrative resources and markets while minimizing risk and investment costs.

To mitigate these risks, PSAS must be structured transparently and equitably. Host governments should be involved in the negotiation process and have a clear understanding of the terms and obligations of the agreement. MNCs should also be aware of the specific needs and concerns of the host country and work to develop a mutually beneficial relationship.

6.2.5. Industrial Lease Agreements

Industrial lease agreements are an alternative model for MNCs to expand their operations in foreign countries without owning physical assets. Instead of investing in the construction of a new plant or acquiring an existing one, the MNCs can lease an industrial facility from an owner, often a government corporation. The owner may be motivated to lease the facility due to a lack of resources or expertise to operate it, or to attract foreign investment and technology transfer to the country.

The lease agreement typically includes a fixed annual rent payment and a scale of payments based on the output of the plant, also known as the throughput rent. This means that the MNC pays a portion of its revenues or profits to the owner, in addition to the fixed rent, as a form of revenue sharing. The throughput rent can be calculated as a percentage of sales, production volume, or profit margins, depending on the agreement. This creates a shared risk and reward system between the MNC and the owner, where both parties benefit from the success of the operation.

Industrial lease agreements are more common in manufacturing industries that require specialized or complex facilities, such as chemical plants, pharmaceutical labs, or semiconductor factories. These industries often require significant capital investments and technological expertise, which may not be available locally. By leasing an existing facility, the MNC can avoid the costs and risks of building a new one and can focus on optimizing the production process and transferring knowledge and skills to local workers.

One advantage of industrial lease agreements is that they provide a flexible and scalable model for MNCs to enter new markets. The MNC can choose the size and location of the facility based on its production needs and market demand, without committing to a long-term investment. The lease term can be negotiated according to the expected lifespan of the technology or product and can be extended or terminated based on performance or market conditions.

Another advantage is that industrial lease agreements can help to mitigate political and legal risks associated with foreign investments. By leasing a facility from a government corporation or other public entity, the MNC can benefit from preferential treatment or incentives, such as tax exemptions or regulatory exemptions that may not be available to foreign-owned companies. The MNC can also leverage the local network and reputation of the owner to navigate bureaucratic hurdles or cultural barriers and to build trust with local stakeholders.

However, industrial lease agreements also pose some challenges and limitations for MNCs. One challenge is to ensure the quality and suitability of the leased facility, which may require upgrades or modifications to meet the MNC's standards or specifications. The MNC may also need to invest in training and development programs for the local workforce to ensure a smooth transfer of knowledge and technology, and to maintain high standards of quality control and safety.

Another challenge is to manage the relationship and expectations between the MNC and the owner, which may have different goals and priorities. The MNC may seek to maximize its profits and market share, while the owner may prioritize the development of local industries and the transfer of technology. This may require frequent communication and negotiation between the parties and a clear understanding of the terms and conditions of the agreement.

6.2.6. Technology Transfer Agreements

Technology Transfer Agreements, also known as TTA, refer to a type of contract that involves the transfer of knowledge, expertise, and proprietary technology from one party to another. Typically, a technology transfer agreement involves a licensor, who owns the technology, and a licensee, who is interested in using the technology for commercial purposes.

TTAs are common in industries such as electronics, aircraft, computers, and biochemicals, where technology plays a crucial role in product development and competitiveness. Host governments in these industries often prioritize indigenous production capabilities, which can lead to JVs between MNCs and indigenous companies. In these cases, the MNC provides the technology, and the indigenous company provides financing, often with government assistance.

In communist countries such as the Russia, Poland, and Romania, negotiations have been spearheaded to obtain technologies from Western firms for high-volume, low-cost products that are internationally competitive in quality. These agreements typically cover the transfer of hard technology, such as patent and trademark rights, as well as efficient adaptation of a product to suit the strategic objectives of the host enterprise, effective development of actual production capacity by long-term enterprise-to-enterprise cooperation after the plant starts production and marketing of the output outside the host country.

While still modest in total business volume compared to equity-based MNCs, industrial leases and technology transfer agreements signify the entrance of technology-based MNCs into the manufacturing sector, which has historically been dominated by equity-based models.

In a typical TTA, the licensor provides the licensee with access to proprietary information, including trade secrets, technical know-how, patents, and copyrights. In exchange, the licensee agrees to pay a fee, often in the form of royalties, for the use of the technology. The licensor may also provide training and support to ensure the successful transfer of the technology.

TTAs can take many forms, depending on the needs of the parties involved. Some TTAs involve the transfer of technology for a specific product, while others may involve the transfer of technology for a broader range of products or services. The parties may also negotiate the duration of the agreement, the geographic scope of the license, and the conditions for termination. Technology transfer agreements allow for the transfer of technology and IPRs from one party to another, often for commercial purposes. The primary benefits of technology transfer agreements include:

1. **Increased Innovation**: Technology transfer agreements can promote innovation by enabling companies to access new technologies, processes, and knowledge that they might not have been able to develop on their own.
2. **Access to New Markets**: Technology transfer agreements can provide companies with access to new markets and customers by enabling them to introduce new products and services based on the transferred technology.
3. **Increased Profitability**: Technology transfer agreements can help companies increase their profitability by giving them access to new technologies and products that can improve efficiency, reduce costs, and increase revenue.
4. **Competitive Advantage**: Technology transfer agreements can give companies a competitive advantage by enabling them to access unique and valuable technologies that their competitors do not have.
5. **Collaboration**: Technology transfer agreements can foster collaboration between companies, academic institutions, and other organizations, leading to new and innovative partnerships.
6. **Economic Growth**: Technology transfer agreements can contribute to economic growth by promoting the commercialization of R&D, and by creating new jobs and business opportunities.

6.2.7. The Structure of MNCs

MNCs are complex organizations with a unique structure that allows them to operate globally. MNCs typically consist of a parent company, which is based in the home country, and various subsidiaries that operate in foreign countries. The subsidiaries may be wholly-owned, partially-owned, or in the form of JVs with local partners.

The structure of MNCs is hierarchical, with the parent company at the top of the chain, followed by intermediate holding companies, and then the subsidiaries. The parent company exercises control over the subsidiaries through ownership, financial control, and management.

In the equity-based model, the parent company owns a controlling interest in the subsidiary. This model allows the parent company to exercise greater control over the operations of the subsidiary and make strategic decisions. The parent company can also benefit from the profits generated by the subsidiary. However, this model can be costly, and the parent company may face regulatory barriers in some countries.

In the technology-based model, the parent company provides technology, expertise, and management know-how to the subsidiary. This model allows the subsidiary to benefit from the expertise of the parent company and access advanced technology. This can help the subsidiary improve its operations and competitiveness. However, the subsidiary may face challenges in adapting to the new technology and may be dependent on the parent company for support.

MNCs may also use a combination of equity-based and technology-based models, depending on the nature of their operations and the regulatory environment in the host country. For example, an MNC may use the equity-based model for its core business operations and the technology-based model for its support functions.

The subsidiaries of MNCs operate as independent entities, with their own management teams, production facilities, and marketing strategies. However, they are subject to the control and coordination of the parent company. The parent company sets the overall strategy for the MNC, including the allocation of resources and the coordination of activities across the subsidiaries.

The structure of MNCs allows them to benefit from economies of scale and scope, access to new markets, and the ability to leverage their expertise and technology across multiple locations. However, it also presents challenges, including the need to manage cultural differences, comply with local regulations, and balance the interests of the parent company and the subsidiaries.

6.3. MNCS CRITICS AND DEFENDERS

MNCs have become increasingly visible and powerful in the global economy. While some defend them for bringing economic growth and job opportunities, others criticize them for their impact on social, environmental, and economic issues. Here, we will examine the criticisms and defenses of MNCs on various grounds.

6.3.1. Challenge to Nation-State Sovereignty

One of the most significant criticisms of MNCs is that they challenge the sovereignty of nation-states. Developing countries want control over their economies to achieve their economic, political, and social objectives. MNCs, with their power and influence, can impede these objectives and force host countries to give up some of their power and independence in exchange for the wealth an MNC may bring. This undermines the sovereignty of the host country and compromises its ability to make independent decisions.

6.3.2. Inequities

Another criticism of MNCs is that they create inequities between developed and developing countries. Allegations of inequities include the pricing of raw materials extracted from developing countries versus the prices of imported manufactured goods from industrialized countries, which leads to a growing inequity. Furthermore, MNCs may avoid taxes in developing countries and give the best management jobs to citizens from their home countries.

6.3.3. Interference with Economic Objectives

Interference with the economic objectives of host countries is another criticism levied against MNCs. This interference can occur in various ways. For example, an MNC may wish to locate a plant in an area of prosperity when the host country would prefer its location in an underdeveloped region. MNC demands local support can add to host-country expenditures for infrastructure. Since MNCs typically do their R&D at home, host countries become technologically dependent on the MNCs for innovation. The MNCs have the strength to attract bank loans that otherwise might be available for local businesses.

6.3.4. Social Disruption

The introduction of different mores, habits, behaviors, and ethical values, new products, management styles, distribution systems, more money, and technology can affect local ways of thinking and doing things. Social disruption is a common criticism of MNCs, especially in areas with traditional cultural values that may not align with the values espoused by MNCs.

6.3.5. Environmental Degradation

MNCs are often criticized for their impact on the environment. Many nations are becoming more concerned about the impact of MNCs on their environment. Environmental concerns are rapidly moving higher in the chain of priorities throughout the world. MNCs are often accused of not taking environmental regulations seriously, leading to environmental degradation in many areas.

6.3.6. Imperialism

Many developing countries view foreign managers with fear and distrust, as they see them as embodying old, exploitative colonialism. This fear and distrust can lead to accusations of imperialism against MNCs.

6.3.7. Symbol of Frustration and Antipathy

MNCs are often viewed as symbols of frustration and antipathy towards the Western world, especially in developing countries. The LDCs have grievances about their position in the world that have nothing to do with the MNC, but the MNC is a convenient visible target for their anger.

6.3.8. MNCs and Technology

MNCs are often criticized for bringing technology that is not suitable for less developed countries. Such technology is highly capital-intensive, but developing countries need a labor-intensive one. Additionally, technology brought in by MNCs is highly expensive. The MNCs charge exorbitantly in the form of fees and royalties, which puts a severe strain on the foreign exchange resources of a developing country. There are also instances of "technology dumping," which implies that MNCs use obsolete technology with the help of turnkey projects shipped down from the principals of other countries.

6.4. MNCS AND HOME SOCIETIES

Labor unions in home countries view MNCs as threats to their job security and wage levels. They argue that MNCs relocate production to countries with lower labor costs, leading to the loss of jobs in the home country. This view is not shared by investors, who benefit from the profits generated by MNCs' foreign investments. Investors also argue that the MNCs' operations benefit the home country's economy by creating new markets for exports and by increasing tax revenues.

Consumers in home countries are also divided in their views of MNCs. Some argue that MNCs bring new products and services to their markets, while others criticize MNCs for engaging in aggressive marketing practices, such as misleading advertising and pricing discrimination. Farmers in home countries also have mixed views of MNCs, as some view MNCs as important buyers of their products, while others criticize MNCs for engaging in practices that undermine local agricultural production.

6.4.1. Host Country Conflicts

Host countries have historically viewed MNCs with suspicion, seeing them as agents of foreign influence and exploitation. However, this view has become more nuanced in recent years. Some host country governments actively court MNCs, viewing them as sources of much-needed foreign investment and technological expertise. These governments offer MNCs incentives such as tax breaks, access to local markets, and subsidies to locate in their countries. Local businesses in host countries, however, often view MNCs as competitors that are given preferential treatment by host country governments. They argue that MNCs' access to capital, technology, and global markets gives them an unfair advantage over local businesses. Environmental groups in host countries also criticize MNCs for engaging in practices that damage the environment, such as deforestation, pollution, and overfishing.

6.4.2. Labor Conflict: Multinationalization and the Threat to Labor Unions

MNCs have transformed the business landscape by taking advantage of new mobility and flexibility to enhance their bargaining power over labor. This newfound power has significantly diminished labor unions' power and bargaining position, threatening their legitimacy and existence.

Historically, labor unions derived their legitimacy and powers through national and local legislation, making them an integral part of the nation-state's internal apparatus. Labor unions focused on countervailing the powers of domestic firms, achieving dominance or equivalence at the bargaining table by effectively organizing and concentrating labor influences into large, well-disciplined unions.

However, as MNCs grew in numbers and international scope, labor unions failed to acquire any international operational capabilities of their own. Their organization and policies remained strictly national or sub-national, while MNCs sourced capital, technology, raw materials, ideas, and labor from anywhere in the world.

This disparity gap between labor unions and MNCs is certain to widen as multinationalization continues. Labor unions' narrow focus on domestic entrenchment provides no possibility of matching the expansion of managerial powers, leaving labor in a position of subservience and subordination that the movement cannot accept or endure.

To address this threat, labor unions attack MNCs as inherently inimical to the domestic economy and seek legislative remedies that would severely restrict multinational corporate operations. Their lobbying campaign charges MNCs with detrimental effects such as investment depression, technology drain, export displacement, low-wage imports, tax evasion, and payment disbalancing.

However, these attacks and restrictions may not be enough to address the larger issue of multinationalization's impact on labor. As MNCs continue to grow in numbers and international scope, labor unions must acquire international operational capabilities to match the expansion of managerial powers. Only then can labor unions effectively counterbalance MNCs' bargaining power and ensure fair labor practices across the globe. The shift in the power balance between management and labor has led to a total struggle, where labor sees MNCs as a new and menacing antagonist. Labor's lobbying campaign charges the MNC with the following detrimental effects:

- **Investment Depression**: MNCs' foreign investments deplete capital resources needed for domestic investment, which undermines economic growth and new job creation in the United States.
- **Technology Drain**: MNCs export U.S. technology to exploit low-cost foreign labor, depriving U.S. workers of their rightful opportunity to share in the utilization and rewards of this technology. Through technology transfers and foreign investments, MNCs replace U.S. workers with foreign workers, exporting jobs.
- **Export Displacement**: MNCs displace U.S. exports with foreign-produced goods, decreasing domestic employment and payrolls, causing the U.S. trade balance to deteriorate and depressing economic conditions at home.
- **Low-Wage Imports**: MNCs substitute imports from their U.S. affiliates in low-wage countries for U.S.-made goods, undermining U.S. wage standards, causing unemployment, and idling plant facilities.
- **Tax Evasion**: MNCs evade taxes by deferring profit repatriation, manipulating transfer prices, and circumventing government regulations. The revenues lost to the national treasury result in a higher tax burden on the general public.
- **Payments Disbalancing**: MNCs' activities have afflicted the United States with the chronic balance of payments deficits, fueled inflation, debased the dollar as a stable currency, and contributed to international monetary disorders.

6.4.3. Offshore Plants

Offshore plants, also known as offshore manufacturing, refer to the process of relocating production facilities to foreign countries, often in search of lower labor and operating costs. This practice has become increasingly common in recent years, particularly among MNCs seeking to remain competitive in the global marketplace.

From the perspective of organized labor, offshore plants are a cause for concern, as they are often viewed as a means of exploiting low-wage workers in developing countries while depriving workers in industrialized nations of job opportunities. Unions have thus pushed for regulatory measures to limit the movement of production facilities offshore and protect domestic jobs. However, it is important to note that the decision to move production offshore is not always motivated purely by a desire to reduce costs. In many cases, MNCs may relocate production facilities in response to changing market conditions or to take advantage of specific comparative advantages offered by certain countries.

For example, a company may choose to locate its capital-intensive, high-tech facilities in industrialized countries where it can benefit from a skilled workforce and advanced infrastructure while outsourcing labor-intensive, low-skill production to less developed areas where wages are lower.

Despite the concerns about organized labor, there are potential benefits to offshore manufacturing for both MNCs and developing countries. For MNCs, it can be a means of maintaining competitiveness and improving profitability, while for developing countries, it can represent an opportunity to attract foreign investment, create jobs, and build infrastructure.

That said, there are also risks associated with offshore manufacturing, particularly when it comes to labor standards and environmental impact. Critics argue that companies operating offshore plants may exploit workers, violate labor laws, and engage in environmentally damaging practices.

To address these concerns, some unions and advocacy groups have pushed for increased regulation of offshore manufacturing, including measures such as the creation of a federal investments commission to oversee transnational capital transactions, restrictions on outward transfers of technology, and the elimination of tax incentives for companies operating offshore.

Finally, offshore manufacturing is a complex and multifaceted issue that requires careful consideration of the various economic, social, and environmental factors at play. While there are potential benefits to this practice, it is important to ensure that workers are not exploited and that environmental standards are upheld, and that regulatory measures are in place to protect the interests of all parties involved.

6.4.4. Ideological Dilemma

The ideological dilemma faced by labor unions in the face of MNCs is a complex and multifaceted issue. On the one hand, unions are committed to promoting international solidarity among workers and combating exploitation wherever it occurs. On the other hand, they often find themselves caught in a difficult position when MNCs operate in multiple countries, as they must balance the interests of workers in their home country with those in the countries where the MNCs have affiliates.

Historically, labor unions have been committed to the ideal of international solidarity. They recognized that workers everywhere faced many of the same challenges and had much in common, and they sought to build cooperative relationships with their counterparts in other countries. The goal was to create a counterforce to exploitation, a means of protecting workers' rights and interests against the power of capital.

In practice, however, achieving this ideal has been difficult. MNCs often operate across borders, creating a complex web of relationships between workers and unions in different countries. For unions in the home country of an MNC, their primary concern is often protecting the jobs and wages of their own members, which can put them in direct conflict with unions in other countries where the MNC has affiliates.

This protectionist offensive, aimed at protecting workers in the home country from the competition with workers in other countries, can create tension and conflict between unions in different parts of the world. Host country unions may view this as an attack on their own members and their right to fair wages and working conditions, while home country unions may see it as necessary to protect the interests of their own members. This conflict between the home country and host country unions can create an unpredictable source of tension in multinational business relations.

Remember

MNCs must navigate the complex and often competing demands of unions in different countries, seeking to balance the interests of workers with the demands of shareholders and the need to remain competitive in a global marketplace.

In this context, unions face a difficult ideological dilemma. On the one hand, they are committed to promoting international solidarity and protecting the rights of workers everywhere. On the other hand, they must balance this commitment with the practical realities of the global economy and the need to protect the interests of their own members.

To navigate this dilemma, some unions have sought to build stronger relationships with unions in other countries, working together to develop common strategies for protecting workers' rights and interests. Others have focused more on protecting the jobs and wages of their own members, sometimes at the expense of workers in other countries.

Ultimately, the ideological dilemma faced by labor unions in the context of MNCs reflects the broader tensions and contradictions of the global economy. As MNCs continue to operate across borders, creating complex relationships between workers and unions in different countries, the need for effective international solidarity and cooperation has never been greater. At the same time, the practical realities of protecting jobs and wages at home often require unions to take a more protectionist stance, creating tension and conflict with unions in other countries.

Finding a way to navigate these competing demands and interests will require ongoing dialogue and cooperation between unions in different parts of the world, as well as a commitment to building a global economy that values the rights and dignity of workers everywhere.

6.5. MNCS EFFECTS ON HOME COUNTRY

6.5.1. Trade and Payments

MNCs can have significant effects on the home country's trade and payments. As MNCs expand their operations overseas, they can increase exports from the home country to foreign affiliates and increase imports of goods and services from those affiliates. At the same time, they can also impact the balance of payments by repatriating profits earned abroad back to the home country.

Research on the impact of MNCs on the domestic economy has been mixed. Some studies have found that MNCs have a positive impact on home-country exports, while others have found little or no effect. Similarly, some studies have found that MNCs increase imports, while others have found no impact.

One potential positive effect of MNCs on the home country's trade is the creation of foreign affiliates. As MNCs set up operations overseas, they often rely on goods and services from the home country to support those operations. This can lead to increased exports from the home country to foreign affiliates, which can help to support jobs and economic growth at home.

On the other hand, MNCs can also impact the balance of payments by repatriating profits earned abroad back to the home country. This can increase the current account deficit, which measures the difference between the value of exports and imports. Additionally, MNCs may engage in transfer pricing, which involves setting prices for goods and services transferred between affiliates in a way that minimizes taxes and maximizes profits. This can lead to reduced tax revenue for the home country and can also distort trade patterns.

The impact of MNCs on the home country's trade and payments is complex and varies depending on a range of factors, including the nature of the MNC's operations, the countries in which it operates, and the broader economic environment. However, it is clear that MNCs have the potential to both positively and negatively impact the home country's economy, and policymakers must carefully consider these effects when crafting trade and investment policies.

In general, the effects of MNCs on the home country's trade and payments are complex and varied. While they can potentially increase exports and support jobs at home, they can also impact the balance of payments and reduce tax revenue through transfer pricing.

6.6. MNCS AND HOST SOCIETIES

The impact of MNCs on host societies has been the subject of much debate and controversy. While many countries have welcomed MNCs for the jobs and economic benefits they bring, others have become increasingly critical of their presence.

Remember

Policymakers must carefully consider these effects when crafting trade and investment policies, and further research is needed to better understand the impact of MNCs on the domestic economy.

One of the most significant impacts of MNCs on host societies is the creation of jobs. MNCs can provide employment opportunities for thousands of people, particularly in areas with high unemployment rates. They can also bring new technologies and skills to the host country, which can help to increase productivity and competitiveness in the local economy.

However, the benefits of MNCs are often accompanied by significant costs. One major concern is that MNCs can exploit cheap labor in developing countries, paying workers low wages and offering poor working conditions. This can contribute to a race to the bottom in terms of labor standards, as countries compete to attract investment by lowering wages and cutting labor protections.

MNCs can also have negative environmental impacts on host societies. Many MNCs operate in industries with high levels of pollution, such as mining, oil and gas, and manufacturing. The extraction of natural resources can also lead to environmental degradation and depletion of local resources.

Another concern is that MNCs can undermine local businesses and industries. They often have access to capital and technology that local businesses cannot match, which can put local producers at a disadvantage. This can lead to the displacement of small-scale producers, who are often the backbone of local economies.

The relationship between MNCs and host societies is complex, and there are no easy solutions to the challenges that arise. However, some steps can be taken to mitigate the negative impacts of MNCs. Host countries can impose regulations on MNCs to ensure that they pay fair wages and operate in an environmentally responsible manner. They can also provide support to local businesses and industries to help them compete with MNCs.

MNCs themselves can also take steps to be more socially responsible. They can adopt codes of conduct that require them to respect human rights and environmental standards. They can also invest in local communities through CSR initiatives, such as funding for education, health care, and infrastructure.

6.6.1. The Adaptability of MNCs to Host Environments

MNCs operate in various countries with different social, economic, and cultural environments. The level of adaptation of MNCs to host environments varies, and it depends on the organizational structure, objectives, and strategies of the company. Some MNCs adapt with ease and become integrated into the host society, while others remain isolated, causing tension and friction. Three categories of MNCs and their adaptability to host environments are described as:

- **Home or Parent Dominated MNCs:** Home-dominated MNCs are organized and managed in a way that their foreign-based subsidiaries and affiliates serve to complement their parent company's operations in the headquarters country. The subsidiaries have no autonomy, and their local interests and needs are subordinate to the parent company's home operations. The management of home-dominated MNCs is highly centralized, run by absentee decision-makers, and serves purposes external to the host countries. Therefore, the MNCs are insensitive to host nation needs, which compounds their ethnocentric managerial behavior. This type of MNC is likely to cause host-country conflict.
- **Federated or Host Dominated MNCs:** The federated MNCs are highly decentralized, and the actual management authority is delegated to individual subsidiaries. The company is set up more like a holding company than a management center. Each subsidiary is run by executives who are local nationals and rely on local methods and decision-making processes. They also adopt leadership styles that derive from indigenous social norms, and their personal standards and loyalties are identified with the host society. Therefore, there is a tight integration of each affiliate with its host country. This makes federated MNCs the least susceptible to social conflict.
- **Internationally Integrated MNCs:** Internationally integrated MNCs are organized to pursue objectives and activities that are worldwide in scope and concept. They are political and national institutions, and their primary loyalty is to the company itself rather than any nation. Their purposes, behavior, values, and operational incentives all derive from their own multinational structure, not from their home country or host country policies or patriotism. These MNCs specialize in production according to the principle of comparative advantage, which means acquiring inputs from countries with the lowest relative costs, locating production facilities for each component in the country best endowed with the necessary resources, and distributing outputs in the markets where the rewards are greatest. This gives them a competitive advantage and productive superiority over domestic or international firms in both developed and developing countries.

- **The Adaptability of MNCs to Host Environments:** The level of adaptation of MNCs to host environments depends on their organizational structure and objectives. Home-dominated MNCs are less adaptable to host environments because they prioritize their parent company's interests over those of the host country. Federated MNCs are more adaptable to host environments because they have high autonomy, and their subsidiaries are run by local nationals who adopt indigenous social norms. The MNCs' decentralized structure also fosters tight integration of each affiliate with its host country. Internationally integrated MNCs are the most adaptable to host environments because they are political and national institutions that specialize in production according to the principle of comparative advantage. They prioritize their multinational structure over their home country or host country policies or patriotism, making them more adaptable to different environments.

6.6.2. Areas of Conflict

These corporations can affect the economies of the countries where they operate and therefore have a degree of power in relation to the governments of those countries. This power is not direct, but rather indirect, and stems from the ability of the MNC to influence certain factors, such as economic policies and regulations. However, this power is not universally welcomed, and some critics view it as a potential source of conflict between the MNC and the host government. This conflict can arise when the MNC's interests are at odds with the interests of the host society. In such cases, the MNC may prioritize its own profit over the well-being of the host society, leading to tension and opposition.

These areas of conflict can manifest in various ways, including disputes over labor practices, environmental standards, taxation, and IPRs. The resolution of these conflicts requires careful negotiation and cooperation between the MNC and the host government, to find a mutually beneficial solution that balances the interests of both parties.

The strategic aspects of a host country's national policy that are subject to the influence of the MNC include:

1. Planning and direction of industrial growth
2. National control of key industries
3. Financial Policy
4. Export-import policy
5. Pricing policy
6. Research and development
7. Human resource policy

1. **Planning and Direction of Industrial Growth:** Planning and directing industrial growth is a critical aspect of economic development, and the host nations need to have control over their industrial strategy. However, many MNCs tend to centralize strategic decisions in their headquarters, which results in the loss of control over industrial strategy by the host government to the foreign-based MNC.

   The MNCs' primary objective is growth and profits globally, rather than in the host economy, and they seek greater efficiency through centralization, which leads to the domination of affiliates by headquarters. Empirical evidence indicates that a high degree of centralization tends to lead to inflexibility of parent company policies, as decisions regarding vital business decisions, such as product mix for each affiliate, the extent of inter-affiliate sales of semi-finished and finished products, export pricing, input procurement, packaging, long-range planning, R&D, and particularly financial management, are made in headquarters.

   When the authority over these vital business decisions is located beyond the jurisdiction of the local authorities, they counter with restrictions on affiliate activities, which extract a price from the MNC. However, a satisfactory method of calculating the price of centralization is yet to be devised, and it may turn out that the operational simplifications gained by centralization may be far lesser than the price of centralization.

   Governments of all nations, particularly those of less developed countries, are assuming more responsibility for the achievement of economic growth and social goals than formerly. To be successful, they need a fairly high degree of certainty in the business sector. The presence of affiliates managed from foreign-based headquarters introduces uncontrollable factors that interfere with the government's planning and policies of economic development.

   With substantial segments of the industry owned and directed from abroad and with home country governments perceiving the affiliates as foreign extremities of their economies, the host governments see a serious challenge to their ability to affect the desired goals. The more responsibility for economic growth and stability the government accepts, the greater its direct involvement in business regulation and direction, and the greater the possibility that the MNC will be perceived as a potential agitator of the national plants.

   Therefore, it is essential to strike a balance between centralization and decentralization of business operations. While centralization may lead to operational simplifications, decentralization may provide local authorities with greater control over industrial strategy and help achieve economic growth and social goals. Governments need to ensure that MNCs follow regulations that are in line with their economic development policies, while MNCs need to recognize and respect the economic and social goals of host nations.

2. **National Control of Key Sectors:** National control of key sectors refers to the ability of a country to regulate and maintain ownership over industries that are critical to its economic development and national security. The fear of losing control over strategic sectors arises when foreign investors, particularly MNCs, acquire ownership and control over these industries. This creates a situation where the country becomes dependent on foreign technology and resources for its growth and development, which may lead to a loss of sovereignty.

   The technology gap between developed and developing nations is one of the factors that contribute to this fear. The headquarters of MNCs have the power to determine whether and how the latest technology is employed by their affiliates. This creates a situation where the host country becomes dependent on foreign technology for its growth and development. The fear of foreign control and ownership of industry arises when a particular industry sector becomes dominated by MNCs, and the host country becomes dependent on the technological in-transfers of the foreign-headquartered MNC for its growth and product development.

   The fear of foreign takeovers is another aspect of national control of key sectors. MNCs may acquire pre-existing indigenous firms, leading to the elimination of local competitors and the creation of foreign monopoly control. The MNCs may use their superior resources to gain a competitive advantage over local firms, making it difficult for them to survive. This can create a situation where there are no nationally owned companies left in a particular industry, leading to a loss of sovereignty.

   To address these fears, many countries have implemented policies aimed at greater independence in technology and ownership of industries critical to their economic development and national security. This includes the establishment of local R&D facilities and the ownership of key industries by national entities. Some countries have also restricted foreign acquisitions to prevent the elimination of local competitors and channel foreign investments into the establishment of new firms.

   National control of key sectors is an essential aspect of a country's economic development and national security. The loss of control over strategic sectors to foreign investors, particularly MNCs, creates a situation where the country becomes dependent on foreign technology and resources for its growth and development. To address this, countries have implemented policies aimed at greater independence in technology and ownership of critical industries. However, there is no feasible alternative to relying on foreign technology, making it necessary to strike a balance between national control and foreign investment.

3. **Financial Policy:** Financial policy is another key area in which conflicts may arise between the MNC and the host country. The MNC has the power to determine where its profits will be allocated, which may or may not be in the host country. This puts the host government in a difficult position because they naturally prefer domestic investment, but they do not have control over the MNC's financial decisions.

   The MNC's contribution to the host country's balance of payments may also vary. On the one hand, the MNC can help relieve a deficit in the balance of payments by investing in the host country. On the other hand, the MNC's investment can contribute to the worsening of the balance of payments if the dividends are transferred outside the host country's borders. Additionally, the increased market share held by the affiliate can conflict with the host country's interests.

   The source of borrowed funds is another area where conflict may arise. The MNC's ability to import larger sums than a national company could threaten the balance of payments position of the host country. Furthermore, the MNC's extension of credit to a foreign subsidiary at a time when the host nation is attempting to dampen domestic purchasing power through import restrictions and exchange controls can easily undermine the host government's domestic monetary policy.

   Even though the magnitudes involved may not be large in comparison to major elements in the balance of payments, the impact of inward foreign investment on a country's balance of payments is often complex and not easily explained. As a result, attitudes toward foreign investment can be formed without taking into account the complexities involved.

   Financial policy is a sensitive area that requires careful consideration and negotiation between the MNC and the host country. The MNC has the power to determine where its profits will be allocated, and this can either benefit or harm the host country's balance of payments position. The source of borrowed funds can also create conflicts, and the MNC's extension of credit to a foreign subsidiary can undermine the host government's domestic monetary policy.

4. **Export-Import Policy:** How a multinational corporation (MNC) conducts its export-import activities can have a significant impact on the balance of payments of the host country. The MNC may make decisions regarding the export activities of its affiliates that prioritize fitting into the overall international marketing strategy of the corporation, rather than meeting the needs of the host government. This can result in the affiliate's exports being redirected to the parent company or other affiliates instead of to the desired customers in the host country. Additionally, the MNC may allocate export markets among its affiliates, limiting the

export potential of the host country and hindering its economic growth.

On the import side, the MNC may direct its affiliates to import resources from the parent company or other affiliates, rather than using resources from the host country. This can contribute to a trade deficit on the part of the host country, further complicating its economic situation.

Furthermore, the fact that the MNC's decision-making center is outside the jurisdiction of the host government increases uncertainty and potential conflict. Even if the MNC contributes to economic growth and stability in the host country, the ability of the parent company to alter the activities of its affiliates adds to the uncertainty facing the host government.

5. **Pricing Policy:** Pricing policies are a critical aspect of MNCs as they impact both the host country's economy and the MNC's overall profitability. There are two major areas of concern regarding MNC pricing policies: Intracompany pricing and pricing policies for customers outside the company. Intracompany pricing, also known as transfer pricing, refers to pricing decisions that affect the transfer of goods or services between different entities of the MNC. Transfer pricing can be used to shift assets among MNC entities, and this can result in a significant impact on the host country's balance of payments.

   Transfer pricing can serve different objectives, including circumventing foreign exchange restrictions, reallocating profits to low-tax countries, and minimizing cash reserves in a host country facing economic or political instability. If used for such purposes, transfer pricing can be detrimental to the host country's economy, and effective government regulations are necessary to prevent such practices.

   In market pricing, local industries may fear that MNC affiliates have the power to undercut local competitors by setting prices low to gain a foothold or increase market share. Large MNCs can afford to absorb significant per-unit losses on sales in small host countries without sacrificing overall profitability. Therefore, local people need to be vigilant in such situations.

   Some MNCs establish a global single-price policy, where the same price applies all over the world. This policy can be problematic when trade barriers and government regulations create incentives to differentiate prices among host country markets. This global single-price policy can also limit the MNC's ability to respond to the demands of individual country markets or maximize its advantage in oligopolistic market structures.

6. **Research and Development:** Research and development (R&D) is a crucial aspect of any modern economy, playing a vital role in fostering innovation, enhancing competitiveness, and driving economic growth.

In this context, MNCs play a critical role in driving R&D, given their vast resources, technical expertise, and global reach. However, MNCs can also cause conflicts of interest with host countries in several ways, as discussed below.

The first issue concerns the location of R&D facilities. Host countries often push MNCs to establish local R&D capacity, as this can help accelerate innovation and scientific research in the host society. However, MNCs tend to concentrate their research efforts in their home countries, primarily due to the availability of advanced educational institutions and scientific talent. This can create tension between the MNC and the host country, as the latter may feel that it is not benefiting sufficiently from the presence of the former. Moreover, the growth of the R&D department in the host country is often dependent on the home office, which can limit the host country's ability to pursue its own scientific agenda.

Even if the affiliate conducts research in the host country, the issue of ownership rights over the findings can create conflicts. Should the company decide to use the results of the research in another country, the benefit to the local economy is minimized. This creates a dilemma for the host country, as it may have invested resources in developing the local R&D capacity, only to see the fruits of its labor benefit the parent company rather than the local economy. As a result, the host country may feel that it is not getting a fair deal from the MNC, which can create tensions between the two parties.

In short, MNCs can help host countries reach a higher level of technology, they may not do so as fast as the host country would like, nor is the technology necessarily the type that the host government deems appropriate for its needs. Additionally, there is the problem of who controls the results of the research. So long as domestic ownership and control over key sectors and key technology have not been achieved, national governments feel threatened. The conflict over ownership of technology is taking on new dimensions as MNCs expand their research bases to host countries, and as more and more host countries assume the dual role of both host and home country.

Despite these conflicts, there are several reasons why MNCs can be beneficial for host countries. First, MNCs bring new technologies and know-how that can help local businesses and industries become more competitive. Second, MNCs often create high-skilled jobs that can improve the standard of living in the host country. Third, MNCs can help integrate local economies into global supply chains, which can enhance their competitiveness and resilience.

To mitigate the conflicts that arise from R&D activities, several strategies can be employed. First, host countries can establish policies and regulations that incentivize MNCs to conduct more R&D activities in the local economy. For example, tax breaks, subsidies, and other forms of financial support can be provided to MNCs that invest in local R&D. Second, host countries can require MNCs to share the results of their R&D activities with local partners, thereby ensuring that the benefits of the research are shared more evenly. Third, host countries can encourage MNCs to collaborate with local universities, research institutions, and businesses to develop joint R&D programs that address local needs and priorities.

7. **Human Resource Policies:** Human Resource Policies are a set of guidelines and procedures that an organization uses to manage its employees. They cover a wide range of areas such as recruitment, selection, training and development, compensation, benefits, performance appraisal, and employee relations (Figure 6.4).

Figure 6.4. Human resource ecosystem.

In the context of international growth, the policy of staffing foreign-based affiliates with headquarters country managers, or home country expatriates, is a common practice. This approach allows for a simpler selection, appointment, and promotion process that is consistent with the firm's established practices and routines. Additionally, this policy promotes uniformity among the managerial cadres throughout the multinational structure, as everyone has the same national and corporate cultures and has progressed within the organization according to the same rules. However, this policy may also create challenges such as cultural misunderstandings and a lack of local expertise. Therefore, organizations need to review and adapt their human resource policies as they expand internationally.

- **Third-Country Expatriates:** Third-country expatriates are managers who work in a foreign country for a company that is headquartered in a third country. These managers often come from Europe or Asia, and many of them have multilingual skills and European education. They are also known to be more adept at adapting to new environments and making friends in foreign social settings than their U.S. counterparts.

  Some U.S. companies prefer third-country expatriates for overseas management positions because of their versatility and potential for mobility toward top management positions. Nestle, a Swiss multinational company, is an example of an establishment that has utilized non-Swiss executives in top corporate posts.

  However, all expatriates are susceptible to conflict with the host country, as they are viewed with mixed reactions by the local society.

  The upper classes may resist expatriates as they threaten local power and prestige structures, while the lower classes may resent them for being foreigners in high-paying positions. These resentments can be compounded by racial or religious biases and can lead to nationalistic and xenophobic feelings, which can range from bureaucratic delays to acts of terrorism and destruction of property. As such, MNCs must be aware of these potential conflicts and take measures to address them.

- **Host Country Nationals:** Established MNCs increasingly rely on host country nationals as a source of executive personnel. There are several reasons for this shift, including the need to better understand the local environment, the need for rapid expansion of management groups due to the growth of overseas operations, the ability to successfully integrate individuals with different national backgrounds into the corporate structure, and pressures from host country authorities to replace expatriate managers with indigenous employees.

  The use of host country nationals is beneficial to MNCs in several ways. These individuals often have a deep understanding of local culture, business practices, and language, which can help MNCs navigate the complexities of the host country's business environment. Host country nationals are also likely to have a network of contacts that can help MNCs establish and maintain business relationships. Additionally, using local talent can help MNCs save on the costs associated with expatriate assignments.

However, there are also challenges associated with relying on host country nationals. One such challenge is the need to address salary discrepancies. Host governments often strongly favor their own people in executive assignments, but they may still object to MNCs' salary policies. MNCs can be criticized for underpaying local nationals in comparison to headquarters executives, or for overpaying them and undermining local firms by poaching their best talent. This presents a real dilemma for MNCs, who must balance their desire to attract and retain top talent with the need to maintain positive relationships with local firms and authorities.

Another challenge associated with using host country nationals is the potential for cultural misunderstandings. While these individuals may have a deep understanding of local culture, they may also have different expectations and approaches to business than their expatriate counterparts. This can lead to conflicts and misunderstandings that must be carefully managed by MNCs.

To address these challenges, MNCs must develop effective human resource policies that promote the recruitment, selection, training, and development of local talent. They must also establish clear communication channels with host country authorities and local firms to ensure that they are aware of local expectations and can respond to concerns in a timely and effective manner.

In summary, the use of host country nationals as a source of executive personnel has become increasingly important for MNCs. While there are benefits associated with this approach, such as a deep understanding of local culture and language, there are also challenges, such as salary discrepancies and cultural misunderstandings. MNCs must develop effective human resource policies and establish clear communication channels with host country authorities and local firms to successfully navigate these challenges and maximize the benefits of using host country nationals.

- **Personnel Practices:** Employment policies of MNCs in foreign countries can be a source of conflict due to differences in social and cultural values. One of the conflicts that can arise is the attempt by MNCs to impose their home country's work methods, mannerisms, and behavior patterns on the host society through their operations. This can lead to resistance from the local workforce, decreased productivity, and potential cultural clashes.

Another source of conflict is the hiring and firing policies of MNCs. In many foreign countries, social values dictate that both managers and labors receive more stable treatment from the firm and are tied to the firm for extended periods of time. However, MNCs often have to shift management personnel, lay off redundant employees, and regroup and retrain labor to meet new tasks, which can be viewed as harsh and contrary to local social values.

In terms of worker recruitment and training, MNCs encounter several problems, particularly in less-developed countries (LCDs) where skilled people are scarce. If the firm imports the needed skills, the host country must forego both the training and the jobs for its own nationals. On the other hand, if the MNC undertakes the required training programs locally, it can be financially prohibitive. Additionally, in some host countries, manual work or sales positions are low in social esteem, making it difficult to interest educated nationals in these positions.

Promotion policies can also be a source of conflict for MNCs. In some countries, there is a rigid social stratification where on-the-job achievement and economic performance are not recognized. Therefore, merit-based promotion of the most competent or deserving personnel to management or supervisory positions can go against expectations and notions of social propriety. For example, promoting a member of a lower caste to a position of supervision over a member of a relatively higher caste in India can cause conflict.

MNCS need to be aware of these potential conflicts and adapt their employment policies to suit the local culture and social values. For example, MNCs can work with local communities to understand their needs and values and develop programs that support the local workforce, such as training and development programs that prioritize local hiring and promotions. Additionally, MNCs can work to create a diverse and inclusive workforce that respects local customs and traditions.

Therefore, successful employment policies in foreign countries require MNCs to be culturally sensitive and adaptable, taking into account the unique social and cultural values of each host country. As a result, MNCs can avoid potential conflicts and build a workforce that is effective and sustainable in the long term.

- **Transborder Data Flow:** Telematics, the convergence of computer and telecommunication technologies, has revolutionized the way we access and process information. With advanced electronic processing capabilities and modern telecommunications facilities, telematics enables transborder data flow, overcoming time and distance as obstacles to large-scale information mobility.

MNCs have played a central role in establishing the required telecommunications infrastructure, producing computer hardware, software, and peripheral equipment, and offering a growing range of data-processing services. This poses a dilemma for LCDs that recognize the significance of telematics for obtaining accurate economic and political information both in their domestic and international spheres but feel vulnerable due to their inability to match the MNCs' capacity with their own facilities of telematics and transborder data transmission.

LCDs fear that the increasing role of telematics and transboundary data flows negatively affects all aspects of relations between poor and rich countries. They fear that their ability to collect, store, process, and access information is inferior, and the lag has been increasing. They fear that their ability to negotiate persuasively and interact effectively with other nations will be eroded.

To address these concerns, LCDs have started promulgating regulatory measures requiring MNCs to share their telematic equipment and software technology with various indigenous installations for the production, processing, transmission, and dissemination of a wide variety of data: economic, scientific, political, social, and legal. However, it is highly doubtful that MNCs will be able to accommodate all these demands.

MNCs are unlikely to be willing to share their proprietary technology and expertise, which they have invested heavily in developing. Moreover, regulatory measures that impose too many restrictions on MNCs could deter foreign investment and hurt the competitiveness of domestic companies, ultimately hindering economic development.

The telematics issue is too new to allow any informed predictions as to the compromises that will ultimately be struck between host governments and MNCs to resolve it. However, one possible solution could be for MNCs to form partnerships with local companies to provide telematics services, thereby leveraging their local knowledge and expertise while also meeting local regulatory requirements.

Another possible solution could be for MNCs to invest in training and education programs to develop local talent, thereby enhancing the local workforce's skills and capacity to use telematics technology. This would also create a more skilled and educated workforce that could attract more foreign investment and contribute to economic growth and development.

6.6.3. National Sovereignty of the Host Country

National sovereignty is the principle that a country is free to govern itself without interference from external forces. It is the fundamental basis for the existence of a state and is central to the concept of nationhood. The erosion of national sovereignty, therefore, is a significant concern for many countries, particularly in the context of the expansion of MNCs.

The growth of MNCs has been accompanied by a corresponding increase in their influence over host countries. This influence can manifest in various ways, such as through the use of foreign technology, industrial dominance, or the MNC's ability to achieve its desired outcomes. This dependence on foreign entities, coupled with the increased international influences, may lead to a loss of sovereignty for the host country. The policies and activities of MNCs have a significant impact on the host country's economy, including its balance of payments, economic planning, and development of technology. The MNC's influence may also extend to other aspects of the host society, which can cause sensitized nationalistic sentiments and reinforce the perception of peril to the host country.

To alleviate these concerns, MNCs must adapt their operations to align with the indigenous needs and sociocultural attitudes of the host societies. This adjustment may include a willingness to work closely with local stakeholders to understand their needs, respect local cultural practices, and contribute to the development of the host country's economy.

For instance, MNCs could adopt strategies such as localized production, which can provide significant benefits to the host country's economy, such as increased employment and transfer of technology. Additionally, MNCs can create mutually beneficial partnerships with local businesses, providing the necessary support and expertise to enable local businesses to compete on a global scale.

Furthermore, MNCs can establish policies that promote ethical practices and social responsibility, ensuring that their operations do not harm the local environment, contribute to corruption or disregard human rights. MNCs can also contribute to the development of the host country's economy by investing in education and training programs that enhance the skills of the local workforce, leading to long-term economic growth.

The importance of preserving national sovereignty cannot be overstated, as it is a fundamental basis for the existence of a state. However, the expansion of MNCs has made it challenging to maintain this sovereignty, leading to fears about the erosion of national identity and power. To address these concerns, MNCs must adapt their operations to align with the host country's needs, promote ethical practices, and contribute to the host country's long-term economic growth. As a result, MNCs can establish mutually beneficial relationships with host countries, creating a sustainable framework for future collaboration.

REVIEW QUESTIONS

1. What are MNCs, and how do they operate in international business?
2. Describe the different types of MNCs.
3. Explain MNCs critics and defenders.
4. What are the advantages and disadvantages of MNCs in international business?
5. What are some of the challenges faced by MNCs in international business?

MULTIPLE CHOICE QUESTIONS

1. Which of the following is not a benefit of MNCs in international business?
   a. Increased investment and economic growth
   b. Increased job opportunities
   c. Improved technology transfer
   d. Increased competition leading to lower prices

2. Which of the following is a characteristic of multinational corporations (MNCs)?
   a. They operate only in their home country
   b. They have a centralized management structure
   c. They do not have any impact on the local economy
   d. They only focus on short-term profits

3. Which of the following is a challenge faced by multinational corporations (MNCs) in international business?
   a. Lack of access to international markets
   b. Difficulty in adapting to local cultures and customs
   c. Limited access to local talent and resources
   d. Lack of government support and regulations

4. Which of the following is an example of a multinational corporation (MNC)?
   a. A small family-owned business
   b. A large chain of coffee shops operating only in one country
   c. A multinational retail corporation with operations in several countries
   d. A government-owned utility company

5. Which of the following is a reason why multinational corporations (MNCs) engage in international business?
   a. To decrease their market share and profitability
   b. To limit their exposure to foreign currencies

c. To take advantage of lower labor costs in other countries
d. To minimize their global reach and influence

Answers to Multiple Choice Questions

1. (d); 2. (b); 3. (b); 4. (c); 5. (c)

REFERENCES

1. Cavusgil, S. T., Knight, G., & Riesenberger, J. R., (2018). *International Business: The New Realities* (5th edn., Vol. 1). Pearson Education, Inc.
2. Chadha, N. K., (2018). *International Business Management: A Managerial Perspective*. Vikas Publishing House.
3. Cherunilam, F., (2017). *International Business Management: Text and Cases*. Himalaya Publishing House.
4. Cullen, J. B., & Parboteeah, K. P., (2018). *International Business: Strategy and the Multinational Company* (2nd edn., Vol. 2). Routledge.
5. Daniels, J. D., Radebaugh, L. H., & Sullivan, D. P., (2018). *International Business: Environments and Operations*. Pearson Education.
6. Deresky, H., (2020). *International Management: Managing Across Borders and Cultures* (10th edn.). Pearson Education.
7. Hill, C. W. L., & Hult, G. T. M., (2019). *Global Business Today* (11th edn., Vol. 1). McGraw-Hill Education.
8. Hill, C. W. L., & Hult, G. T. M., (2021). *International Business: Competing in the Global Marketplace* (12th edn., Vol. 2). McGraw-Hill Education.
9. Kuthiala, B. K., & Kuthiala, D., (2017). *International Business Management: Theory and Practice*. Excel Books.
10. Luthans, F., & Doh, J. P., (2020). *International Management: Culture, Strategy, and Behavior* (10th edn., Vol. 2). McGraw-Hill Education.
11. Sharma, K., & Dubey, A., (2017). *International Business Management: Globalization and Beyond*. Pearson India.
12. Wild, J. J., Wild, K. L., & Han, J. C. Y., (2017). *International Business: The Challenges of Globalization* (9th edn., Vol. 1). Pearson Education, Inc.

CHAPTER 7

MARKETING RESEARCH IN INTERNATIONAL BUSINESS

UNIT INTRODUCTION

The globalization of business has been a major development in recent decades, as companies expand into new foreign markets and trade across borders. In order to succeed in these markets, companies require extensive information about foreign markets and consumers, which has made international marketing research (IMR) an essential tool for companies seeking to compete in today's global economy.

IMR involves the systematic gathering, recording, and analysis of data to provide information that is relevant to making marketing decisions in foreign markets. This information includes consumer behavior, market trends, and other factors that may affect a company's marketing strategy in different countries. By understanding the needs and preferences of consumers in foreign markets, as well as the challenges and opportunities that exist in these markets, companies can develop effective marketing strategies.

The globalization of business has led companies to expand into not only developed markets such as Europe, the United States, and Japan, but also into the unstable but growing markets of Latin America, the politically uncertain markets of the Middle East and Russia, and the rapidly changing markets of South East Asia and emerging African markets. The development of new communication and information technologies has further accelerated the globalization of business, changing lifestyles, consumer behavior, and purchasing patterns of different nations. Several factors influence the marketing research process in different countries. Cultural, political, and economic factors all play a role in shaping consumer behavior and market trends in different countries. For example, cultural differences can affect consumer behavior, while political factors such as regulations and trade policies can impact a company's ability to enter and operate in foreign markets. Economic factors such as exchange rates, inflation, and income levels can also affect a company's marketing strategy in foreign markets.

The purpose of this chapter is to give the definition of IMR and describe the factors which influence marketing research in different countries. The chapter also deals with the steps of the IMR process and its main categories.

Learning Objectives

After completing this chapter, you will be able to:

- Understand the concept and framework of international market research
- Learn to design and implement effective research methods for international markets
- Understand the unique challenges and opportunities of conducting marketing research in the global marketplace
- Develop skills in collecting and analyzing data from diverse sources
- Learn to use marketing research findings to develop effective international marketing strategies and tactics.
- Develop skills in presenting marketing research findings to diverse audiences, including global stakeholders and decision-makers.
- Understand the importance of ethical considerations in IMR.

Key Terms

- Cross-cultural research
- Cultural factors
- Data analysis
- Data collection
- Economic factors
- Ethical considerations
- Political factors
- Primary research
- Technology

7.1. CONCEPT OF MARKET RESEARCH

Marketing research is a critical component of successful businesses in today's globalized economy. It involves the systematic gathering, analysis, and interpretation of information to help businesses make informed decisions about their products and services. Through marketing research, companies can better understand consumer needs and behaviors, identify market trends, and stay competitive in an ever-changing business landscape.

Marketing research is a well-planned and systematic process that uses scientific methods to provide accurate and authentic information. It is an objective process that attempts to provide unbiased and factual information that decision-makers can use to make informed decisions. The main task of marketing research is to gather and analyze information in a systematic and organized way.

While marketing research is conducted for a specific purpose, marketing information systems (MIS) are set up to generate, analyze, store, and distribute information to marketing decision-makers on an ongoing basis. MIS is a continuous entity, whereas marketing research is an ad-hoc system that generates information when it is conducted. MIS information is more rigid and structured, while marketing research is more flexible and adaptable to specific purposes. Marketing research is a growing and widely used business activity, as companies need to know more about their customers to stay competitive. It is a necessary link between marketing decision-makers and the markets in which they operate. The principles of marketing research include the importance of timeliness and the significance of defining objectives cautiously and clearly. Decision-makers should avoid researching to support decisions already made (Figure 7.1).

Figure 7.1. Market research.

Marketing research is a growing and widely used business activity, and its principles are critical to generating useful information for managers.

7.1.1. Defining Marketing Research

Marketing research is defined in different ways by various institutions. Here are some examples:

- **American Marketing Association (AMA):** "Marketing research is the function that links the consumer, customer, and public to the marketer through information—information used to identify and define marketing opportunities and problems; generate, refine, and evaluate marketing actions; monitor marketing performance; and improve understanding of marketing as a process."
- **Market Research Society (MRS):** "Marketing research is the systematic gathering, recording, and analysis of data about issues relating to marketing products and services. The goal is to identify and assess how changing elements of the marketing mix impact customer behavior."
- **European Society for Opinion and Marketing Research (ESOMAR):** "Marketing research is the systematic gathering and interpretation of information about individuals or organizations using statistical and analytical methods and techniques of the applied social sciences to gain insight or support decision making."
- **International Chamber of Commerce (ICC):** "Marketing research involves the gathering, analysis, and interpretation of information relating to a particular market or markets, as well as the preparation and presentation of reports containing findings and recommendations for management action."

These definitions highlight the importance of systematically gathering and analyzing data to inform decision-making related to marketing products and services. Marketing research involves a range of techniques and methods, including surveys, focus groups, data analysis, and statistical modeling. The goal is to understand consumer behavior, preferences, and attitudes to develop effective marketing strategies and improve business performance.

TIPS

Marketing research is an essential tool for businesses to stay competitive in today's globalized economy. It helps companies better understand consumer needs and behaviors, identifies market trends, and stay ahead of the competition. By using scientific methods to gather, analyze, and interpret information, marketing research provides decision-makers with accurate and authentic information they can use to make informed decisions.

7.2. A FRAMEWORK OF INTERNATIONAL MARKETING RESEARCH

International marketing research (IMR) is a term used to refer to research carried out in different countries and cultures for various purposes. It can include research for true international products, foreign research, multinational research, and cross-cultural research. While cross-cultural research may not cross national boundaries, it can be challenging, as shown in the example of ethnic minority communities in London. However, methodologically, there is no difference between domestic and IMR since researchers must adapt their techniques to their target respondents, whether in their home country or abroad.

Despite this, IMR is a distinct subject area that requires attention. Mary Goodyear, an experienced international marketing researcher, supports this view. She argues that while there may be no fundamental difference between domestic and international research, the latter has unique challenges that require specialized knowledge and skills. For instance, cultural differences can be subtle but crucial, such as different attitudes towards advertising, promotions, and pricing. Language barriers and translation issues can also complicate the research process.

Furthermore, IMR often involves dealing with unfamiliar legal and regulatory frameworks, different distribution channels, and varying levels of economic development. Researchers need to be aware of these factors and adjust their research design and methodology accordingly. They may also need to collaborate with local partners, such as research firms or consultants, who have the necessary expertise and networks in the target countries.

Goodyear emphasizes that conducting IMR requires a deep understanding of the cultures and markets involved. Researchers need to be familiar with the history, customs, values, and beliefs of the target audience to develop relevant and effective research questions, methods, and instruments. They need to be sensitive to cultural nuances, avoid ethnocentrism, and ensure that the research respects the local norms and practices.

7.2.1. IMR

The rapidly changing global environment presents both opportunities and challenges for organizations. Advancements in technology, increasing international trade and investment, and the convergence of consumer preferences are compelling businesses to expand their globalization strategies. However, differences in political, legal, economic, social, and cultural factors across countries make it challenging to conduct meaningful market research. IMR follows a similar process as domestic research, including problem definition, methodology design, fieldwork, and final report and recommendations. However, the challenge lies in addressing the differences between countries and ensuring the comparability of research results. This requires a deep understanding of local cultures and customs, as well as a thorough analysis of the political, legal, and economic conditions in each market.

As companies become more global in their operations, they need to be able to carry on a meaningful dialog with their customers, regardless of where they are located. This requires designing consumer-based strategies that are customized for international market segments. Market research is the key link between marketing management and an organization's ultimate customer base.

To better utilize market research approaches that enable them to stay close to worldwide and diverse customer segments, firms need to adapt to the continual change and uncertainty in the global market. They need to stay up-to-date with the latest technological advancements and develop a deep understanding of the political, legal, and economic conditions in each market. They also need to be able to quickly adjust their strategies and tactics to address the constantly changing market conditions.

7.2.2. Defining International Marketing Research

IMR refers to the process of gathering, recording, and analyzing data about markets, consumers, and competitors in different countries or regions around the world. It involves the application of research methods and techniques to identify and evaluate marketing opportunities and challenges, generate and refine marketing actions, monitor marketing performance, and improve the understanding of marketing processes in the context of global markets. IMR helps companies make informed decisions about market entry, product development, pricing, promotion, and distribution strategies that are customized to the needs and preferences of consumers in different cultures and economic environments.

Here Are Some Definitions of International Marketing Research:

"IMR is the systematic and objective search for, and analysis of, information relevant to the identification and solution of any international marketing problem or opportunity." – *Philip Kotler*

"IMR is the process of planning, collecting, and analyzing data relevant to marketing decision-making in a global context." – *Naresh Malhotra*

"IMR is the process of gathering, analyzing, and interpreting information about a company's overseas markets and competitors in order to identify opportunities and threats and to make informed decisions about marketing strategies." – *Michael R. Czinkota*

"IMR is the systematic and objective search for information and analysis of data relevant to international marketing decisions." – *Warren J. Keegan*

"IMR is the systematic and objective identification, collection, analysis, and dissemination of information and insights to support international marketing decisions." – *V. Kumar and Rohit Deshpande.*

7.2.3. International Marketing Research Process

IMR is a crucial component of any global marketing strategy. It involves gathering and analyzing data to understand foreign markets, consumer behavior, and competition. The process of conducting IMR can be complex, with many different factors to consider.

1. **Conduct Preliminary Research:** Before you begin your IMR, it is essential to conduct some preliminary research on your topic of interest. This can involve going online and searching for existing survey reports related to your topic. The searched reports may not be specific to your requirement, but they can give you some ideas on how to go about your primary research. Additionally, conducting a SWOT analysis of your business and industry can help you identify potential opportunities and threats in foreign markets.
2. **Develop a Research Brief:** Developing a research brief is a critical step in the IMR process. A research brief is a statement setting out the objectives and background of the case in sufficient detail to enable the researcher to plan an appropriate study. A good research brief must include a background to the problem, a description of the product or service to be researched, a description of the market to be researched, and a statement of the objectives, timing, and budget constraints.
3. **Identify the Right Marketing Research Agency:** Using a professional market research agency can ensure that you get the information you need so that you can make strategic decisions based on reliable evidence. First, you need to find some marketing research agencies with the help of trade associations, business contacts, market research societies, business intelligence groups, independent consultant groups, local or online directories, etc. Once you have a list of potential agencies, draw up a market research agency shortlist. As long as you understand your own research needs, a quick check of what each agency offers will allow you to eliminate unsuitable ones.
4. **Choosing a Marketing Research Agency:** Ask each marketing research agency to provide a brief proposal, setting out what kind of research

they would suggest, their timelines and costs, and enclosing examples of past projects. Choose an agency that understands what you need to know, and has shown that they know how to get the right information within your budget.

5. **Determine Data Collection Model:** The data collection mode you use will impact both the type of data you collect and how it is collected. There are two categories of data, qualitative and quantitative. Qualitative data is unstructured and is often exploratory by nature, while quantitative research is the mathematical approach to collecting data. It is essential to understand the different modes of data collection and what type of data they can collect. You also need to consider how robust and agile the different modes of data collection are.
6. **Conduct Data Analysis:** The most important aspect of market research is being able to analyze the data once it has been collected. A thorough analysis should guide you on how to act on the insights you have gathered. It is therefore crucial that the research agency, through their insights report, address the questions you had set out at the start of your survey.
7. **Complete a Post Project Review:** Having a session with the research team after the completion of your project to share feedback and discuss the project's execution is sometimes overlooked. Such an undertaking involves various departments but is important to understand why a project did or did not go as smoothly as planned. A post-project review session helps both parties know what areas worked and which ones the agency or the client will need to improve for their next project.

7.2.4. Importance of International Marketing Research

Market research plays a crucial role in the success of an organization. It serves as the bridge between the company and its customers, enabling the organization to understand consumer behavior and gain insights into their needs and preferences. Without market research, companies risk launching products that fail to resonate with their target market, leading to significant financial losses. Effective market research enables companies to tailor their marketing strategies to specific micro-niches of the larger macro market, allowing them to gain a competitive edge in an increasingly crowded marketplace.

The growth of the international research business in recent years highlights the importance of market research in a global context. Companies pursuing global business strategies require specialized, targeted information about buyers in dispersed international markets to compete effectively in the 21st century. This demand for international market research is driven by the need for companies to understand the fundamental needs of foreign customers and the interaction of the four P's (product, price, place, and promotion) in foreign markets. Before pursuing international marketing strategies, companies must ask a series of strategic questions to determine their need for international market research. These questions include assessing the growth of international sales as a percentage of overall revenue, comparing the growth rates of international and domestic markets, evaluating the company's competitive position outside the US, and understanding the interaction of the four P's in foreign markets. The answers to these questions can help organizations prioritize their need for international market research and make informed decisions regarding target markets, brands, and other strategic marketing mix variables.

One of the key benefits of market research is that it enables companies to stay in touch with their best customers. It is estimated that it costs six times as much to attract a new customer as it does to keep a current customer. Therefore, companies must focus on retaining their existing customers by understanding their changing preferences and needs. Market research provides an actionable method for companies to keep a pulse with their valued customers and gain insights into subtle shifts in buying preferences that could ultimately lead to brand defection.

Remember

In today's consumer environment of over-choice and over-communication, companies must be skilled at crafting well-targeted strategies directed at specific micro-niches of the larger macro market.

This requires a deep understanding of customer behavior and preferences, which can only be gained through effective market research. Companies that go to market without first uncovering specific segment needs and perceptions risk facing the monumental cost of marketing failure. For example, a new product launch can cost $125 million or more, and the risk of not incorporating consumer behavior into the marketing strategy is significant.

Finally, while the internet has rapidly grown and gained acceptance by certain consumers, it may not necessarily be the optimum medium for conducting international market research projects. The challenges of deploying research tactics in developing foreign markets require specialized expertise and a deep understanding of local cultures and consumer behaviors. Therefore, companies must carefully evaluate their options when it comes to conducting international market research and seek out specialized expertise when necessary.

Market research is the vital link between the organization and its customers. It enables companies to gain a deep understanding of consumer behavior and translate this into actionable marketing strategies. The growth of the international research business highlights the importance of market research in a global context, as companies require specialized, targeted information about buyers in dispersed international markets. By prioritizing their need for market research and seeking out specialized expertise when necessary, companies can gain a competitive edge in an increasingly crowded marketplace.

7.3. TECHNIQUES OF INTERNATIONAL MARKETING RESEARCH

IMR is a crucial component of any company's strategy that intends to compete globally. It enables organizations to identify and evaluate market opportunities, assess competition, evaluate demand, determine market entry barriers, and formulate effective marketing strategies. The techniques of conducting IMR can be divided into two broad categories, which are complementary in practice. These are Desk Research and Survey Research (which is also called field research).

7.3.1. Desk Research

Desk research is a technique of collecting information from documentary sources or other published and unpublished sources. In other words, information and data already exist in published or unpublished form. Through desk research, the sources of such data are searched, and relevant documents, publications, etc., are collected. This stage of searching for sources of published or what is also called secondary data is also referred to as bibliography research or library research. The actual desk research involves the compilation, processing, and analysis of secondary data following the objectives of the research. In IMR, desk research plays a crucial role. In most countries, a good amount of general economic, political, and market information is available from secondary sources. Information on the country's industrial and economic profile, government policies and regulations, size, composition, and destination of foreign trade, and a host of other general information is often available for desk research. Desk research provides background information for selecting the most promising foreign markets for in-depth investigation. It can also point out specific factors that should be carefully looked into. Desk research, therefore, could be used for general and limited information on foreign markets as well as the preliminary step for effective planning and conducting survey research in foreign countries.

7.3.2. Sources of Data

The key to successful desk research is the knowledge of how to find out relevant sources of required data and how to collect and make use of them.

The principal sources of information can be classified under specific categories like government sources, semi-government sources, private sources, and international sources.

- **Government Sources:** Governments in all countries generate a wide variety of information and data that are useful and relevant to marketing. Information provided by governments covers wide areas like population, economy, policies, programs, industries, institutions, rules and regulations, etc., and is published in the forms of reports, documents, journals, notifications, etc. The governments in different countries are the largest generators of information and data useful for international marketing.
- **Semi-Government Sources**: In many countries, there are specialized semi-government agencies or institutions charged with specific tasks such as monitoring consumption trends, foreign trade, industrial development, income distribution, purchasing power of people, health, education, etc. These institutions usually carry out regular studies primarily to help and guide government policy-making. The reports and publications of these institutions contain valuable information relevant to marketing.
- **Private Sources:** There are research institutions, publishing houses, banking and financial institutions, chambers of commerce, trade associations, and a host of other similar organizations which collect, process, and disseminate different kinds of information in their respective areas of concern which could be relevant to international marketing.
- **International Sources:** International organizations within and outside the UN system publish a wealth of statistical data and information relating to markets. The important among these organizations are the Food and Agricultural Organizations (FAO), International Labor Organization (ILO), United Nations Conference on Trade and Development (UNCTAD), UN Economic Commission; International Monetary Fund (IMF), Organization for Economic Cooperation and Development (OECD), International Trade Center (ITC), and several others. Many developed countries have set up an `Import Promotion Office' (IPO) to assist developing countries to export their goods to the developed country markets. Valuable information on foreign markets is available from the IPOs of different countries. The diplomatic missions located in the exporter's country can often provide a great deal of information about their respective countries and guide the researcher on other sources of information.

Many developed countries have set up Import Promotion Offices (IPOs) to assist developing countries in exporting their goods to developed country markets. IPOs can provide valuable information on foreign markets, including product trends, consumer behavior, and cultural differences. These offices can also guide researchers on other sources of information. For instance, diplomatic missions located in the exporter's country can provide a great deal of information about their respective countries.

7.3.3. Criteria for Evaluating Sources of Secondary Data

There are several criteria that businesses can use to evaluate the sources of secondary data. These criteria include:

- **Coverage**: Is the source likely to cover the subject of research comprehensively and precisely?
- **Level**: Is the level of information too high, too low, or just right for research?
- **Emphasis**: Does the material focus on the most relevant aspects of the subject?
- **Timeliness**: Is the material up-to-date or outdated for research?
- **Accuracy**: How accurate and reliable is the information? Who originally collected it, and for what purpose?
- **Web Sources**: The internet is a valuable resource for businesses looking to conduct market research. Most of the leading newspapers and magazines are available in some form on the internet and can be used as an invaluable resource for companies and markets. Additionally, the internet provides access to libraries, government statistics, company information, product design, and much more. Businesses can use general search engines like Google, Yahoo, and Excite to search for relevant information on the internet.

Did you Know?

In 1951, the FAO's headquarters was moved from Washington, D.C., United States, to Rome, Italy. The agency is directed by the Conference of Member Nations, which meets every two years to review the work carried out by the organization and to plan on and budget for the next two-year period.

7.3.4. Survey Research

Survey research, also known as field research, is different from desk research. In desk research, the data is already available, while in survey research, data is generated in the course of doing the research. Most of the desk research on foreign markets can be done in the exporter's country itself, but survey research has to be carried out with the potential markets abroad through direct contact with people there. Desk research provides the general background or framework for planning and conducting survey research for the collection of primary information specific to the exporter's needs.

Conducting Survey Research:

Conducting survey research or field research involves the following steps:

- **Scope of the Research**: The scope of research has to be clearly described, covering the purpose of research, information to be collected and from whom, geographic areas to be covered, and the like.
- **Definition of the Universe**: It spells out the 'universe' or 'population' selected for the survey. For example, the survey may be carried out among the end-users/consumers, importers, distributors, retailers, industrial buyers, representatives of chambers, trade associations, government departments, agencies, or any other group of people concerned with the subject matter of research.
- **Methods of Sample Selection**: When doing survey research, it is usually not possible to interview every user or importer, distributor, etc., of a company's product. There must, therefore, be some methods of selecting respondents. This is done by sampling. The usual practice is to draw smaller samples from the relevant 'universe' selected for the survey.

7.3.5. Techniques of Interviewing

These techniques include personal interviews, telephone interviews, mail or postal surveys, and online surveys (Figure 7.2).

Figure 7.2. Techniques of interviewing.

- **Personal Interviews:** The face-to-face personal interview is considered the most effective and reliable method of collecting information in market research, both at the consumer and industrial levels. Personal interviews allow for a more in-depth and detailed understanding of the respondents' attitudes, beliefs, and behaviors.

To conduct personal interviews, businesses first select the interviewee or respondent using one of the sampling methods available. The interview can then be conducted in a structured, semi-structured, or unstructured manner.

A structured interview follows a structured questionnaire, mostly using closed-ended questions. The questions are asked in the same language and sequence, with appropriate answers marked/ticked as pre-coded on the questionnaire or recorded verbatim in the case of open-ended questions.

An unstructured interview allows for a free exchange between the interviewer and the respondent, without sticking to a set list of questions as in the case of structured interviews. The semi-structured interview is a combination of the two types mentioned above.

- **Telephone Interviews:** Telephone interviews are limited to those who can be contacted over the phone and are more suitable for asking a few short and simple questions. They are quick and less time-consuming, making them ideal for identifying the right kind of respondents for subsequent personal interviews or for contacting busy executives for quick interviews.
- **Mail Surveys:** Mail or postal surveys can be conducted in a foreign market from the researcher's home country. The mailing list of respondents, such as importers, can be prepared and questionnaires sent by mail for filling in and returning by the respondents.

While the method is the least expensive, it is the most unreliable, and the response rate is usually very low. This technique is best used for conducting surveys with highly targeted audiences or for conducting surveys over a more extended period.

- **Online Surveys:** Online surveys are similar to mail surveys in that they use self-administered questionnaires. However, online surveys differ in the means through which they are carried out. They can be conducted through email or posted on the web, with the URL provided to respondents.

Online surveys are highly cost-effective, and their reach can be broadened to include respondents worldwide. They are quick and easy to complete and can offer a high response rate if the survey is appropriately designed.

7.4. FACTORS INFLUENCING MARKETING RESEARCH IN DIFFERENT COUNTRIES

Marketing research is a crucial process for companies seeking to expand their reach and target new markets. It involves gathering and analyzing data about the market, including consumer behavior, preferences, and attitudes, as well as the economic and social factors that affect demand for products or services. However, marketing research must be adapted to the specific context of different countries, which presents unique challenges and opportunities. Here, we will explore the main factors that influence marketing research in different countries, including cultural, racial, climatic, economic, religious, historical, and language differences.

1. **Cultural Differences:** Culture is a fundamental factor that influences consumer behavior and preferences in different countries. Cultural differences can lead to misunderstandings or blunders that can harm a company's reputation or sales. For example, the use of symbols or colors that have negative connotations in a particular culture can offend and reduce the appeal of a product. Companies must be aware of the cultural norms and values in each country and adapt their marketing strategies accordingly. This may involve changes to the product, price, promotion, or distribution channels.
2. **Racial Differences:** Racial differences can affect consumer preferences and the way products or services are marketed. For example, beauty products may need to be adapted to the skin tones and hair types of different racial groups. Companies must also be sensitive to racial stereotypes and avoid using language or imagery that can be perceived as offensive or discriminatory.
3. **Climatic Differences:** Climatic differences can affect the demand for products and the way they are designed or marketed. For example, products that are suitable for cold or rainy climates may not be appropriate for hot or dry climates. Companies must adapt their products to the local climatic conditions and ensure that they are suitable for the target market.
4. **Economic Differences:** Economic differences are a major factor that affects consumer behavior and preferences in different countries. Economic factors include the level of income, purchasing power, and infrastructure of the market. Companies must adapt their products and pricing strategies to the local economic conditions and ensure that they are affordable and accessible to the target market. This may involve changes to the product features or packaging, as well as the distribution channels and marketing tactics.
5. **Religious Differences:** Religious differences can have a significant

impact on consumer behavior and preferences in different countries. Companies must be aware of the religious norms and values in each country and adapt their products and marketing strategies accordingly. For example, food products that are not certified as Halal may not be acceptable in Islamic countries.

6. **Historical Differences:** Historical differences can also affect consumer behavior and preferences in different countries. For example, products that are associated with a particular country or culture may be more appealing in other countries. Companies must be aware of the historical context and cultural heritage of each country and adapt their marketing strategies accordingly.
7. **Language Differences:** Language differences can also present challenges for marketing research in different countries. Companies must ensure that their marketing messages are translated accurately and appropriately for the target market. This may involve hiring local translators or adapting the language and messaging to suit the local context.

7.5. CHALLENGES OF CONDUCTING INTERNATIONAL MARKETING RESEARCH

IMR is a crucial element for organizations that want to expand their operations beyond their borders. However, conducting IMR comes with its own set of challenges. The following are some of the major challenges that researchers face while conducting IMR:

7.5.1. Cultural Differences

Cultural differences are a significant challenge that researchers face when conducting IMR. Culture is a fundamental component of the environment in which markets exist, and it affects how people respond to products and services. Therefore, researchers must take cultural differences into account when conducting market research across borders. Social institutions, gender roles, language, religion, aesthetics, education, and time orientation are some of the cultural components that are closely related to national culture. Researchers must be aware of these cultural differences and adapt their research methods accordingly (Figure 7.3).

1. **Language Differences:** Language is another significant challenge that researchers face when conducting IMR. While many organizations have command over the English language, not everyone can understand English. Furthermore, there are variations within the same language, which can make it difficult to communicate effectively. For instance,

Americans and British have some variations in the way they speak English. Researchers must take language differences into account when designing their questionnaires.

Figure 7.3. Cultural differences in marketing.

2. **Translation and Conversion:** Translating questionnaires from one language to another can be challenging because of differences in idioms, concepts, syntax, and vocabulary. Therefore, researchers must ensure that the translation and conversion of their questionnaires are accurate. They may also need to have their questionnaires translated by a professional translation service to ensure that they are correctly translated.
3. **Language Rules:** Syntax is a significant challenge when it comes to language in IMR. Translating English into grammar-based languages can be challenging because of sentence constructions. Therefore, researchers must ensure that their questionnaires are phrased correctly, to avoid misinterpretations by respondents.
4. **Traditional and Cultural Norms:** Cultural norms are another significant challenge when it comes to IMR. These norms are not always transparent, and this makes it challenging to analyze the international market. Ignoring cultural norms can lead to significant problems in IMR. For instance, the U.S. Ketchup Company failed to investigate why ketchup was not available in Japan and invested a significant amount to launch their product. Later, they found out that soy sauce was preferred in Japan. Understanding cultural norms is critical for the success of IMR.
5. **Period and Time Zone:** Differences in time zones can have a significant impact on communication and the timing

of the project. Extra time is required for communication to take place across the world. Time of day also matters in countries like Japan where business is only done during business hours. Researchers must keep time zones in mind when conducting IMR.

6. **International Holidays:** Foreign holidays are another factor that researchers must keep in mind when conducting IMR. Different countries have different holidays depending on their culture, religion, and beliefs. It is essential to check the holiday schedule before starting research in another country.

7.5.2. Sampling Collecting Issues and Sampling Framework

Sampling is a common practice in IMR. However, collecting data from samples can be challenging, especially in countries like China, where the population is vast. In China, only 32 cities have a population of at least one million, while 42 have a population between 500,000 and one million, and the remaining 548 have a population of less than 500,000. Researchers may have difficulty collecting data from every sampling.

1 **Local Interviews:** Local interviews are a complicated communication process that researchers may use to understand the customers' point of view about product quality. However, this technique can have some problems due to language barriers among the countries.

2. **Questionnaire Period:** It is possible that the time it takes to complete a questionnaire can vary based on the language it is translated into. This may be due to a variety of factors, including differences in syntax, grammar, and vocabulary between languages. Additionally, cultural differences and context-specific language usage can also play a role in the length of time it takes to complete a questionnaire.

However, it is important to note that the length of time it takes to complete a questionnaire can also be influenced by a variety of other factors, including the complexity of the questions, the level of detail required in responses, and the respondent's level of familiarity with the topic being addressed in the questionnaire. Therefore, it is not always accurate to assume that a questionnaire will take a specific amount of time to complete based solely on the language it is translated into.

7.5.3. Measurement and Dimension Issues

In IMR, it is crucial to ensure that the scales and measures used to obtain data from different countries are equivalent. This is because the equivalence of data is one of the major issues that must be dealt with early in the international market research process. To achieve equivalence of data, three factors must be considered. Firstly, the same phenomena should be used in both countries in the study of equivalence. Secondly, the phenomena should be measured consistently in each country. Finally, the samples used in each country must be equivalent to each other. These factors are critical in ensuring the reliability and validity of data collected from different countries. The perception of reliability, which describes consistency over time, and validity, which is responsible for the type of instrument used for measurement, are also crucial in any market research effort.

7.5.4. Market Research Infrastructure

Another factor that affects the measurement and dimension issues in IMR is the market research infrastructure. The quality of media and internet control is crucial in ensuring the success of any market research project. In countries where there is no proper media technology, market research projects may face numerous challenges, resulting in unsuccessful research. Additionally, the widespread use of print and broadcast media in western countries and the internet's diffusion may result in a skewed sample that may not be representative of the population.

7.5.5. Data Collection Complications

Data collection is more challenging in international markets than in domestic markets. The process of carrying out sales in international markets is more complicated and more expensive. Additionally, unreliable mailing services in developed countries may pose a significant challenge in carrying out international mail surveys (Figure 7.4).

Figure 7.4. *Representation of data collection techniques.*

7.5.6. Legal Restrictions

Privacy and legal restrictions pose a significant challenge in IMR. Different countries have different privacy policies, with some countries having strict privacy policies that may shut down marketing activities that collect and portray personal information. For instance, European countries have strict privacy policies, while the Chinese government monitors the questionnaire structure and the endorsement of the final data, which is in direct conflict with the American approach of non-disclosure of proprietary client results.

7.6. SCOPE OF RESEARCH IN THE INTERNATIONAL MARKET

IMR is an essential tool for marketers to make informed decisions in the global marketplace. IMR facilitates marketing management to carry out marketing functions consistently, effectively, and smoothly.

7.6.1. Product Research

Product research is a critical part of IMR as it studies the individual product. The research focuses on the making and marketing of the product, including its color, size, shape, quality, packaging, brand name, and price. Product research also deals with product modification, product innovation, and product life cycles. The product is modified as per the needs and wants of the consumers to ensure that it does not fail in the market.

7.6.2. Consumer Research

Consumer research is another important aspect of IMR as it studies consumer behavior. The research analyzes the consumer's needs, wants, likes, dislikes, attitude, age, sex, income, location, buying motives, etc. This data is used to make decisions about the product, its price, place, and promotion.

7.6.3. Packaging Research

Packaging research is a subset of product research that studies the package of the product. The research aims to improve the quality of the package, make it more attractive and convenient for consumers, and reduce the cost of packaging. It also selects a suitable method for packaging and the appropriate packaging material.

7.6.4. Pricing Research

Pricing research studies the pricing of the product. It selects a suitable method of pricing and fixes the price for the product. It also compares the companies' prices with the competitor's prices and fixes the discount and commission given to middlemen. The research studies the market price trends and future price trends.

7.6.5. Advertising Research

Advertising research studies the advertising of the product. It fixes the advertising objectives, budget, message, layout, copy, slogan, headline, etc. The research selects suitable media for advertising and evaluates the effectiveness of advertising and other sales promotion techniques.

7.6.6. Sales Research

Sales research studies the selling activities of the company. The research studies the sales outlets, sales territories, sales forecasting, sales trends, sales methods, the effectiveness of the sales force, etc.

7.6.7. Distribution Research

Distribution research studies the channels of distribution. It selects a suitable channel for the product and fixes the channel objectives. The research identifies the channel functions like storage, grading, etc., and evaluates the competitor's channel.

7.6.8. Policy Research

Policy research studies the company's policies, including marketing policies, sales policies, distribution policies, pricing policies, inventory policies, etc. The research evaluates the effectiveness of these policies and makes necessary changes if required.

7.6.9. International Marketing

Research IMR studies the foreign market. It collects data about consumers from foreign countries, the economic and political situation of different countries, and data about foreign competitors. This data is very useful for exporters.

7.6.10. Motivation Research

Motivation research studies consumers' buying motives. It analyzes those factors that motivate consumers to buy a product and finds out why consumers buy a particular product. The research also finds out the causes of consumer behavior in the market.

7.6.11. Market Research

Market research studies the markets, market competition, and market trends. The research does sales forecasting and estimates the demand for new products. It also fixes the sales territories and sales quotas.

7.6.12. Media Research

Media research studies various advertising media such as television (TV), radio, newspapers, magazines, the internet, etc. The research studies the merits and demerits of each media selects a suitable media for advertising does media planning, and studies media cost. It helps in sales promotion and avoids wastage in advertising.

7.7. IDENTIFYING MARKET OPPORTUNITIES FOR BUSINESS GROWTH

In today's rapidly changing business environment, sustaining growth and profitability is never a guarantee. Technological and scientific advances shorten the life cycles of products and services, business models change, and new competitors appear from outside the industry. This constant instability makes it necessary to seek new business opportunities. There can be different ways to identify market opportunities for business growth as follows:

7.7.1. Consumer Segmentation

To understand your target audience, you must identify consumer segments that share common characteristics. These characteristics can be "hard" variables such as age, gender, place of residence, educational level, occupation, and level of income, or "soft" variables such as lifestyle, attitude, values, and purchasing motivations. By analyzing these variables, businesses can estimate the number of potential customers and identify motivations that lead to purchasing decisions.

For instance, Aguas Danone, a bottled water company in Argentina, identified two drivers behind non-alcoholic drink consumption: health and flavor. Bottled water was perceived as healthy but did not offer the attribute of good taste. Soft drinks and juices tasted good but were perceived as highly caloric. The company realized there was an opportunity for healthy drinks offering both taste and flavor. As a result, they launched flavored bottled water, Ser, with great success. According to data from Euromonitor International, Aguas Danone has been the leader of Reduced Sugar Flavored Bottled Water in Argentina since launching in 2002, beating giants such as Coca-Cola and Nestlé.

7.7.2. Purchase Situation Analysis

Purchase situations must also be examined to uncover expansion opportunities. Businesses should ask themselves when people buy their product or service, where people make the purchase, and how they pay. Looking at distribution channels, payment methods, and all other circumstances that involve purchasing decisions can teach you how consumers buy and how you can position your product appropriately.

For example, vending machines offering snacks like yogurt and individual juices have been introduced in the hallways of the subway of Santiago de Chile, promoting on-the-go consumption. Another aspect to explore is the acceptance of different means of payment. For example, Amazon recently launched Amazon Cash in the US, enabling consumers without credit cards to shop online by adding credit to their personal Amazon accounts.

7.7.3. Direct Competition Analysis

In addition to analyzing demand and purchasing situations, it is important to analyze supply. Knowing the existing players in the market where you are competing or going to compete is important when evaluating opportunities. Relevant questions, in this case, are: what are the products and brands of our industry that are growing more significantly, and why? What is their value proposition? What competitive advantage do we have over them? For example, SKY airline, competing in the Chilean market against a notably positioned brand such as LAN, found there was an opportunity to differentiate itself with a low-cost model, which until then had not existed in Chile. SKY lowered its costs, by eliminating complimentary food and beverages for all passengers during flights and in doing so lowered its ticket prices. This helped the company increase its share of carried passengers from 10% in 2008 up to 20% in 2017, according to Euromonitor International.

7.7.4. Indirect Competition Analysis

Analyzing indirect competition can help businesses identify opportunities in substitute industries. For instance, with the decrease in airfares, airlines may want to explore opportunities in consumer segments currently served by other means of transportation. To do this, air carriers need to research the number of people who travel on long-distance buses and trains, popular routes, ticket prices, occupancy rates of long-distance buses and trains, and what it would take to convince a bus or train passenger to travel by plane. This type of analysis helps establish competitive advantages against indirect competitors and provides insight into additional opportunities for growth.

7.7.5. Analysis of Complementary Products and Services

Businesses should monitor the performance of products that are complementary to their own. For example, a packaging company should monitor sales of products that it could potentially package, while a company producing coffee machines should gather insights into the evolution of different types of coffee sales. Trends in complementary markets should be taken into account when making investment decisions.

7.7.6. Analysis of Other Industries

Sometimes, businesses want to expand a certain business model or philosophy beyond their current industrial sector. To do this, they need to analyze competition, market sizes, market shares, growth rates, unit prices, per capita sales, and brand positioning in other industries. For example, Easy Group maximized the occupancy rate of flights with the airline Easy Jet and then applied the same model to cinemas and buses for Easy Cinema and Easy Bus, respectively.

7.7.7. Foreign Markets Analysis

Exploring foreign markets can lead to additional opportunities when a company operates in a mature or saturated market. Markets in different countries grow at different paces due to disparities in the level of economic development and local habits. Knowing the evolution of per capita consumption of a given product in a given country can serve as an indicator of the maturity of the product's life cycle. Having information on the size of the market and competitors in other countries will help to estimate the business potential. Monitoring what happens in more developed countries in terms of consumption habits can also serve as indicators of potential indexes in their own country.

7.7.8. Environment Analysis

Analyzing changes in the environment with technological and scientific developments can generate new business opportunities. For instance, the growth of the internet and smartphone penetration has enabled the arrival of companies with new business models such as Airbnb and Uber. Beyond mobile and the internet, artificial intelligence, robotization, the internet of things, biotechnology, and renewable energy sources also provide multiple business opportunities.

Regulatory changes and other transformations in the business environment can create new market opportunities for businesses. One example of such a change is Chile's new labeling requirements for products high in calories, sodium, sugars, and saturated fats. This change may represent an opportunity for healthier products that are not affected by the new labels. To identify new market opportunities, it is essential to conduct market research on the local business environment.

Conducting a variety of analyzes will provide a comprehensive view of the market and help create long-term strategic business plans. Once new market opportunities have been identified, companies must move quickly to develop a plan. This involves developing a value proposition, planning the commercialization chain, and estimating costs, revenues, cash flows, and financing needs. Not all market opportunities will succeed, but experimentation through pilot testing can help determine their potential.

Pilot testing of new products, services, or business models can be performed in controlled areas to minimize the cost of failed opportunities. However, there is a risk of alerting the competition about the company's strategy. This risk must be compared against the risk and cost of launching a new product at a global scale and failing. Many experiments will fail during pilot testing, but some will succeed and be developed on a larger scale.

The example of Coca-Cola's launch of Coca-Cola Life in 2013 illustrates the importance of pilot testing. The pilot test started in Argentina and Chile, followed by launches in other countries like the UK, Sweden, Australia, Switzerland, Japan, and New Zealand. However, sales of Coca-Cola Life did not grow as much as expected in many of these markets. As a result, Coca-Cola discontinued the brand in Australia and the UK. Pilot testing helped Coca-Cola determine the success of Coca-Cola Life, and a failure at a global scale would have had higher costs in terms of expenditure and brand image.

7.8. ETHICAL CONSIDERATIONS IN INTERNATIONAL MARKETING RESEARCH

Marketing research is an important tool that helps companies to understand consumer behavior, preferences, and trends. It provides valuable insights that enable businesses to make informed decisions and develop effective marketing strategies. However, the ethical considerations in marketing research are of utmost importance. Conducting marketing research abroad can present unique ethical challenges that require careful consideration.

7.8.1. ESOMAR Code of Conduct

The ESOMAR produces a code of conduct that guides professional practice and protects the interests of all research stakeholders. This code of conduct outlines the ethical responsibilities of the four stakeholders involved in marketing research: the client, researcher, respondent, and public. The code provides guidelines for maintaining confidentiality, obtaining informed consent, and ensuring that research is conducted ethically and respectfully.

7.8.2. Professional Associations

In addition to the ESOMAR Code of Conduct, individual countries may have their codes of practice that reflect their cultural and industrial heritage. The development of professional associations in many countries has been a key development in promoting the ethical practice in marketing research. These associations provide guidance to researchers on ethical issues and may introduce or discuss quality standard systems for fieldwork. For example, in the Czech Republic, Hungary, Poland, and Russia, major market research suppliers are forming associations and investing in training their staff to meet Western standards.

7.8.3. Ethical Challenges in International Markets

While ethical considerations in marketing research are similar across borders, some ethical issues become more challenging when conducting research in international markets. One of the most significant challenges is dealing with cultural and language differences. For instance, some cultures may be more sensitive to certain topics or questions, which can affect the validity of the research. Language barriers can also create challenges in obtaining informed consent, ensuring confidentiality, and maintaining accurate translations of research materials.

Another challenge in IMR is ensuring that research is conducted ethically and respectfully, particularly in countries with different legal systems and social norms. For example, in some countries, bribery and corruption may be common practices, and researchers may be tempted to offer incentives to respondents to participate in research. This can compromise the integrity of the research and raise ethical concerns.

David Mendoza, Director of Gobi International, an Anglo-Russian industrial research company, faced a dilemma when conducting research in Russia. Some respondents, influenced by the Soviet-style system, refused to answer any questions, while others, disillusioned with the system, were willing to provide information for a fee. Mendoza acknowledged that this practice was highly unsatisfactory and tried to avoid it whenever possible. However, in some cases, there may be no choice but to offer incentives to obtain information.

REVIEW QUESTIONS

1. Define international marketing research.
2. What are the unique challenges of conducting marketing research in the global marketplace?
3. What are the different research methods that can be used for international markets and how can they be implemented effectively?
4. How can data be collected and analyzed from diverse sources for international marketing research?
5. How can ethical considerations be addressed in international marketing research?

MULTIPLE CHOICE QUESTIONS

1. What is the first step in conducting marketing research in the global marketplace?

a. Developing a research plan
b. Collecting data
c. Analyzing data
d. Identifying research objectives

2. What type of research is often used in cross-cultural marketing research?

a. Secondary research
b. Qualitative research
c. Quantitative research
d. Experimental research

3. Which of the following is an example of a cultural factor that can impact international marketing research outcomes?

a. Tariffs
b. Language barriers
c. Economic instability
d. Technological advancements

4. What is the purpose of conducting market analysis in international marketing research?

a. To identify potential customers
b. To determine market size
c. To assess the market competition
d. All of the above

5. How can technology be leveraged in international marketing research?

a. By automating data collection

b. By improving data analysis

c. By facilitating cross-cultural communication

d. All of the above

Answers to Multiple Choice Questions

1. (d); 2. (b); 3. (b); 4. (d); 5. (d)

REFERENCES

1. Cavusgil, S. T., Knight, G., & Riesenberger, J. R., (2018). *International Business: The New Realities* (5th edn., Vol. 1). Pearson Education, Inc.
2. Chadha, N. K., (2018). *International Business Management: A Managerial Perspective*. Vikas Publishing House.
3. Cherunilam, F., (2017). *International Business Management: Text and Cases*. Himalaya Publishing House.
4. Cullen, J. B., & Parboteeah, K. P., (2018). *International Business: Strategy and the Multinational Company* (2nd edn., Vol. 2). Routledge.
5. Daniels, J. D., Radebaugh, L. H., & Sullivan, D. P., (2018). *International Business: Environments and Operations*. Pearson Education.
6. Deresky, H., (2020). *International Management: Managing Across Borders and Cultures* (10th edn.). Pearson Education.
7. Hill, C. W. L., & Hult, G. T. M., (2019). *Global Business Today* (11th edn., Vol. 1). McGraw-Hill Education.
8. Hill, C. W. L., & Hult, G. T. M., (2021). *International Business: Competing in the Global Marketplace* (12th edn., Vol. 2). McGraw-Hill Education.
9. Kuthiala, B. K., & Kuthiala, D., (2017). *International Business Management: Theory and Practice*. Excel Books.
10. Luthans, F., & Doh, J. P., (2020). *International Management: Culture, Strategy, and Behavior* (10th edn., Vol. 2). McGraw-Hill Education.
11. Sharma, K., & Dubey, A., (2017). *International Business Management: Globalization and Beyond*. Pearson India.
12. Wild, J. J., Wild, K. L., & Han, J. C. Y., (2017). *International Business: The Challenges of Globalization* (9th edn., Vol. 1). Pearson Education, Inc.

INDEX

S

W

Z

Printed in the United States
by Baker & Taylor Publisher Services